Exam Ref 70-764
Administering a SQL
Database Infrastructure

Victor Isakov

Exam Ref 70-764 Administering a SQL Database Infrastructure

Published with the authorization of Microsoft Corporation by:
Pearson Education, Inc.

Copyright © 2018 by Pearson Education

ISBN-13: 978-1-5093-0383-0
ISBN-10: 1-5093-0383-9

Library of Congress Control Number: 2017953072
8 2019

Trademarks

Microsoft and the trademarks listed at https://www.microsoft.com on the "Trademarks" webpage are trademarks of the Microsoft group of companies. All other marks are property of their respective owners.

Warning and Disclaimer

Special Sales

For information about buying this title in bulk quantities, or for special sales opportunities (which may include electronic versions; custom cover designs; and content particular to your business, training goals, marketing focus, or branding interests), please contact our corporate sales department at corpsales@pearsoned.com or (800) 382-3419.

For government sales inquiries, please contact governmentsales@pearsoned.com.

For questions about sales outside the U.S., please contact intlcs@pearson.com.

Editor-in-Chief	Greg Wiegand
Acquisitions Editor	Trina MacDonald
Development Editor	Troy Mott
Managing Editor	Sandra Schroeder
Senior Project Editor	Tracey Croom
Editorial Production	Backstop Media
Copy Editor	Christina Rudloff
Indexer	Julie Grady
Proofreader	Christina Rudloff
Technical Editor	Martin 'MC' Brown
Cover Designer	Twist Creative, Seattle

Contents at a glance

Introduction

First and foremost, thank you for your purchase and all the best of luck in your endeavor to become certified and an expert in the SQL Server data platform. The 70-764 exam is intended for database professionals who perform installation, maintenance, and configuration tasks on the SQL Server platform. Other responsibilities include setting up database systems, making sure those systems operate efficiently, and regularly storing, backing up, and securing data from unauthorized access.

This book is geared toward database administrators who are looking to train in the administration of SQL Server 2016 infrastructure. To help you prepare for the exam you can use Microsoft Hyper-V to create SQL Server virtual machines (VMs) and follow the examples in this book. You can download an evaluation copy of Windows Server 2016 from *https://www.microsoft.com/en-us/evalcenter/evaluate-windows-server-2016/*. SQL Server 2016 can be downloaded for free from *https://www.microsoft.com/en-us/sql-server/sql-server-downloads*. You can download the AdventureWorks databases from *https://msftdbprodsamples.codeplex. com/*. The Wide World Importers database can be downloaded from *https://github.com/Microsoft/sql-server-samples/releases/tag/wide-world-importers-v1.0*.

This book covers every major topic area found on the exam, but it does not cover every exam question. Only the Microsoft exam team has access to the exam questions, and Microsoft regularly adds new questions to the exam, making it impossible to cover specific questions. You should consider this book a supplement to your relevant real-world experience and other study materials. If you encounter a topic in this book that you do not feel completely comfortable with, use the "Need more review?" links you'll find in the text to find more information and take the time to research and study the topic. Great information is available on MSDN, TechNet, and in blogs and forums.

Organization of this book

This book is organized by the "Skills measured" list published for the exam. The "Skills measured" list is available for each exam on the Microsoft Learning website: *https://aka.ms/examlist*. Each chapter in this book corresponds to a major topic area in the list, and the technical tasks in each topic area determine a chapter's organization. If an exam covers six major topic areas, for example, the book will contain six chapters.

Microsoft certifications

Microsoft certifications distinguish you by proving your command of a broad set of skills and experience with current Microsoft products and technologies. The exams and corresponding certifications are developed to validate your mastery of critical competencies as you design and develop, or implement and support, solutions with Microsoft products and technologies both on-premises and in the cloud. Certification brings a variety of benefits to the individual and to employers and organizations.

> **MORE INFO   ALL MICROSOFT CERTIFICATIONS**
>
> For information about Microsoft certifications, including a full list of available certifications, go to *https://www.microsoft.com/learning*.

Acknowledgments

Victor Isakov   I would like to dedicate this book to Christopher, Isabelle, Marcus and Sofia. With your love and "infinite patience" I am the luckiest guy on this planet! It would be remiss of me not to also thank Trina MacDonald and Troy Mott for their "infinite patience" in helping me complete this "impossible task."

Microsoft Virtual Academy

Build your knowledge of Microsoft technologies with free expert-led online training from Microsoft Virtual Academy (MVA). MVA offers a comprehensive library of videos, live events, and more to help you learn the latest technologies and prepare for certification exams. You'll find what you need here:

https://www.microsoftvirtualacademy.com

Quick access to online references

Throughout this book are addresses to webpages that the author has recommended you visit for more information. Some of these addresses (also known as URLs) can be painstaking to type into a web browser, so we've compiled all of them into a single list that readers of the print edition can refer to while they read.

Download the list at *https://aka.ms/exam764administersql/downloads*.

The URLs are organized by chapter and heading. Every time you come across a URL in the book, find the hyperlink in the list to go directly to the webpage.

Errata, updates, & book support

We've made every effort to ensure the accuracy of this book and its companion content. You can access updates to this book—in the form of a list of submitted errata and their related corrections—at:

https://aka.ms/exam764administersql/errata

If you discover an error that is not already listed, please submit it to us at the same page.

If you need additional support, email Microsoft Press Book Support at mspinput@microsoft.com.

Please note that product support for Microsoft software and hardware is not offered through the previous addresses. For help with Microsoft software or hardware, go to *https://support.microsoft.com*.

We want to hear from you

At Microsoft Press, your satisfaction is our top priority, and your feedback our most valuable asset. Please tell us what you think of this book at:

https://aka.ms/tellpress

We know you're busy, so we've kept it short with just a few questions. Your answers go directly to the editors at Microsoft Press. (No personal information will be requested.) Thanks in advance for your input!

Stay in touch

Let's keep the conversation going! We're on Twitter: *http://twitter.com/MicrosoftPress*.

Important: How to use this book to study for the exam

Certification exams validate your on-the-job experience and product knowledge. To gauge your readiness to take an exam, use this Exam Ref to help you check your understanding of the skills tested by the exam. Determine the topics you know well and the areas in which you need more experience. To help you refresh your skills in specific areas, we have also provided "Need more review?" pointers, which direct you to more in-depth information outside the book.

The Exam Ref is not a substitute for hands-on experience. This book is not designed to teach you new skills.

We recommend that you round out your exam preparation by using a combination of available study materials and courses. Learn more about available classroom training at *https://www.microsoft.com/learning*. Microsoft Official Practice Tests are available for many exams at *https://aka.ms/practicetests*. You can also find free online courses and live events from Microsoft Virtual Academy at *https://www.microsoftvirtualacademy.com*.

This book is organized by the "Skills measured" list published for the exam. The "Skills measured" list for each exam is available on the Microsoft Learning website: *https://aka.ms/examlist*.

Note that this Exam Ref is based on publicly available information and the author's experience. To safeguard the integrity of the exam, authors do not have access to the exam questions.

Important: How to use this book to study for the exam.

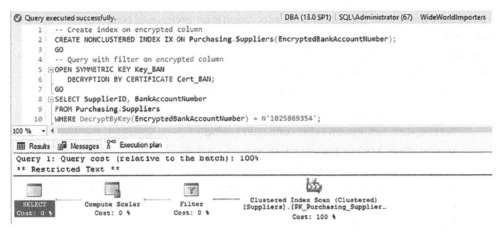

```
  Query executed successfully.                    DBA (13.0 SP1)   SQL\Administrator (67)   WideWorldImporters
  1    -- Create index on encrypted column
  2    CREATE NONCLUSTERED INDEX IX ON Purchasing.Suppliers(EncryptedBankAccountNumber);
  3    GO
  4    -- Query with filter on encrypted column
  5  ⊟OPEN SYMMETRIC KEY Key_BAN
  6      DECRYPTION BY CERTIFICATE Cert_BAN;
  7    GO
  8  ⊟SELECT SupplierID, BankAccountNumber
  9    FROM Purchasing.Suppliers
 10    WHERE DecryptByKey(EncryptedBankAccountNumber) = N'1025869354';

100 %  ▼ ◀

  ▦ Results   ▨ Messages   ⚇ Execution plan
  Query 1: Query cost (relative to the batch): 100%
  ** Restricted Text **

                                                    Clustered Index Scan (Clustered)
   SELECT         Compute Scalar        Filter       [Suppliers].[PK_Purchasing_Supplier…
   Cost: 0 %       Cost: 0 %          Cost: 0 %              Cost: 100 %
```

FIGURE 1-4 Execution plan for search on encrypted, indexed column

---

NEED MORE REVIEW?   EXTENSIBLE KEY MANAGEMENT (EKM)

SQL Server's EKM enables third party EKM/HSM vendors to integrate the solutions with the database engine. This allows you to store both asymmetric keys and symmetric keys in the EKM solution, taking advantage of advanced capabilities such as key aging and key rotation. For more information on SQL Server's EKM visit *https://docs.microsoft.com/en-us/sql/relational-databases/security/encryption/extensible-key-management-ekm*.

SQL Server can take advantage of Microsoft's EKM solution in Azure. The SQL Server Connector for Microsoft Azure Key Vault enables encryption within the database engine to use the Azure Key Vault service. For more information visit *https://docs.microsoft.com/en-us/sql/relational-databases/security/encryption/extensible-key-management-using-azure-key-vault-sql-server*.

Implement Always Encrypted

Always Encrypted (AE) is a new feature in SQL Server 2016 that allows you encrypt both data at rest and data in flight. This differentiates it from column-level encryption and transparent database encryption, which we will look at in the next section. Perhaps its most important capability is its ability to secure the data with your database outside of the database engine in the client application. This effectively means that the database administrator can no longer get access to the encrypted data within any database because the keys needed for decryption are kept and controlled outside of their domain.

AE was designed so that encryption and decryption of the data happens transparently at the driver level, which minimizes the changes that have to be made to existing applications. However, existing applications will have to be changed to leverage AE. AE's primary use case is to separate the duties of the database administrator from your application administrators. It can be used where both the data and the application is on-premise, or both are in the cloud. But it really shines where the data is in the cloud and the application is on-premise. In this use case the cloud database administrators will not be able to access your sensitive data. The data remains until it is decrypted by your client application, that you control!

At a high level the AE architecture works as shown in Figure 1-5:

1. The client application issues a parameterized query. It uses the new Column Encryption Setting=Enabled; option in the connection string.

2. The enhanced ADO.NET driver interrogates the database engine using the [sp_describe_parameter_encryption] system stored procedure to determine which parameters target encrypted columns. For each parameter that will require encrypting the driver retrieves the encryption algorithm and other information that will be used during the encryption phase

3. The driver uses the Column Master Key (CMK) to encrypt the parameter values before sending the ciphertext to the database engine.

4. The database engine retrieves the result set, attaching the appropriate encryption metadata to any encrypted columns, and sends it back to the client application. The data is encrypted both at rest within the database and in flight from the database engine to the client application.

5. The client application's driver decrypts any encrypted columns in the result set and returns the plaintext values to the application.

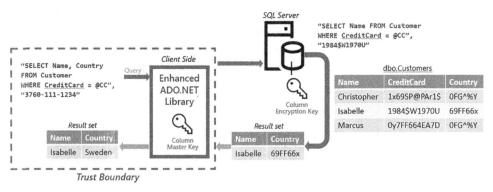

FIGURE 1-5 Always Encrypted architecture

> **NEED MORE REVIEW?** **SP_DESCRIBE_PARAMETER_ENCRYPTION**
>
> The [sp_describe_parameter_encryption] system stored procedure analyses the specified query and its parameters to determine which parameters correspond to database columns that are protected by AE. It is used by the database engine to return the encryption metadata for the parameters that correspond to encrypted columns. For more information visit *https://docs.microsoft.com/en-us/sql/relational-databases/system-stored-procedures/sp-describe-parameter-encryption-transact-sql*.

AE supports the following two types of encryption:

- **Deterministic** Deterministic encryption uses a method that always generates the same ciphertext for any given plaintext value.
    - It allows for the transparent retrieval of data through equality comparisons. Point lookups, equality joins, grouping and indexing are all supported through deterministic encryption.
    - With deterministic encryption a BINARY2 collation, such as Latin1_General_BIN2, must be used for character columns.
    - Users might be able to guess encrypted columns values for columns with a small domain of values, such as an example of the[Gender] or [State] fields.
- **Randomized** With randomized encryption, different ciphertext will be generated for the same plaintext. This makes randomized encryption much more secure than deterministic encryption.
    - Effectively no search/comparison operations are allowed.
    - Use randomized encryption for columns that you want to retrieve.

Being a first release technology in SQL Server 2016, AE has a number of limitations:

- Only the AEAD_AES_256_CBC_HMAC_SHA_256 encryption algorithm is supported.
- The following data types are not supported:
    - FILESTREAM
    - GEOGRAPHY
    - GEOMETRY
    - HIERARCHYID
    - IMAGE
    - NTEXT
    - ROWVERSION
    - SQL_VARIANT
    - TEXT
    - TIMESTAMP
    - XML
- You cannot alter a column and encrypt it. You must add a new column and add/import the data. SQL Server Management Studio supports such functionality.
- Queries can perform equality comparison on columns encrypted using deterministic encryption.
    - All other operations (like greater/less than, pattern matching using the LIKE operator, or arithmetical operations) are not supported.
- Queries on columns encrypted by randomized encryption cannot perform operations on those columns.

- Indexing columns encrypted using randomized encryption is not supported.
- Temporal tables cannot include encrypted columns.
- Triggers may fail if they reference encrypted columns.
- Queries must be passed with properly typed parameters, such as SqlCommand and SqlParameter.
- Ad-Hoc queries against encrypted data will raise an exception.
- Only ADO.NET, through the .NET 4.6 framework is supported.
  - The initial release only supported the SQL Server client driver. Support for ODBC and JDBC will released later.
- Change Data Capture (CDC) does not work on encrypted columns.
  - Change tracking is supported, although it only tracks changes of encrypted values.
- Replication is not officially supported.
  - Availability Groups and Log Shipping is supported.
- Performance will be potentially impacted. Expect performance to be significantly slower compared to non-encrypted inserts and updates.
  - More space will be consumed by encrypted columns when compared to unencrypted columns. Compressions benefits will be minimal.

AE uses the following two types of keys:

- **Column Master Key (CMK)**   The CMK is used to protect the keys used to encrypt the column encryption keys.
  - CMKs must be stored in a trusted key store such as the Azure Key Vault, Windows Certificate Store, or Hardware Security Modules (HSMs). More information can be found at *https://docs.microsoft.com/en-us/sql/relational-databases/security/encryption/create-and-store-column-master-keys-always-encrypted.*
  - The CMKs need to be accessible by client applications that will encrypt or decrypt data.
  - Information about the CMKs, including their location is stored in the database's [sys]. [column_master_keys] system catalog view.
- **Column Encryption Key (CEK)**   The CEK is used to encrypt sensitive data stored in table's columns.
  - All values in a column can be encrypted using a single CEK.
  - You should store column encryption keys in a secure/trusted location for backup.
  - Each CEK can have 2 encrypted values from 2 CMKs to allow master key rotation. Rotating AE keys is a complicated process that you can get5 more information on at *https://docs.microsoft.com/en-us/sql/relational-databases/security/encryption/rotate-always-encrypted-keys-using-powershell.*
  - Encrypted values of column encryption keys are stored in the [sys].[column_encryption_key_values] system catalog views.

6. In the Summary page of the Always Encrypted Wizard you can review the summary of your configuration, as shown in Figure 1-11. Select Finish.

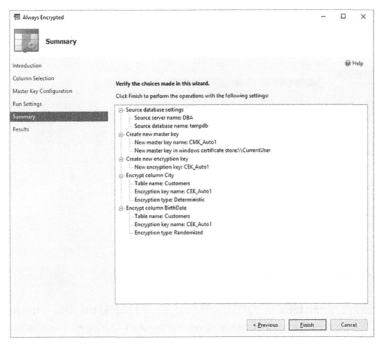

FIGURE 1-11 Always Encrypted Wizard

7. Once the Always Encrypted Wizard completes its task, review the summary information, as shown in Figure 1-12, and click on close.

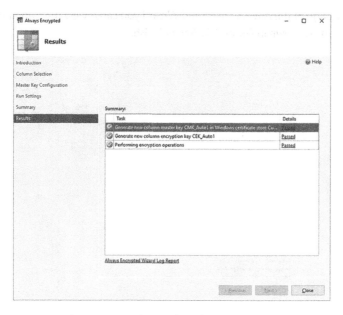

FIGURE 1-12 Always Encrypted Wizard Results page

If you query the encrypted table in SQL Server Management Studio the data in the AE en-crypted columns will be shown as ciphertext, as shown in Figure 1-13. You may notice that four customers have the same ciphertext for the [City] field. This is because they all live in the same city, and we used deterministic encryption. This highlights the potential vulnerability of using deterministic encryption.

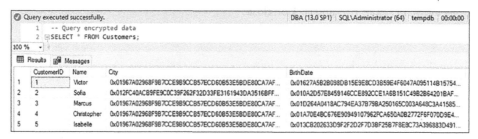

FIGURE 1-13 Always Encrypted column ciphertext

To transparently query the AE encrypted columns in SQL Server Management Studio you can use the **column encryption setting = enabled** connection string parameter as shown in Figure 1-14.

Troubleshoot encryption errors

Troubleshooting encryption errors can be difficult due to the inherent complexity of encryption architectures and the multiple actors involved. Performing a root cause analysis might require you to examine your SQL Server instances, client computers, Active Directory Domain Services, (ADDS), Windows operating system, or even hardware.

The root cause for encryption errors can included wrong or changed passwords, missing or expired certificates, SQL Server configuration being changed, encryption algorithm issues, time not being synchronized, key length, password complexity, EKM issues and a plethora of other problems.

When troubleshooting encryption errors, examine the following potential sources for error messages:

- **Error log**   SQL Server's error log should generally be your first port of call.
- **Windows event logs**   The Windows application, security or system event logs will also generally have useful information that you can leverage in your troubleshooting efforts.
- **sys.asymmetric_keys**   This DMV returns information about asymmetric keys. Pay attention to the encryption algorithm being used and how the asymmetric key was encrypted (master key, password, or service master key).
- **sys.certificates**   This system catalog view will have more information about the certificates within the database, including their issuer, and the expiry date.
- **sys.column_encryption_keys**   Returns information about column encryption keys (CEKs) created with the CREATE COLUMN ENCRYPTION KEY statement.
- **sys.column_encryption_key_values**   This DMV returns information about encrypted values of column encryption keys (CEKs) created with either the CREATE COLUMN EN-CRYPTION KEY or the ALTER COLUMN ENCRYPTION KEY (Transact-SQL) statement.
- **sys.column_master_keys**   Returns a row for each database master key added by using the CREATE MASTER KEY statement. Each row represents a single column master key (CMK).
- **sys.crypt_properties**   This is a system catalog view that returns each cryptographic property associated with a securable.
- **sys.cryptographic_providers**   Another system catalog view that returns information about each registered cryptographic provider.

- **sys.dm_database_encryption_keys**   Another important DMV for troubleshooting encryption problems as discussed earlier in this section.

- **sys.key_encryptions**   This system catalog view contains a row for each symmetric key encryption specified by using the ENCRYPTION BY clause of the CREATE SYMMETRIC KEY statement.

- **sys.dm_exec_connections**   The [sys].[dm_exec_connections] DMV will have information about each current connection being made to the database engine. It contains the [encrypt_option] column, describing whether encryption is enabled for a particular connection.

- **sys.openkeys**   This system catalog view returns information about encryption keys that are open in the current session.

- **sys.security_policies**   Returns a row for each security policy in the database.

- **sys.symmetric_keys**   This DMV returns information about symmetric keys. Again, pay attention to the encryption algorithm being used.

When writing exam items you might look at issues caused by trying to restore a TDE-enabled database on another server, or issues caused by key rotation.

If you get a difficult exam question on troubleshooting encryption errors, mark the question for review and move on. Avoid spending too much time on any one question so you can get through the entire exam. Your exam technique is just as important as your knowledge of SQL Server.

Skill 1.2 Configure data access and permissions

We will now examine how you give users access to the databases contained within your SQL Server environment. Given SQL Server's history, there are multiple ways in which you can grant or deny users access to your databases. You do not have to use all of the techniques that will be covered here. A good approach with security modelling is to keep it simple.

In examining Skill 1.2 we will take a layered approach. Initially we will have a look at how you can grant users login access to your SQL Server environment and how you can make them a member of roles at the server level that have a number of implied permissions. Once a user can connect to your SQL Server instance they will then need to be granted access to your databases. Each database has its own set of roles that users can be a member of and we will examine what permissions those roles have. We will also examine how you can control access to individual objects within your database. Finally we will look at two new features that were introduced in SQL Server 2016 to further help you control access to your data: row-level security and dynamic data masking.

This skill represents a massive domain for the exam. In the exam you might get asked a question that requires a knowledge of the syntax to control security within SQL Server. You might get asked an exam question that will test your knowledge of the implied and explicit permission that will need to be given to a user to achieve a particular requirement. Pay close attention to the new features introduced in SQL Server 2016 and specifically what they protect against.

This section covers how to:

- Create and maintain users
- Create and maintain custom roles
- Manage database object permissions
- Configure row-level security
- Configure dynamic data masking
- Configure user options for Azure SQL Database

Create and maintain users

Before a user can access a database within SQL Server you will need to grant them a login and authorize them to access the appropriate databases. Although you can give access to individual objects in a database, it is easier to take advantage of database roles. In this section, we will go through the initial process of creating and maintaining users.

SQL Server supports the following two different types of logins:

- **SQL Authentication**   With SQL authentication login names and password are stored by the database engine in the [master] system database. Users wanting to connect to SQL Server will explicitly need to provide their login name and password. Connections formed using SQL authentication are also referred to as non-trusted connections.

- **Windows Authentication**   With Windows accounts are explicitly given permission to log into SQL Server. When users log into Active Directory (AD) or Windows and try to connect to SQL Server they will be implicitly granted access. Such connections are also referred to as trusted connections.

When SQL Server is set up you configure whether you want to want the database engine to support only Windows authentication or both Windows and SQL authentication. This can be reconfigured at any time, although a restart will be required for the change to take effect.

Figure 1-18 shows the options available for creating a new login for SQL Server.

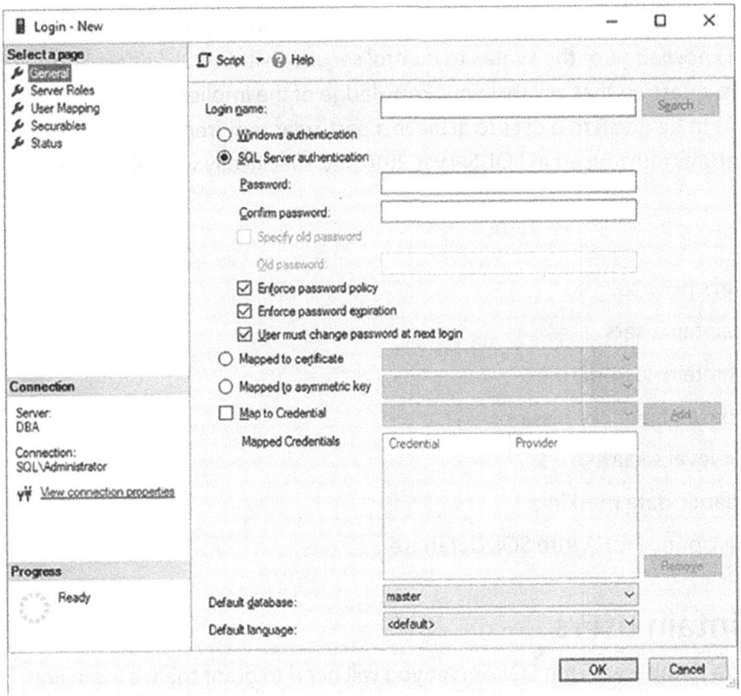

FIGURE 1-18 Creating a new login

Use the following syntax to create a login:

```
CREATE LOGIN login_name { WITH <option_list1> | FROM <sources> }
<option_list1> ::=
    PASSWORD = { 'password' | hashed_password HASHED } [ MUST_CHANGE ]
    [ , <option_list2> [ ,... ] ]


<option_list2> ::=
    SID = sid
    | DEFAULT_DATABASE = database
    | DEFAULT_LANGUAGE = language
    | CHECK_EXPIRATION = { ON | OFF}
    | CHECK_POLICY = { ON | OFF}
    | CREDENTIAL = credential_name


<sources> ::=
    WINDOWS [ WITH <windows_options>[ ,... ] ]
    | CERTIFICATE certname
    | ASYMMETRIC KEY asym_key_name


<windows_options> ::=
    DEFAULT_DATABASE = database
    | DEFAULT_LANGUAGE = language
```

Listing 1-9 shows examples of how to create a login.

LISTING 1-9 Creating logins

```
USE master;
-- Create Windows login
CREATE LOGIN [SQL\Marcus] FROM WINDOWS
GO
-- Create SQL login
CREATE LOGIN Isabelle
    WITH PASSWORD = 'A2c3456$#',
    CHECK_EXPIRATION = ON,
    CHECK_POLICY = ON;
GO
-- Create login from a certificate
CREATE CERTIFICATE ChristopherCertificate
    WITH SUBJECT = 'Christopher certificate in master database',
    EXPIRY_DATE = '30/01/2114';
GO
CREATE LOGIN Christopher FROM CERTIFICATE ChristopherCertificate;
GO
```

EXAM TIP

For the exam make sure you understand orphaned users, how to use the sp_change_users_login system stored procedure, and how to troubleshoot orphaned users. For more information visit: *https://docs.microsoft.com/en-us/sql/sql-server/failover-clusters/troubleshoot-orphaned-users-sql-server.*

EXAM TIP

Introduced in SQL Server 2012, contained databases were designed to solve a number of problems with moving databases between SQL Server instances. This feature has never evolved from SQL Server 2012. However, you might still get an exam question on it. For more information about contained databases visit: *https://docs.microsoft.com/en-us/sql/relational-databases/databases/contained-databases* and *https://docs.microsoft.com/en-us/sql/relational-databases/security/contained-database-users-making-your-database-portable.*

SQL Server supports the ability of grouping logins into a role, against which permissions can be set. The following types of roles are supported:

- **Server Roles** Server roles exist at the server scope and consequently allow you to control permissions at the database engine level.

- **Database roles** Database roles exist at the database scope and help control permissions within only that database.

> **NEED MORE REVIEW? CROSS-DATABASE OWNERSHIP CHAINING**
>
> Although cross-database ownership chaining is not recommended, you should make sure you understand the concepts involved for the exam. For more information visit: *https://docs. microsoft.com/en-us/dotnet/framework/data/adonet/sql/enabling-cross-database-access-in-sql-server.*

You can add logins to fixed server roles, which will grant the user a number of server-wide security privileges. The privileges will depend on what fixed server role you use. Table 1-2 shows the fixed server roles available in SQL Server, along with their description.

TABLE 1-2 Fixed server roles

Fixed Server Role	Description
dbcreator	Members can create, alter, drop, and restore any database.
bulkadmin	Members can run the BULK INSERT statement
diskadmin	Members can manage disk files.
processadmin	Members can end processes that are running in an instance of SQL Server.
public	Every login within SQL Server belongs to this fixed server role.
securityadmin	Members can manage logins and their properties, including resetting password for SQL Server logins. Members can GRANT, DENY, and REVOKE server-level permissions and database-level permissions if they have access to a database.
serveradmin	Members can change server-wide configuration options and shut down the server.
setupadmin	Members can add and remove linked servers by using Transact-SQL statements.
sysadmin	Members can perform any activity in the server

Figure 1-19 shows the permissions assigned to these fixed server roles: © Microsoft Corporation, SQL Server documentation, *https://docs.microsoft.com/en-us/sql/relational-databases/security/authentication-access/server-level-roles*.

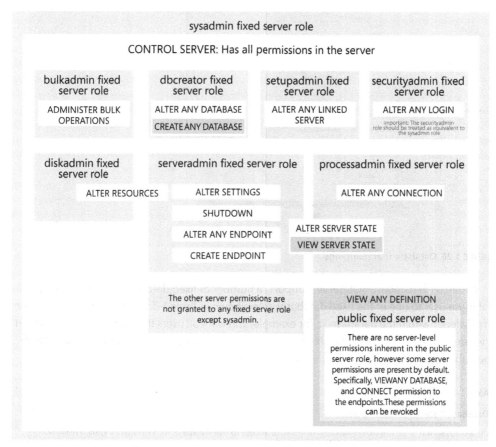

FIGURE 1-19 Fixed server role permissions

To give a login access to a database you need to create a user mapping between the login and the users within the database. Although you can have a different login name from a user name within the database, a best practice is to keep them identical. Figure 1-20 shows how you can create a database user account for a login in the User Mapping page of the Login Proper-ties dialog box.

FIGURE 1-20 Database user mappings

Within each database SQL Server supports a number of fixed database roles. By adding a database user to one of the fixed databases roles shown in Table 1-3, you grant them a number of privileges within the database. If, for example, you want all users that can log into SQL Server and connect to a database to be able to read all of the data within that database, you can add the public role to the [db_datareader] fixed database role.

TABLE 1-3 Fixed database roles

Database Role	Description
db_accessadmin	Members can add or remove access to the database for Windows logins, Windows groups, and SQL Server logins.
db_backupoperator	Members can back up the database.
db_datareader	Members can read all data from all user tables.
db_datawriter	Members can add, delete, or change data in all user tables.
db_ddladmin	Members can run any Data Definition Language (DDL) command in a database.
db_denydatareader	Members cannot read any data in the user tables within a database.
db_denydatawriter	Members cannot add, modify, or delete any data in the user tables within a database.
db_owner	Members can perform all configuration and maintenance activities on the database, and can also drop the database.
db_securityadmin	Members can modify role membership and manage permissions. Adding principals to this role could enable unintended privilege escalation.
public	Every user within the database belongs to this fixed database role. Consequently, it maintains the default permissions for all users within the database.

There are a number of additional database roles in the [msdb] system database, as shown in Table 1-4. Make sure you know what they do for the exam because you may get a question that asks which one of these roles needs to be granted for a particular administrative task.

TABLE 1-4 [msdb] roles

[msdb] Role	Description
db_ssisadmin db_ssisoperator db_ssisltduser	Members can administer and use SSIS.
dc_admin dc_operator dc_proxy	Members can administer and use the data collector.
PolicyAdministratorRole	Members can perform all configuration and maintenance activities on Policy-Based Management policies and conditions.
ServerGroupAdministratorRole ServerGroupReaderRole	Members can administer and use registered server groups.
dbm_monitor	Members can view database mirroring status, but not update it but not view or configure database mirroring events.

Listing 1-10 shows examples of how to create and maintain roles.

LISTING 1-10 Creating and maintaining roles

```
-- Add Windows login to fixed server role
USE master;
GO
ALTER SERVER ROLE sysadmin ADD MEMBER [SQL\Marcus]
GO
-- Add database user
USE [WideWorldImporters]
GO
CREATE USER [Isabelle] FOR LOGIN [Isabelle]
GO
-- Add database user to fixed database roles
ALTER ROLE [db_datareader] ADD MEMBER [Isabelle]
GO
ALTER ROLE [db_datawriter] ADD MEMBER [Isabelle]
GO
```

EXAM TIP

Make sure you remember the different fixed server-level and database-level roles and what permissions they give the user. The exam might ask you a question that requires you make a user a member of multiple roles.

Create and maintain custom roles

The permissions associated with the fixed server and databases roles we have looked at so far cannot be modified. They represent an easy way for you to quickly grant a set of permissions to users. For more complex requirements you will have to take advantage of custom roles.

SQL Server supports the following custom roles:

- **Application roles**   Introduced in SQL Server 7.0, application roles allow you to restrict user access to data based on the application that the user is using. Application roles allow the application to take over the responsibility of user authentication.

- **User-defined database roles**   These roles have been available with SQL Server since it was released on the Windows NT platform, although they used to be called groups before.

- **User-defined server roles**   These roles were introduced in the SQL Server 2012. They allow you to create a custom role at the server scope with a customized set or permissions. Server roles can be nested in scope.

> *MORE INFORMATION*   **APPLICATION ROLES**
>
> Although this is an old feature, there is a possibility that you might get asked a question on the exam about application roles. For more information on what application roles are and how to configure them using the [sp_setapprole] system stored procedure visit: *https://docs. microsoft.com/en-us/sql/relational-databases/security/authentication-access/application-roles* and *https://docs.microsoft.com/en-us/sql/relational-databases/system-stored-procedures/sp-setapprole-transact-sql.*

Figure 1-21 shows you how to create a new user-defined server role. The General page allows you to control which permissions are assigned to which securables. The Members page allows you to control which logins belong to the role. The Memberships page allows you to control which other server roles are a member of this role.

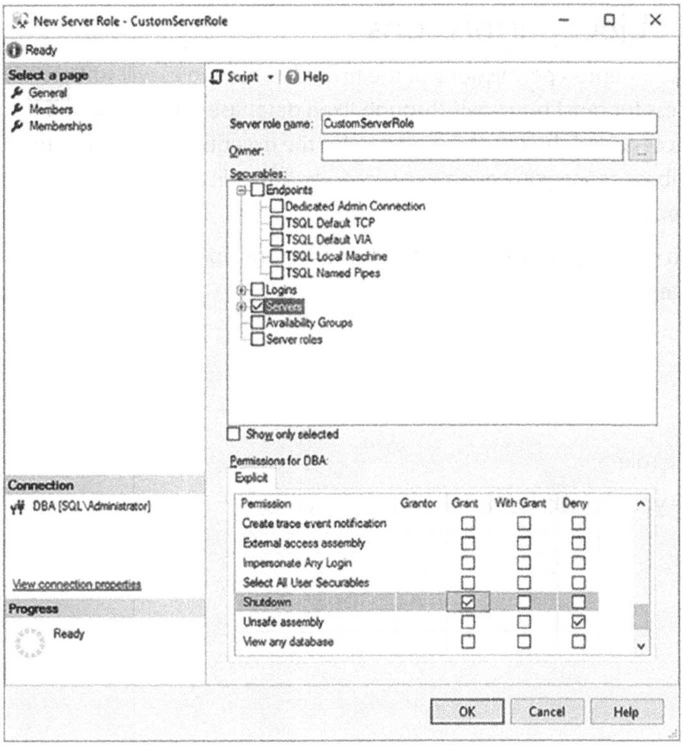

FIGURE 1-21 Creating new user defined server role

Listing 1-11 shows examples of how to a create user-defined server role.

LISTING 1-11 Creating and maintaining user-defined server roles

```
-- Create user-defined server role
USE master;
GO
CREATE SERVER ROLE CustomerServeRole
GO
-- Add members to user-defined server role
ALTER SERVER ROLE CustomerServeRole ADD MEMBER Christopher
ALTER SERVER ROLE processadmin ADD MEMBER CustomerServeRole
ALTER SERVER ROLE securityadmin ADD MEMBER CustomerServeRole
--
GRANT SHUTDOWN TO CustomerServeRole
GRANT VIEW SERVER STATE TO CustomerServeRole
GO
-- Deny control to logins
DENY CONTROL ON LOGIN::[NT SERVICE\SQLSERVERAGENT] TO CustomerServeRole
DENY CONTROL ON LOGIN::sa TO CustomerServeRole
DENY CONTROL ON LOGIN::[NT SERVICE\MSSQLSERVER] TO CustomerServeRole
DENY CONTROL ON LOGIN::[SQL\Administrator] TO CustomerServeRole
GO
```

Manage database object permissions

In a lot of cases leveraging the inherited permissions of the fixed database roles will suffice. So try to control security access for most principals through fixed database roles because it is then easier to manage that access, and then control security for the exceptions through other mechanisms. Within the database scope you have a very granular capability to control permission against all database objects.

Within a database you can control permissions for the following principals that we have, as looked at earlier in this chapter:

- Application role
- Database User
- Fixed database role
- User-defined database role
- At the database scope you can secure the following securables:
- Application role
- Assembly
- Asymmetric key
- Certificate
- Contract
- Fulltext catalog
- Fulltext stoplist
- Message type
- Remote Service Binding
- (Database) Role
- Route
- Schema
- Search property list
- Service
- Symmetric key
- User

Although schemas are mostly used in the industry to provide a namespace in a database, they also represent a container against which permissions can be controlled. At the schema scope you can secure the following securables:

- Type
- XML schema collection

- The following objects:
  - Aggregate
  - External Table
  - Function
  - Procedure
  - Queue
  - Synonym
  - Table
  - View

Use the following statements to control permissions against the securables:

- **GRANT** Grants permissions on a table, view, table-valued function, stored procedure, extended stored procedure, scalar function, aggregate function, service queue, or synonym.

- **DENY** Denies permissions on tables, views, table-valued functions, stored procedures, extended stored procedures, scalar functions, aggregate functions, service queues, and synonyms. A DENY takes precedence over all other permissions at the same object level.

- **REVOKE** Revokes permissions on a table, view, table-valued function, stored procedure, extended stored procedure, scalar function, aggregate function, service queue, or synonym.

Use the following statement to grant permissions to a database object:

```
GRANT <permission> [ ,...n ] ON
    [ OBJECT :: ][ schema_name ]. object_name [ ( column [ ,...n ] ) ]
    TO <database_principal> [ ,...n ]
    [ WITH GRANT OPTION ]
    [ AS <database_principal> ]

<permission> ::=
    ALL [ PRIVILEGES ] | permission [ ( column [ ,...n ] ) ]

<database_principal> ::=
        Database_user
    | Database_role
    | Application_role
    | Database_user_mapped_to_Windows_User
    | Database_user_mapped_to_Windows_Group
    | Database_user_mapped_to_certificate
    | Database_user_mapped_to_asymmetric_key
    | Database_user_with_no_login
```

The types of permissions that can be granted, denied, or revoked depends on the securable. Granting ALL is equivalent to granting all ANSI-SQL92 permissions applicable to the object as shown in Table 1-5.

TABLE 1-5 ALL permissions

Object	Permissions
Scalar function	EXECUTE, REFERENCES.
Stored procedure	EXECUTE.
Table	DELETE, INSERT, REFERENCES, SELECT, UPDATE.
Table-valued function	DELETE, INSERT, REFERENCES, SELECT, UPDATE.
View	DELETE, INSERT, REFERENCES, SELECT, UPDATE.

Figure 1-22 shows an example of how to configure object level permissions in SQL Server Management Studio. In this example the UPDATE and SELECT permissions have been granted to the [Sales].[Orders] table. Furthermore, the DELETE permission has been denied.

FIGURE 1-22 Configuring object level permissions

It is also possible to configure permissions at the column level in SQL Server as shown in Figure 1-23.

```
INSERT Wards VALUES( 1, N'Emergency');
INSERT Wards VALUES( 2, N'Maternity');
INSERT Wards VALUES( 3, N'Pediatrics');
GO
-- Insert patient data
INSERT Patients VALUES ( 1001, N'Victor', 101, 1, '20171217',  '20180326')
INSERT Patients VALUES ( 1002, N'Maria', 102, 1, '20171027',  '20180527')
INSERT Patients VALUES ( 1003, N'Nick', 107, 1, '20170507',  '20170611')
INSERT Patients VALUES ( 1004, N'Nina', 203, 2, '20170308',  '20171214')
INSERT Patients VALUES ( 1005, N'Larissa', 205, 2, '20170127',  '20170512')
INSERT Patients VALUES ( 1006, N'Marc', 301, 3, '20170131',  NULL)
INSERT Patients VALUES ( 1007, N'Sofia', 308, 3, '20170615',  '20170904')
GO
-- Inset nurses' duties
INSERT StaffDuties VALUES ( 101, 1, '20170101', '20171231')
INSERT StaffDuties VALUES ( 101, 2, '20180101', '20181231')
INSERT StaffDuties VALUES ( 102, 1, '20170101', '20170630')
INSERT StaffDuties VALUES ( 102, 2, '20170701', '20171231')
INSERT StaffDuties VALUES ( 102, 3, '20180101', '20181231')
-- Insert doctors' duties
INSERT StaffDuties VALUES ( 200, 1, '20170101', '20171231')
INSERT StaffDuties VALUES ( 200, 3, '20180101', '20181231')
INSERT StaffDuties VALUES ( 201, 1, '20170101', '20181231')
GO
-- Query patients
SELECT * FROM patients;
-- Query assignments
SELECT d.StaffID, StaffName, USER_NAME(DatabasePrincipalID) as DatabaseUser, WardID,
StartTime, EndTime
FROM StaffDuties d
INNER JOIN Staff s ON (s.StaffID = d.StaffID)
ORDER BY StaffID;
GO
-- Implement row level security
CREATE SCHEMA RLS;
GO
-- RLS predicate allows access to rows based on a user's role and assigned staff duties.
-- Because users have both SELECT and UPDATE permissions, we will use this function as a
-- filter predicate (filter which rows are accessible by SELECT and UPDATE queries) and
-- a block predicate after update (prevent user from updating rows to be outside of
-- visible range).
-- RLS predicate allows data access based on role and staff duties.
CREATE FUNCTION RLS.AccessPredicate(@Ward INT, @StartTime DATETIME, @EndTime DATETIME)
    RETURNS TABLE
    WITH SCHEMABINDING
AS
RETURN SELECT 1 AS Access
FROM dbo.StaffDuties AS d JOIN dbo.Staff AS s ON d.StaffId = s.StaffId
WHERE ( -- Nurses can only see patients who overlap with their wing assignments
    IS_MEMBER('Nurse') = 1
    AND s.DatabasePrincipalId = DATABASE_PRINCIPAL_ID()
    AND @Ward = d.WardID
    AND (d.EndTime >= @StartTime AND d.StartTime <= ISNULL(@EndTime, GETDATE()))
)
OR ( -- Doctors can see all patients
```

```
        IS_MEMBER('Doctor') = 1
);
GO
-- RLS filter predicate filters which data is seen by SELECT and UPDATE queries
-- RLS block predicate after update prevents updating data outside of visible range
CREATE SECURITY POLICY RLS.PatientsSecurityPolicy
ADD FILTER PREDICATE RLS.AccessPredicate(WardID, StartTime, EndTime) ON dbo.Patients,
ADD BLOCK PREDICATE RLS.AccessPredicate(WardID, StartTime, EndTime) ON dbo.Patients
AFTER UPDATE;
GO
-- Test RLS
-- Impersonate a nurse
EXECUTE ('SELECT * FROM patients;') AS USER = 'NurseIsabelle';
-- Only 3 patient records seen
GO
-- Impersonate a doctor
EXECUTE ('SELECT * FROM patients;') AS USER = 'DoctorChristopher';
-- All 7 patient records returned
GO
-- Attempt by nurse to move patient to another ward
EXECUTE ('UPDATE patients SET WardID = 1 WHERE patientId = 1006;') AS USER =
'NurseIsabelle'
-- Filtered, consequently 0 rows affected
EXECUTE ('UPDATE patients SET WardID = 3 WHERE patientId = 1001;') AS USER =
'NurseIsabelle'
-- Blocked from changing wing, with following error:
/*
Msg 33504, Level 16, State 1, Line 156
The attempted operation failed because the target object 'Hospital.dbo.Patients' has
a block predicate that conflicts with this operation. If the operation is performed
on a view, the block predicate might be enforced on the underlying table. Modify the
operation to target only the rows that are allowed by the block predicate.
The statement has been terminated.
*/
```

As discussed earlier in this section, the TVF used by RLS will introduce an overhead to your queries. Figure 1-24 shows the execution plan for the SELECT * FROM patients query from Listing 1-13.

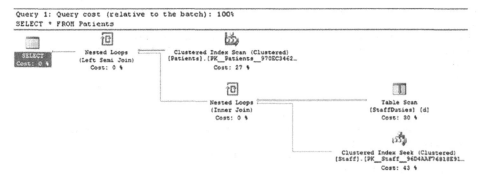

FIGURE 1-24 Row level security execution plan overhead

Configure dynamic data masking

Dynamic data masking (DDM) is the last of the three major security features added in SQL Server 2016. DDM helps prevent unauthorized users from accessing data that is deemed sensitive. It is important to understand that it is a masking technology and not an encryption technology, so the data in the database is not changed. Designated fields in the result sets of queries are masked. As the mask is added to the schema of the table, DDM is completely transparent to the application and requires no changes. It also means that users can use inference or brute-force techniques to deduce the data.

DDM is a powerful new feature that can be used in a number of use cases including:

- Masking sensitive data in production environments. Examples include:
    - Call center staff not being able to see customer's credit card details. In this example, a masking rule could mask all but the first 4 and last 3 digits of the credit card.
    - All sensitive information being masked from a contractor has been engaged to tune the performance of the database solution.
- Masking sensitive data in development and testing environments where production databases have been restored is another example. Again, developers and testers should not be privy to personally identifiable information (PII) such as email addresses, phone numbers, and addresses.

DDM supports the following types of masks:

- **Custom string**   A masking method that shows the first and last letters and adds a custom padding string in the middle.
- **Default**   Full masking depending on the field's data type:
    - For binary data types use a single byte of ASCII value 0 (binary, varbinary, image).
    - For date and time data types use 01.01.1900 00:00:00.0000000 (date, datetime2, datetime, datetimeoffset, smalldatetime, time).
    - For numeric data types use a zero value (bigint, bit, decimal, int, money, numeric, smallint, smallmoney, tinyint, float, real).
    - For string data types, use XXXX or fewer Xs if the size of the field is less than 4 characters (char, nchar, varchar, nvarchar, text, ntext).
- **Email**   Masks email addresses by showing only the first letter and a constant .com suffix in the following format: aXXXX@XXXX.com.
- **Random**   A masking method that will substitute a random value within a specified range for a numeric type.

Masking rules cannot be defined for the following:

- Always Encrypted encrypted columns.
- COLUMN_SET or a sparse column that is part of a column set.
- FILESTREAM data.
- Computed column:

- If a computed column depends on a masked column the computed column will return masked data.

- A column with data masking cannot be a key for a FULLTEXT index.

Listing 1-14 shows an example of where the email address and phone number have been masked for a non-privileged user.

LISTING 1-14 Implementing DDM

```
USE WideWorldImporters
GO
-- Create non-privileged user
CREATE USER NonPrivilegedUser WITHOUT LOGIN
GO
ALTER ROLE db_datareader ADD MEMBER NonPrivilegedUser
GO
-- Mask email address
ALTER TABLE Application.People
ALTER COLUMN EmailAddress ADD MASKED WITH (FUNCTION = 'EMAIL()')
-- Mask phone number
ALTER TABLE Application.People
ALTER COLUMN PhoneNumber ADD MASKED WITH (FUNCTION = 'PARTIAL(0,"XXX-XXX-",4)')
GO
-- Query table as dbo
SELECT TOP 5 FullName, PhoneNumber, FaxNumber, EmailAddress FROM Application.People;
-- Query table as non-privileged user
EXECUTE AS USER = 'NonPrivilegedUser';
SELECT TOP 5 FullName, PhoneNumber, FaxNumber, EmailAddress FROM Application.People;
REVERT;
GO
```

Figure 1-25 shows the result set for the query executed by the dbo and non-privileged user in Listing 1-14:

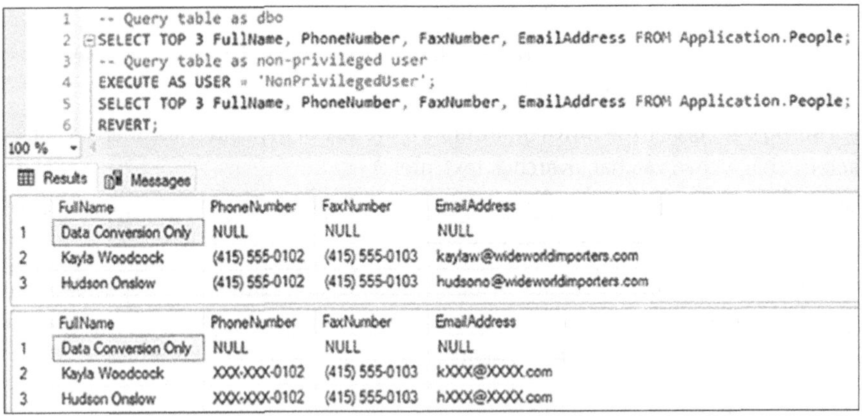

FIGURE 1-25 Dynamic data masking result set

Configure user options for Azure SQL Database

Within Azure SQL Database there multiple security levels. First, there are firewall rules limiting connectivity by IP address. Note that the Azure SQL Database service is only available through TCP port 1433. Second, there are authentication mechanisms that require users to prove their identity. Finally there are authorization mechanisms limiting users to specific actions and data. Although, it is similar to what we have covered so far in Skill 1.2, there are some subtle differences.

> **NEED MORE REVIEW?** **AZURE SQL DATABASE SERVER-LEVEL AND DATABASE-LEVEL FIREWALL RULES**
>
> The Azure SQL Database service helps protect your data through firewalls that prevent all access to your database server until you specify IP addresses have permission. To learn about how to grant access through the firewall visit: *https://docs.microsoft.com/en-us/azure/sql-database/sql-database-firewall-configure.*

Azure SQL Database supports the following types of authentication:

- **SQL Authentication**   Requires a user name and password combination.
- **Azure Active Directory Authentication**   Uses identities managed by the Azure Active Directory. Both managed and integrated domains are supported.

To use Azure Active Directory Authentication you need to create another server admin called the **Azure AD admin**, which is allowed to administer Azure AD users and groups. This administrator will be able to perform all operations that a regular server administrator can.

Azure SQL Database will close connections that have been idle for more than 30 minutes and the connection will have to login again. As a safety precaution, continuously active connections will require reauthorization at least every 10 hours. The database engine triggers the reauthorization process by using the originally submitted password. No end user input is required.

Azure SQL Database potentially has the following two administrative accounts, depending on how you have configured it:

- **Server admin**   A Server admin login is required when you create an Azure SQL Database. This account connects using SQL Server authentication. Only one of these accounts can exist.
- **Azure AD admin**   One Azure Active Directory account, either an individual or security group account, can be optionally configured as an administrator. It is required if you want to use Azure AD accounts to connect to Azure SQL Database.

Azure SQL Database has the following additional database roles in the virtual master system database that are not relevant in the on-premise version:

- **dbmanager**   Members of this role will be able to create and delete databases. After creating a database, the user becomes the owner of that database and be able to connect to the database as a dbo. Members of the dbmanager role do not necessarily have permission to access databases that they do not own.

- **loginmanager**   Members of this role will be able to create and delete logins in the virtual master system database.

NEED MORE REVIEW?   **AZURE SQL DATABASE SECURITY TUTORIAL**

If you have not worked with Azure SQL Database and want to familiarize yourself with Azure SQL Database security for the exam, you can go through the tutorial located at: *https://docs. microsoft.com/en-us/azure/sql-database/sql-database-security-tutorial*.

Skill 1.3: Configure auditing

The final section in this security chapter examines the skills required to implement auditing in SQL Server. Auditing is an important capability in the security context. It helps you understand database activity,it maintains regulatory compliance, and it provides insights into discrepancies or anomalies that might indicate business concerns or suspected security violations.

In Skill 1.3 we will have a look at how you configure, query, and manage auditing with SQL Server via its native auditing capabilities. We will then look at the equivalent capabilities within Azure SQL Database.

For the exam, make sure you understand the capabilities and limitations of SQL Server's native auditing. In some use cases it will not be sufficient to meet your auditing requirements. You might also have to take advantage of other technology such as Change Data Capture (CDC), Change Tracking, Data Definition Language (DDL) triggers, Data Manipulation Language (DML) triggers, logon triggers, SQL Trace, and related technologies. So you also need to understand these technologies' capabilities.

This section covers how to:

- Configure an audit on SQL Server
- Query the SQL Server audit log
- Manage a SQL Server audit
- Configure an Azure SQL Database audit
- Analyze audit logs and reports from Azure SQL Database

Configure an audit on SQL Server

Auditing has been available since SQL Server 2008 and allows you to track and log specific events at the database engine or database level. Auditing was designed to have a minimal impact on the database engine. Consequently, auditing leverages extended events and can only write to high performance targets such as files and the Windows event logs.

Potentially, there are a lot of different events in SQL Server that you can audit. There are also potentially governmental or industry standards that you might have to comply with for governance reasons. SQL Server audit simply provides the tools that enable you to enable, store, and view audits configured at the database engine or database scope.

EXAM TIP

SQL Server still supported Common Criteria compliance and the deprecated C2 audit mode. Although you should no longer be using these in the field, make sure you understand then for the exam. You can find more information about Common Criteria compliance at: *https://docs.microsoft.com/en-us/sql/database-engine/configure-windows/common-criteria-compliance-enabled-server-configuration-option*. For C2 level auditing visit: *https://docs.microsoft.com/en-us/sql/database-engine/configure-windows/c2-audit-mode-server-configuration-option*.

An audit is made up of a number of different elements that you will need to configure:

- **SQL Server audit**   Represents a collection of server and database level events that you want to explicitly audit. You can have multiple audits per SQL Server instance. When you create a SQL Server audit you will need to specify the following properties:

  - A name for the audit.

  - The audit destination that can be a file or the Windows security or application log. For the file destination you can configure a number of properties including the maximum file size, maximum rollover files, and whether you want to reserve disk space. To minimize overhead SQL Server audit writes to text files that can quickly grow in size depending on how many events you have configured to be audited.

  - The action that you can take if the database engine cannot write to the audit destination. Valid actions are: continue, fail operation, or shut down the SQL Server instance.

- **Server Audit Specification**   The server audit specification allows you to control which server-level events will be written to the SQL Server audit. These events are actually server-level action groups that can be raised by extended events. You can only have one server audit specification per SQL Server audit.

- **Database Audit Specification**   The database audit specification collects database-level audit actions potentially raised by extended events. Again, you can only have one server audit specification per SQL Server audit.

You can also audit the actions in the auditing process. These can be at either the server or database level. For a complete list of server-level, database-level, and audit-level action groups visit: *https://docs.microsoft.com/en-us/sql/relational-databases/security/auditing/sql-server-audit-action-groups-and-actions*. You will not need to remember them for the exam. However it might be worth your while to familiarize yourself with the types of events that can potentially be audited.

NOTE **AUDITING FEATURES IN SQL SERVER EDITIONS**

When SQL Server 2016 was released Standard Edition only supported basic (server-level) auditing. Enterprise Edition supporting enhanced (server-level and database-level) auditing. However, with the release of SQL Server 2016 Service Pack 1 Standard Edition also supports enhanced auditing. For more information visit: *https://www.linkedin.com/pulse/microsoft-changes-feature-support-between-editions-sql-victor-isakov*.

To configure auditing in SQL Server, perform the following steps:

1. Open SQL Server Management Studio, connect to your SQL Server instance, and expand the Security folder.

2. Right click on the Audits folder and select New Audit.

3. Configure the audit properties as shown in Figure 1-26:

   ■ Audit name

   ■ File destination

FIGURE 1-26 SQL Server audit

4. Right-click on the audit that you have just created and enable it.

5. Right-click on the Server Audit Specifications folder and select New Server Audit Specification.

6. Configure the server audit specification to audit the following action types as shown in Figure 1-27:

    ■ FAILED_LOGIN_GROUP

    ■ SUCCESSFUL_LOGIN_GROUP

    ■ LOGOUT_GROUP

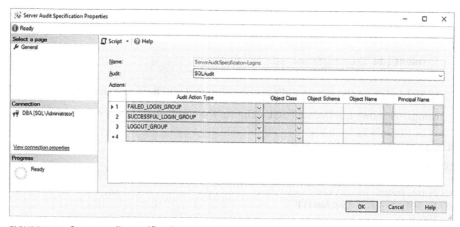

FIGURE 1-27 Server audit specification properties

7. Right click on the server audit specification that you have just created and enable it.

8. Expand the security folder in database that you want to audit.

9. Right-click on the Database Audit Specification folder and select New Database Audit Specification.

10. Configure the database audit specification to audit the following action types as shown in Figure 1-28:

    ■ SELECT on table for a specific database user

    ■ UPDATE on table for the public role

    ■ SUCCESSFUL_LOGIN_GROUP

    ■ BACKUP_RESTORE_GROUP

    ■ AUDIT_CHANGE_GROUP

    ■ USER_CHANGE_PASSWORD_GROUP

    ■ DATABASE_PERMISSION_CHANGE_GROUP

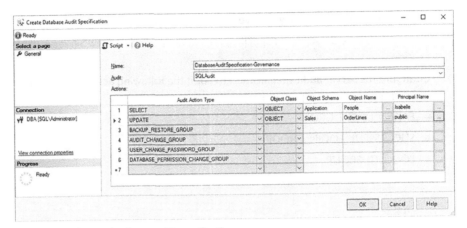

FIGURE 1-28 Create database audit specification

11. Right-click on the server audit specification that you have just created and enable it.

Listing 1-15 shows the Transact-SQL script for the audit we have just created.

LISTING 1-15 Implementing auditing

```
USE [master]
GO
-- Create audit
CREATE SERVER AUDIT [SQLAudit]
TO FILE (
    FILEPATH = N'C:\SQLAudit\',
    MAXSIZE = 4096 MB,
    MAX_ROLLOVER_FILES = 2147483647,
    RESERVE_DISK_SPACE = OFF
)
WITH (
    QUEUE_DELAY = 1000,
    ON_FAILURE = CONTINUE,
AUDIT_GUID = '4ab952ef-97c4-4e02-8a9e-1b4324499705'
)
ALTER SERVER AUDIT [SQLAudit] WITH (STATE = ON)
GO
-- Create server audit specification
CREATE SERVER AUDIT SPECIFICATION [ServerAuditSpecification-Logins]

FOR SERVER AUDIT [SQLAudit]
ADD (FAILED_LOGIN_GROUP),
ADD (SUCCESSFUL_LOGIN_GROUP),
ADD (LOGOUT_GROUP)
WITH (STATE = ON)
GO
-- Create database audit specification
USE [WideWorldImporters]
GO
CREATE DATABASE AUDIT SPECIFICATION [DatabaseAuditSpecification-Governance]
FOR SERVER AUDIT [SQLAudit]
```

```
ADD (BACKUP_RESTORE_GROUP),
ADD (AUDIT_CHANGE_GROUP),
ADD (DATABASE_PERMISSION_CHANGE_GROUP),
ADD (USER_CHANGE_PASSWORD_GROUP),
ADD (UPDATE ON OBJECT::[Sales].[OrderLines] BY [public]),
ADD (SELECT ON OBJECT::[Application].[People] BY [Isabelle])
WITH (STATE = ON)
GO
```

Query the SQL Server audit log

As we saw in the previous section, SQL Server audits can be written to either a binary file or the Windows Event log. In most cases your destination will be the binary file as opposed to the Windows Event log, because it is self-contained and sufficient for most use cases.

SQL Server Management Studio has the capability of viewing the audit logs. Figure 1-29 shows an example of a user attempting to perform a backup of the database. Note that the user did not have the appropriate permissions and the backup operation failed. But the SQL Server audit has captured their attempt in any case.

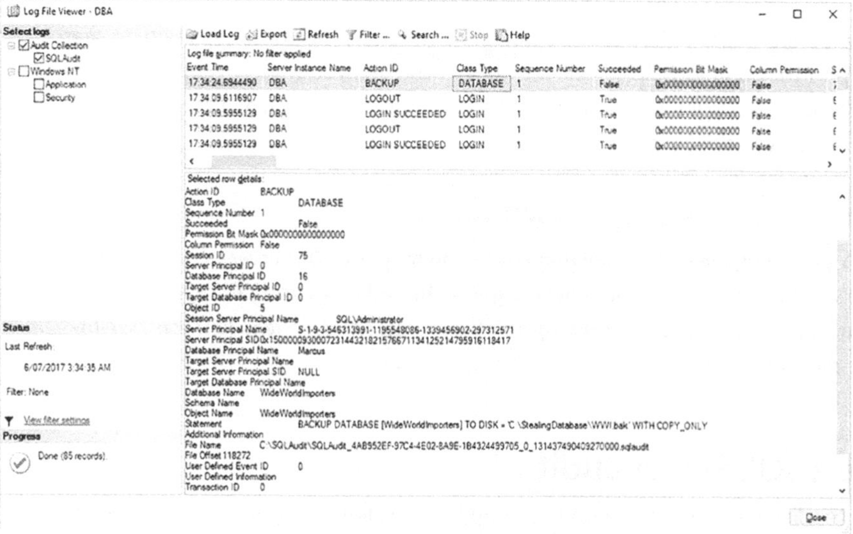

FIGURE 1-29 BACKUP operation audited

Figure 1-30 shows an example of a user modifying a column with the table that we set up auditing against in the previous section. The update operation has succeeded in this case. Note that the audit has not captured the state of the data before and after the update operation. Likewise, auditing select statements will not capture what the user saw at the time.

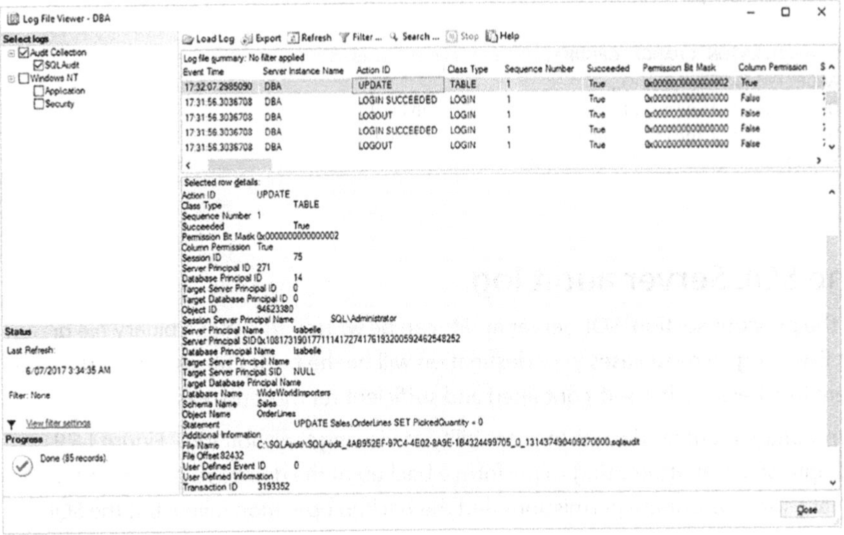

FIGURE 1-30 UPDATE operation audited

The audit log file viewer in SQL Server Management Studio has some capability to search, filter and export the audit logs. In certain instances, however, you want to read the log file programmatically. You might want to import the contents of the log file into a database for example. In this case use the sys.fn_get_audit_file system function.

> **NEED MORE REVIEW?**   **SYS.FN_GET_AUDIT_FILE**
>
> The sys.fn_get_audit_file system function allows you to query SQL Server's and Azure SQL Database's audit files. To learn about how to query the audit files using this system function visit: *https://docs.microsoft.com/en-us/sql/relational-databases/system-functions/sys-fn-get-audit-file-transact-sql.*

Manage a SQL Server audit

As discussed earlier, the SQL Server audit is designed to be light-weight, and consequently has a very simple architecture. Most of the management is done during the configuration of the SQL Server audit. Otherwise you can enable and disable the SQL Server audit, server audit specification, or database audit specification through SQL Server Management Studio.

The following options, available at the SQL Server audit level, represent the key management configuration options:

- **Queue delay (in milliseconds)**   This option controls how audit actions will be processed and can potentially impact performance in edge cases. A value of 0 indicates that audit actions will be processed synchronously. A non-zero value indicates asynchronous processing and has potentially less of an impact on performance, but events might be

C. Incorrect: DDL triggers will only be able to track schema changes to objects made with a database.

D. Correct: DML triggers will be able to track the before and after image of changes made to the tables within the database.

Chapter summary

- The Service Master Key is the root of the SQL Server encryption hierarchy and is generated automatically the first time it is needed to encrypt another key.
- Column-level encryption can be protected by either passwords, passphrases, asymmetric keys, symmetric keys or certificates.
- You should not use asymmetric keys to protect column level encryption due to performance and administration overhead.
- Always Encrypted protects data at the column level and allows you to protect data access from the database administrator.
- Always Encrypted protects data at rest and in flight. All encryption and decryption is performed outside of SQL Server.
- Always Encrypted supports deterministic and randomized encryption at the column level.
- Randomized encryption is more secure, because it prevents all users from being able to deduce other values in the same column.
- Randomized encryption prevents all comparison operations against the encrypted column.
- Transparent database encryption (TDE) only protects data at rest, which helps prevents malicious users from stealing the database files or database backups only.
- Backup compression is compatible with TDE.
- SQL Server supports the creation of user defined server roles.
- Row-level security (RLS) is highly customizable as it supports predicate based access control.
- One of RLS's primary use cases is to implement multi-tenant database solutions.
- Dynamic data masking (DDM) does not encrypt the data, it only masks the result set.
- SQL Server supports auditing at the server scope and database scope.
- SQL Server auditing can write to external files or the Windows event logs.
- SQL Server auditing does not audit what the user saw or the data before and after any modifications.

- **Whether point-in-time recovery is required**   If your organization requires a database to be recovered to a specific point-in-time you will have no choice but to implement log backups. Furthermore, the database will have to use the full recovery model.

- **The recovery objectives defined by your organization**   Quantifying your RPO, RTO, and RLO are critical to your backup strategy.

- **How the transaction log is managed**   Some databases experience substantial transaction log growth. You might also have limited storage dedicated to the transaction log. As a result, you might have to take more frequent log backups than planned to manage the transaction log.

- **The database's recovery model**   Different recovery models impact whether transaction log backups can be taken. If your database is using the simple recovery model, you will not be able to leverage log backups.

- **The importance of the data within the database**   Some databases might not be important to your organization, they may be used in a staging or development environment, or they can be a replica of a production system. In such cases there might be no business requirement to back up the database at all.

In the exam you might be given a scenario where you will have to determine the RTO and the RPO. Watch out for statements in the questions that stipulate that only "fifteen minutes' worth of data can be lost," or that "the database needs to be recovered in two hours." Pay attention to the factors discussed above, and in particular the sizes of the databases and the implied duration of any backup operations, because this will help you in the formulation of the backup strategy.

Evaluate potential backup strategies

Let's examine a number of simple scenarios and what backup strategy could potentially be used for them. The purpose of these scenarios is to show you the types of considerations that help you design your backup strategy.

The first scenario is for a data warehouse solution where a read-only database is used for analytical and reporting purposes. At the end of each day a process changes the database to read/write mode, populates the database with that day's transactions, and then changes the database back to read-only mode. This process starts at midnight and takes 1-2 hours to complete. The database uses the simple recovery model. Users query the database between 08:00 and 18:00. Management has stipulated a RTO of 4 hours and a RPO of 0 minutes.

For this data warehouse solution a full database backup at 03:00 every day can be used as the backup strategy. Our full backup completes within 2 hours. There is no need for differential backups.

The second scenario is for a transactional database used by a customer relations management (CRM) solution. Users are continually modifying the database during business hours (08:00 and 18:00) by adding new customer, activity, and opportunity records. Management requires a RTO of 4 hours and a RPO of 2 hours. The database will also potentially need to be recovered to any specific point in time. A number of re-indexing jobs start at midnight and take 2 hours to complete. You notice that after 75 minutes, the transaction log fills up 95% of the storage allocated to it.

For this CRM solution the following strategy can be used. Although management requires a RPO of 2 hours, the transaction log will consume all of its allocated storage within that time frame. Differential backups cannot be used, because they do not support point-in-time recovery.

- Full database backup at 03:00 every day
- Incremental backups every hour during business hours from 08:00 and 18:00

The final scenario is for a large, mission-critical, 24x7 database used in a manufacturing context. The existing tables are continually being updated by a variety of sensors in the manufacturing process. The transaction log grows rapidly in size. Although new records are also added to the database, it does not grow substantially in size. A full database backup cannot be performed daily since there is insufficient storage. The database needs to be restored to any point-in-time up to 3 months back. Management has indicated a RTO of 5 minutes.

For this manufacturing database the following backup strategy can be used. Differential backups are used to minimize the amount of storage consumed by backups. Transaction log backups allow you to recover to a point-in-time and only lose 5 minutes' worth of data.

- Full database backup at 03:00 every Monday
- Incremental backups every five minutes
- A differential backup at the end of each day at 23:00

Back up databases

Earlier we discussed the different high-level backup operations that potentially make up your backup strategy. In reality, SQL Server supports more types of backup operations. These different types of backup operations allow you to further customize your backup strategy and potentially capture any data modifications made to the database since the last backup operation after a disaster incident.

In this section we will cover the different types of database backup operations supported by SQL Server. We will also have a look at various techniques that can be used to back up larger databases where you might not have an appropriate maintenance window.

SQL Server supports the following types of backup operations:

- **Full**   This contains the entire contents of the database and any changes made to the database during the backup operation. Consequently, a full backup represents the database at the point in time when the backup operation finished.
- **Differential**   This contains only the differences between the last full database backup and the point in time when the differential backup operation was executed.
- **Log**   This contains all of the log records that were performed since the last log backup.
- **File**   This contains either a file or filegroup that makes up the database.

- **Partial**   This is similar to a full backup, but it excludes all read-only filegroups by default. For a read-write database, a partial backup contains the primary filegroup and all read-write filegroups. For a read-only database, a partial backup contains only the primary filegroup.

- **Tail-Log**   This contains all the transaction log records that have not been backed up since the last log backup. A tail-log backup operation is typically performed as the first task in a disaster recovery process. This ensures that no data is lost up to the point-in-time when the disaster incident occurred. For the tail-log backup to be successful the database's transaction log file must be available.

The exam will most likely cover only full, differential, and log backups. However, you need to be prepared for some of the less commonly used backup operations that are designed more for edge and border cases. Make sure you understand the use cases of where file and partial backups are used.

When you perform a backup operation you need to specify a backup destination. Although tape devices are supported they are rarely used in the industry today due to their speed. Most organizations back up directly to a disk based destination and then potentially backup these database backups to tape.

Unfortunately, the legacy of using tapes as a destination still exists in the backup operation. Consequently, for the exam you will need to understand the following concepts used by SQL Server backup operations:

- **Backup device**   A disk or tape device to which the database engine performs a backup operation.

- **Media family**   A backup created on a single non-mirrored device, or a set of mirrored devices in a media set.

- **Backup set**   This represents a successful backup operation's content.

- **Media set**   A set of backup media that contains one or more backup sets.

- **Log sequence number (LSN)**   An internal numbering sequence used for each operation within the transaction log. This is used internally by the database engine and typically not used by database administrators.

- **Sequence number**   This indicates the order of the physical media within a media family. Also, media families are numbered sequentially according to their position within the media set.

NEED MORE REVIEW?   **LOG SEQUENCE NUMBER (LSN)**

To learn about log sequence numbers visit *https://docs.microsoft.com/en-us/sql/relational-databases/backup-restore/recover-to-a-log-sequence-number-sql-server*.

Every backup device starts with a media header that is created by the first backup operation and remains until the media is reformatted. The media header contains information about the backup device's contents and the media family it belongs to. The information includes:

- The name of the media
- The unique identification number of the media set
- The number of media families in the media set
- The sequence number of the media family containing this media
- The unique identification number for the media family
- The sequence number of this media in the media family
- Whether the media description contains an MTF media label or a media description
- The Microsoft Tape Format media label or the media description
- The name of the backup software that wrote the label
- The unique vendor identification number of the software vendor that formatted the media
- The date and time the label was written
- The number of mirrors in the set (1-4); 1 indicates an un-mirrored device

EXAM TIP

Make sure you understand what sequence numbers are represented in backup devices and how they are ordered. The exam might ask you to restore a series of backups in order using Transact-SQL and the sequence number will be important to the answer.

Consider the following series of backup operations that perform a full, differential, and incremental backup to four backup devices concurrently as shown in Listing 2-1.

LISTING 2-1 Multiple backups to four backup devices

```
-- Initial full backup
BACKUP DATABASE AdventureWorks  TO
DISK = 'R:\SQLBackup\AdventureWorks_BackupDevice1.bak''
DISK = 'R:\SQLBackup\AdventureWorks_BackupDevice2.bak ''
DISK = 'R:\SQLBackup\AdventureWorks_BackupDevice 3.bak ''
DISK = 'R:\SQLBackup\AdventureWorks_BackupDevice 4.bak '
WITH
```

```
FORMAT'
MEDIANAME = ' AdventureWorksMediaSet1';
GO
-- Differential backup
BACKUP DATABASE AdventureWorks TO
DISK = 'R:\SQLBackup\AdventureWorks_BackupDevice1.bak''
DISK = 'R:\SQLBackup\AdventureWorks_BackupDevice 2.bak ''
DISK = 'R:\SQLBackup\AdventureWorks_BackupDevice 3.bak ''
DISK = 'R:\SQLBackup\AdventureWorks_BackupDevice 4.bak '
WITH
NOINIT'
MEDIANAME = 'AdventureWorksMediaSet1''
DIFFERENTIAL;
GO
-- Incremental backup
BACKUP LOG AdventureWorks TO
DISK = 'R:\SQLBackup\AdventureWorks_BackupDevice1.bak''
DISK = 'R:\SQLBackup\AdventureWorks_BackupDevice 2.bak ''
DISK = 'R:\SQLBackup\AdventureWorks_BackupDevice 3.bak ''
DISK = 'R:\SQLBackup\AdventureWorks_BackupDevice 4.bak '
WITH
NOINIT'
MEDIANAME = 'AdventureWorksMediaSet1';
GO
```

These three backup operations result in the following media set, as shown in Figure 2-1.

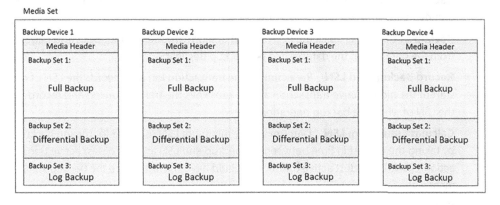

FIGURE 2-1 Backup media set

Now that we have covered the different types of backup operations and destinations let's look at these operations in more detail. Understanding how these backup operations work will help you design an appropriate backup strategy.

Performing full backups

Full backups form the baseline of your backup strategy. Differential and log backups do not work unless they have a baseline full database backup. If a full backup is corrupted or lost you will not be able to restore any subsequent differential and log backups. This highlights the need to periodically perform a full database backup.

A full backup contains a copy of the database and the transaction log operations performed during the database backup phase. The backup operation only backs up the allocated pages within the database. Unallocated pages are not backed up. For a 100GB database that only has 10GB of data, the full database backup is only approximately 10GB in size uncompressed.

> **NEED MORE REVIEW?** **SQL SERVER INTERNAL ARCHITECTURE**
>
> Understanding the database engine's internal architecture will help you understand how the different backup operations work internally. To learn about extents and pages visit *https://docs.microsoft.com/en-us/sql/relational-databases/pages-and-extents-architecture-guide.*

With a full database backup, the database engine performs the following high-level actions:

- **Checkpoint**   Performs a database checkpoint. The checkpoint process flushes all dirty data from the buffer pool to disk to minimize the amount of work required by the restore process.

- **Record backup start LSN**   Examines the transaction log and records the log sequence number (LSN) of when the backup operation started.

- **Backup data**   Backs up all the extents (unit of eight physically contiguous 8KB pages) from the data files in the database to the backup destination.

- **Record backup end LSN**   Re-examines the transaction log and records the LSN of the start of the oldest active transaction and re-examines the transaction log and records the LSN of when the backup operation started.

- **Calculate minimum LSN**   Determines the minimum LSN required for the log backup by taking the earliest in time between the backup end LSN and the oldest active transaction's LSN. The oldest active transaction could have started before the backup statement was executed.

- **Backup log**   Backs up the transaction log between the calculated minimum LSN and the backup end LSN. This ensures that the recovered database will be consistent as of the time of the backup operation's completion.

Consider the following sequence of events, as shown in Figure 2-2.

1. Transaction A begins
2. Transaction A changes page 100
3. A full backup begins
4. Backup checkpoint occurs
5. Backup reads page 100
6. Backup reads page 200
7. Backup reads page 300
8. Transaction B begins
9. Transaction B changes page 200
10. Transaction C begins
11. Transaction A modifies page 300
12. Transaction B commits
13. Transaction A commits
14. Transaction C modifies page 200
15. Backup database read ends

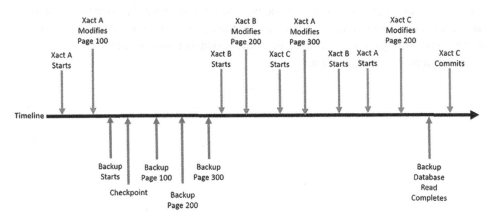

FIGURE 2-2 Backup example timeline

In this example, the Backup Data phase captures the modification to page 100 by transaction A, but not the subsequent modification to pages 200 and 300 made by transactions A, B, and C. The Backup Data phase neither re-reads pages that have been backed up but then modified, nor does it block transactions by reading the page before allowing the modification. The Backup Log phase has to read enough of the transaction log so as to be able to recover the database to a consistent state as of the end of the Backup Data phase. Consequently, the Backup Log phase would have to capture the modifications made to pages 200 and 300. If you were to restore this database backup it would not include the changes made to page 200 by transaction C, because it did not commit before the Backup Data phase completed. This modification would be undone (rolled back) by the recovery phase of the restore operation.

EXAM TIP

It is very likely that the exam will have a question with a similar timeline of scheduled backup operations and what has gone wrong. For you to be able to answer the exam question correctly you will have to understand the importance of events and incidents in the time line and be able to formulate the correct recovery plan. Watch out in particular of when transactions commit.

Figure 2-3 shows the internal operations that were performed during a full database against a timeline. You can see how the database engine initially allocates a number of resources to the backup operation. You can control some of these resources such as the maximum transfer size and buffer count. Note how the full backup operation clears the differential bitmaps before performing the initial backup discussed above. It then scans the allocation bitmaps so as to predict the size of the backup file. This estimation is used to create the backup destination file before it can start writing to it. At the very end, after the data copy phase it backups up the transaction log and closes off the backup set. The resultant backup set file can be shorter than the initial estimation.

Load Log | Export | Refresh | Filter ... | Search ... | Stop | Help

Log file summary: No filter applied

Date	Source	Message
1/03/2017 6:51:12 AM	spid52	Backup(WideWorldImporters): BACKUP DATABASE finished
1/03/2017 6:51:12 AM	Backup	BACKUP DATABASE successfully processed 72194 pages in 1.643 seconds (343.284 MB/sec).
1/03/2017 6:51:12 AM	spid52	Backup(WideWorldImporters): Writing history records is complete (elapsed = 14 ms)
1/03/2017 6:51:12 AM	spid52	Backup(WideWorldImporters): Writing history records
1/03/2017 6:51:12 AM	Backup	Database backed up. Database: WideWorldImporters, creation date(time): 2017/03/01(06:17:26), pages dumped: 72203, first LSN: 623:16776:37, last LSN: 623:16808:1, number of dump
1/03/2017 6:51:12 AM	spid52	Backup(WideWorldImporters): Writing the end of backup set
1/03/2017 6:51:12 AM	spid52	Backup(WideWorldImporters): BackupStream(0): Writing trailing metadata to the device L:\SQL_BACKUP\WideWorldImporters.BAK
1/03/2017 6:51:12 AM	spid52	Backup(WideWorldImporters): Writing the trailing metadata
1/03/2017 6:51:12 AM	spid52	Backup(WideWorldImporters): Copying transaction log is complete
1/03/2017 6:51:12 AM	spid52	Backup(WideWorldImporters): MediaFamily(0): FID=2, VLFID=623, DataStreamSize=65536 bytes
1/03/2017 6:51:12 AM	spid52	Backup(WideWorldImporters): Copying transaction log
1/03/2017 6:51:12 AM	spid52	Backup(WideWorldImporters): Copying data files is complete
1/03/2017 6:51:12 AM	spid52	Backup(WideWorldImporters): Last LSN: 623:16808:1
1/03/2017 6:51:12 AM	spid52	Backup(WideWorldImporters): TotalSize=591396364 bytes
1/03/2017 6:51:12 AM	spid52	Backup(WideWorldImporters): FID=3, ExpectedExtents=8851, IsDifferentialMapAccurate=0
1/03/2017 6:51:12 AM	spid52	Backup(WideWorldImporters): FID=1, ExpectedExtents=173, IsDifferentialMapAccurate=0
1/03/2017 6:51:12 AM	spid52	Backup(WideWorldImporters): Calculating expected size of total data
1/03/2017 6:51:12 AM	spid52	Backup(WideWorldImporters): InitialExpectedSize=591396364 bytes, FinalSize=591396364 bytes, ExcessMode=0
1/03/2017 6:51:12 AM	spid52	Backup(WideWorldImporters): BackupStream(0): Total MSDA size = 9024 extents
1/03/2017 6:51:12 AM	spid52	Backup(WideWorldImporters): MediaWriter is expecting completion
1/03/2017 6:51:12 AM	spid52	Backup(WideWorldImporters): TotalSize=591396364 bytes
1/03/2017 6:51:12 AM	spid52	Backup(WideWorldImporters): FID=3, ExpectedExtents=8851, IsDifferentialMapAccurate=0
1/03/2017 6:51:12 AM	spid52	Backup(WideWorldImporters): FID=1, ExpectedExtents=173, IsDifferentialMapAccurate=0
1/03/2017 6:51:12 AM	spid52	Backup(WideWorldImporters): Calculating expected size of total data
1/03/2017 6:51:12 AM	spid52	Backup(WideWorldImporters): Completed reading the data file D:\SQL_DATA\WideWorldImporters_UserData.ndf
1/03/2017 6:51:10 AM	spid52	Backup(WideWorldImporters): Reading the data file D:\SQL_DATA\WideWorldImporters_UserData.ndf
1/03/2017 6:51:10 AM	spid52	Backup(WideWorldImporters): Completed reading the data file D:\SQL_DATA\WideWorldImporters.mdf
1/03/2017 6:51:10 AM	spid52	Backup(WideWorldImporters): Reading the data file D:\SQL_DATA\WideWorldImporters.mdf
1/03/2017 6:51:10 AM	spid52	Backup(WideWorldImporters): BackupStream(0): Writing MSDA of size 9024 extents
1/03/2017 6:51:10 AM	spid52	Backup(WideWorldImporters): Number of data file readers = 1
1/03/2017 6:51:10 AM	spid52	Backup(WideWorldImporters): Copying data files
1/03/2017 6:51:10 AM	spid52	Backup(WideWorldImporters): TotalSize=591396364 bytes
1/03/2017 6:51:10 AM	spid52	Backup(WideWorldImporters): FID=3, ExpectedExtents=8851, IsDifferentialMapAccurate=0
1/03/2017 6:51:10 AM	spid52	Backup(WideWorldImporters): FID=1, ExpectedExtents=173, IsDifferentialMapAccurate=0
1/03/2017 6:51:10 AM	spid52	Backup(WideWorldImporters): Calculating expected size of total data
1/03/2017 6:51:10 AM	spid52	Shared Backup BufferQ count: 7
1/03/2017 6:51:10 AM	spid52	Backup(WideWorldImporters): BackupStream(0): Writing leading metadata to the device L:\SQL_BACKUP\WideWorldImporters.BAK
1/03/2017 6:51:10 AM	spid52	Backup(WideWorldImporters): Writing the leading metadata
1/03/2017 6:51:10 AM	spid52	Backup(WideWorldImporters): Last LSN: 623:16808:1
1/03/2017 6:51:10 AM	spid52	Backup(WideWorldImporters): Work estimation is complete
1/03/2017 6:51:10 AM	spid52	Backup(WideWorldImporters): Estimated total size = 591413248 bytes (data size = 591396364 bytes, log size = 16384 bytes)
1/03/2017 6:51:10 AM	spid52	Backup(WideWorldImporters): TotalSize=591396364 bytes
1/03/2017 6:51:10 AM	spid52	Backup(WideWorldImporters): FID=3, ExpectedExtents=8851, IsDifferentialMapAccurate=0
1/03/2017 6:51:10 AM	spid52	Backup(WideWorldImporters): FID=1, ExpectedExtents=173, IsDifferentialMapAccurate=0
1/03/2017 6:51:10 AM	spid52	Backup(WideWorldImporters): Calculating expected size of total data
1/03/2017 6:51:10 AM	spid52	Backup(WideWorldImporters): Scanning allocation bitmaps is complete
1/03/2017 6:51:10 AM	spid52	Backup(WideWorldImporters): Scanning allocation bitmaps
1/03/2017 6:51:10 AM	spid52	Backup(WideWorldImporters): Start LSN: 623:16776:37, SERepl LSN: 0:0:0
1/03/2017 6:51:10 AM	spid52	Backup(WideWorldImporters): Checkpoint is complete (elapsed = 3 ms)
1/03/2017 6:51:10 AM	spid52	Backup(WideWorldImporters): Writing a checkpoint
1/03/2017 6:51:10 AM	spid52	Backup(WideWorldImporters): Differential bitmaps are cleared
1/03/2017 6:51:10 AM	spid52	Backup(WideWorldImporters): Clearing differential bitmaps
1/03/2017 6:51:10 AM	spid52	Backup(WideWorldImporters): Effective options: Checksum=1, Compression=1, Encryption=0, BufferCount=7, MaxTransferSize=1024 KB
1/03/2017 6:51:10 AM	spid52	Backup(WideWorldImporters): The media set is ready for backup
1/03/2017 6:51:10 AM	spid52	Backup(WideWorldImporters): Preparing the media set for writing
1/03/2017 6:51:10 AM	spid52	Encode Buffer count: 7
1/03/2017 6:51:10 AM	spid52	Media Buffer size: 1024 KB
1/03/2017 6:51:10 AM	spid52	Media Buffer count: 7
1/03/2017 6:51:10 AM	spid52	Filesystem i/o alignment: 512
1/03/2017 6:51:10 AM	spid52	TXF device count: 0
1/03/2017 6:51:10 AM	spid52	Filestream device count: 0
1/03/2017 6:51:10 AM	spid52	Fulltext data device count: 0
1/03/2017 6:51:10 AM	spid52	Tabular data device count: 1
1/03/2017 6:51:10 AM	spid52	Total buffer space: 21 MB
1/03/2017 6:51:10 AM	spid52	Min MaxTransferSize: 64 KB
1/03/2017 6:51:10 AM	spid52	MaxTransferSize: 1024 KB
1/03/2017 6:51:10 AM	spid52	Sets Of Buffers: 3
1/03/2017 6:51:10 AM	spid52	BufferCount: 7
1/03/2017 6:51:10 AM	spid52	Memory limit: 3071 MB
1/03/2017 6:51:10 AM	spid52	Backup/Restore buffer configuration parameters
1/03/2017 6:51:10 AM	spid52	Backup(WideWorldImporters): The backup media set is open
1/03/2017 6:51:10 AM	spid52	Backup(WideWorldImporters): Opening the backup media set
1/03/2017 6:51:10 AM	spid52	Backup(WideWorldImporters): Synchronizing with other operations on the database is complete
1/03/2017 6:51:10 AM	spid52	Backup(WideWorldImporters): Acquiring bulk-op lock on the database
1/03/2017 6:51:10 AM	spid52	Backup(WideWorldImporters): Opening the database with S lock
1/03/2017 6:51:10 AM	spid52	Backup(WideWorldImporters): BACKUP DATABASE started

FIGURE 2-3 Backup media set

Use the following statement to perform a full backup:

```
BACKUP DATABASE { database_name | @database_name_var }
  TO <backup_device> [ '...n ]
  [ <MIRROR TO clause> ] [ next-mirror-to ]
  [ WITH <general_WITH_options> [ '...n ] ] ]
[;]
```

Performing differential backups

Differential backups represent a delta within the database between the time of the differential backup and the last full backup. The database engine keeps track of all changes made to the database, at the extent level, via an internal bitmap called a Differential Change Map (DCM). Performing a full database backup clears the DCM by default.

Although a single row in a table might be modified, the differential backup will back up the entire 64KB extent. This is done for performance reasons, but results in backup sizes being larger than they strictly need to be. Figure 2-4 shows how a differential backup backs up Database Extents via the DCM.

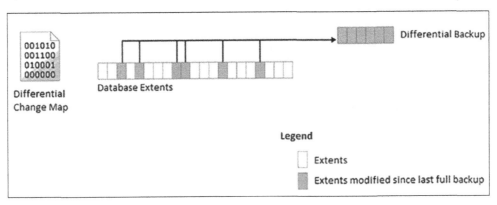

FIGURE 2-4 Differential backup high-level internals

Typically, differential backups get larger in size as more time passes between subsequent differential backup operations and the baseline full backup. At some point in time this size increase impacts your RTO. Don't forget that it takes longer to restore the full and differential backups when compared to restoring a standalone full backup.

Perform differential database backups when any of the following apply:

- You want to reduce the time taken by the backup operation as compared to the full backup and you do not need point-in-time recovery.
- You want to reduce the size of the database set as compared to the full backup and you do not need point-in-time recovery.

Use the following statement to perform a differential backup:

```
BACKUP DATABASE { database_name | @database_name_var }
  TO <backup_device> [ '...n ]
  [ <MIRROR TO clause> ] [ next-mirror-to ]
WITH DIFFERENTIAL
  [ WITH  <general_WITH_options> [ '...n ] ] ]
[;]
```

The size, or potential size of the differential backup will be the determining factor in any potential exam question. So pay attention to how records are being modified in any exam questions. A lot of insert operations within the database imply that the differential backups will get larger in size as time progresses. A lot of update operations to existing data implies that a "steady state" will be achieved with respect to the size of the differential backups as time elapses. You will need to compare both the size and recovery impact of differential backups to transaction log backups, and we will look at them next.

Performing log backups

Log backups represent an incremental backup as discussed earlier as they capture all changes made to the database since the last full or previous log backup. By default, the log backup also reclaims the space within the transaction log by removing records that are no longer required for recovery purposes. This is typically called "truncating the log". A log backup cannot be performed unless the database is in full recovery model and an initial full backup has been performed. We will cover recovery models in detail later in the "Configure database recovery models" section in this chapter.

Log backups are the primary mechanism used to manage the transaction log so that it does not grow too large. For busy databases, it is common to back up the transaction log more frequently. The log backup frequency directly impacts your RPO. Backing up the log every 15 minutes means that you lose a maximum of 15 minutes of committed transaction in the worst case scenario, where you cannot perform a tail-log backup. Tail-log backups are discussed in more detail later in the "Perform tail-log backups" section of this chapter.

> **IMPORTANT** **CONTROLLING LOGGING OF SUCCESSFUL BACKUP OPERATIONS**
>
> By default, every successful backup operation records an entry in the database engine's error log. If log backups are performed very frequently, these messages can result in excessive error log growth and make troubleshooting errors more difficult due to the size of the error log. Consider suppressing these messages using trace flag 3226. This trace flag applies to all backup operations. Unsuccessful backup operations are still logged to the error log.
>
> For more information on trace flags and trace flag 3226 visit *https://docs.microsoft.com/en-us/sql/t-sql/database-console-commands/dbcc-traceon-trace-flags-transact-sql*

Perform transaction log backups when any of the following apply.

- Your database has smaller RPO than the frequency of your full/differential backups.

- You need to recover the database up until the time that it crashed.

- You need point-in-time recovery.

- You need to ensure that the database's transaction log does not grow too large.

Use the following statement to perform a log backup:

```
BACKUP LOG { database_name | @database_name_var }
  TO <backup_device> [ '...n ]
  [ <MIRROR TO clause> ] [ next-mirror-to ]
  [ WITH { <general_WITH_options> | <log-specific_optionspec> } [ '...n ] ]
[;]
```

For most databases a combination of full, differential and log backups are sufficient. However, for more "exotic" use cases you can leverage file backups that do not backup the entire database. Such use cases make great exam questions although they are not commonly "seen in the wild." Let's have a look at how you can perform file and partial backups of your databases next. Remember that they typically all require log backups so as to synchronize the database to a consistent state.

Performing file backups

File backups are typically used where a multi-file database is very large and cannot be completely backed up in the existing maintenance window. Consequently, you rotate the backup of the various files that make up your database at different time intervals.

Perform file backups in the following scenarios:

- You have a very large database and plan to rotate the backups of the files that make up the database.

- Your database is made up of different files, some of which might contain read-only data, or data that is rarely modified. In this case you can back up the different files at different frequencies.

Use the following statement to perform a file/filegroup backup:

```
BACKUP DATABASE { database_name | @database_name_var }
 <file_or_filegroup> [ '...n ]
  TO <backup_device> [ '...n ]
  [ <MIRROR TO clause> ] [ next-mirror-to ]
  [ WITH { DIFFERENTIAL | <general_WITH_options> [ '...n ] } ]
[;]
```

File backups have been supported in SQL Server for a very long time and were probably designed for large databases. We will examine how you can backup very large databases in the "Backup VLDBs" section later in this chapter.

Performing partial backups

Partial backups were introduced in SQL Server 2012 to make backing up very large databases that contain one or more read-only filegroups easier. By default, partial backups do not backup up the read-only filegroups, although read-only file groups can be optionally added to a partial backup. SQL Server Management Studio and the Maintenance Plan Wizard do not support partial backups.

A typical scenario is a very large database that has a read-only filegroup used to store archive data. That archive data is substantial in size and modified only annually. As a result there is no need to back up the read-only filegroup at the same frequency as the full backups.

Use the following statement to perform a partial backup:

```
BACKUP DATABASE { database_name | @database_name_var }
 READ_WRITE_FILEGROUPS  [ ' <read_only_filegroup> [ '...n ] ]
  TO <backup_device> [ '...n ]
  [ <MIRROR TO clause> ] [ next-mirror-to ]
  [ WITH { DIFFERENTIAL | <general_WITH_options> [ '...n ] } ]
[;]
```

Use backup options

Now that we have covered the different types of backups supported in SQL Server we need to examine the important backup options. The exam is going to test your ability to understand these options and use them in the appropriate circumstances. Backup questions in the exam typically have Transact-SQL statements as answer choices and not screen captures.

The BACKUP statement has a large number of WITH options. For the exam, make sure you understand what the following options do and when to use them:

- **CHECKSUM | NO_CHECKSUM**   These options help ensure that your backup can be successfully restored without errors. The CHECKSUM option specifies that the backup operation verifies that each page of the database does not have a checksum or torn page error, if those database options are enabled and available. It also generates a checksum for the entire backup. The default behavior is NO_CHECKSUM, which does not validate pages and does not generate a backup checksum. Page validation and checksum generation consumes more processor resources during the backup operation. But their value is important in disaster recovery scenarios.

- **CONTINUE_AFTER_ERROR | STOP_ON_ERROR**   These options tell the database engine what to do in the case of a backup operation encountering a page checksum error. The CONTINUE_AFTER_ERROR option tells the backup operation to continue on if it encounters any page validation errors. The default option is STOP_ON_ERROR, which instructs the backup operation to stop.

- **COPY_ONLY**   This specifies that the backup is a copy only backup, which means your backup sequence is not affected. For all intents and purposes the backup operation did not occur. For a full backup, a copy only option does not reset the DMC, so subsequent differential backups are not affected. For a log backup the copy only option does not truncate the transaction log, so the log chain is not broken. Copy only backups are typically used to refresh non-production environments with production backups when the existing backup sequence should not be impacted. A copy only backup is still recorded in the ERRORLOG.

- **COMPRESSION | NO_COMPRESSION**   Backup compression has been available since the SQL Server 2008 Enterprise Edition and the SQL Server 2008 R2 Standard Edition. The COMPRESSION option enables backup compression. The NO_COMPRESSION option explicitly disables backup compression. The compression level cannot be controlled. Backup compression can consume extra processor resources so be careful with its usage in high-performance environments. The default behavior of the database engine is not to use backup compression. Setting the backup compression default server configuration option can change this default.

- **DESCRIPTION**   This option allows you to describe the backup set using up to 255 characters.

- **ENCRYPTION | NO_ENCRYPTION**   These options controls whether the backup should be encrypted. The default behavior is the same as the NO_ENCRYPTION option, which is not to encrypt. When you encrypt a backup you need to specify which encryption algorithm to use. The following encryption algorithms are supported:

  - AES_128

  - AES_192

  - AES_256

  - TRIPLE_DES_3KEY

When you encrypt a backup you also have to specify the encryptor using one of the following options:

- **SERVER CERTIFICATE** = Encryptor_Name

- **SERVER ASYMMETRIC KEY** = Encryptor_Name

- **EXPIREDATE | RETAIN_DAYS**   These two options allow you to control when the backup set expires and can be subsequently overwritten. RETAINSDAYS takes precedence over EXPIREDATE.

- **FORMAT | NO FORMAT**   The FORMAT option is destructive as it causes a new media set to be created. All existing backup sets are unrecoverable. If you format a single tape that belongs to an existing striped media set, the entire media set is useless. The default option, NOFORMAT, preserves the existing media header and backup sets on the media volumes used by the backup.

- **INIT | NOINIT**   The INIT option specifies that all backup sets should be overwritten. The media header is preserved. The existing backup sets are not overwritten if the EXPIRYDATE/RETAINDAYSA have not expired, or if the backup set name provided does not match the one in the backup media. The NOINIT option, which is the default, specifies that the backup set be appended to the existing ones in the media set.

- **NAME**   This option gives the backup set a name. Up to 128 characters can be used.

- **MEDIADESCRIPTION**   This option allows you to describe the media set. It is limited to 255 characters.

- **MEDIANAME**   This allows you to use up to 128 characters to give the media set a name.

- **RETAINDAYS**   This option allows you to control when the backup set expires and can be subsequently overwritten.

- **SKIP | NOSKIP**   The SKIP option specifies that the backup operation should ignore the "safety check" that normally checks the backup set's expiration date or name before overwriting it.

- **STATS**   This controls at what percentage intervals the database engine should display a message indicating the progress of the backup operation. The default value is 10, which means you are notified whenever another 10 percent of the backup operation completes.

Furthermore, the BACKUP statement supports the ability to back up the same data/log to a number of mirrored backup devices via the MIRROR TO clause. The MIRROR TO clause must have the same type and number of the backup devices as the TO clause. A maximum of three MIRROR TO clauses can be used, so a total of four mirrors is possible per media set. The primary reason for using mirrored media sets is to provide redundancy at the backup device level.

Listing 2-2 shows a full backup operation that has been mirrored to a number of different servers.

LISTING 2-2 Mirrored backups

```
BACKUP DATABASE WorldWideImporters
TO DISK = 'B:\SQLBackup\WorldWideImporters.bak'
MIRROR TO DISK = '\\DEVSERVER\SQLBackup\SQLBackup\WorldWideImporters.bak''
MIRROR TO DISK = '\\TESTSERVER\SQLBackup\SQLBackup\WorldWideImporters.bak''
MIRROR TO DISK = '\\STAGINGSERVER\SQLBackup\SQLBackup\WorldWideImporters.bak''
WITH FORMAT;
```

When backing up a large database it can be useful to know how far an executing backup operation has come and how long it will take to complete. You can query the [sys].[dm_exec_requests] dynamic management view (DMV) to monitor a backup operation's progress. Use the query in Listing 2-3 to show the progress of a running BACKUP operation:

LISTING 2-3 Progress of backup operation

```
SELECT session_id' db_name(database_id) as database_name'
        start_time' command' percent_complete' estimated_completion_time
FROM sys.dm_exec_requests
WHERE command LIKE 'backup %';
```

Perform database snapshots

Database snapshots are a read-only, static view of a database at the point-in-time when the database snapshot was taken. A database snapshot is a sparse file that is created separately from the database. This snapshot file holds the old versions of the database's pages as data in the database is modified. A database can have multiple database snapshots, and each database snapshot has a unique name. Database snapshots have to be removed explicitly.

Database snapshots make great questions in the exam. If you don't know how database snapshots work at the database engine level, you might easily choose them as an answer when they are clearly not the correct answer choice. Database snapshots work at the page level. Whenever a page is modified its pre-modified version is written to the snapshot file. Consequently, the database snapshot will consume more disk space as more data is modified within the database. A database can have multiple database snapshots. Although the predominant use case for database snapshots is for reporting purposes, they can be used for safeguarding against user mistakes. Reverting a database snapshot is quicker in most cases than restoring a database and replaying all log backups, up until the user mistake is made. For example, you might want to take a database snapshot before you execute some sort of end-of-day batch process. If an error occurs, or you decide you need to roll back this batch process, you can simply revert the database back to the time of the database snapshot. All data modifications after the database snapshot are to be expunged.

> **IMPORTANT   DATABASE SNAPSHOT DEPENDENCY**
>
> Database snapshots are dependent on the parent database. If the parent database's data files are corrupted or lost, queries against the database snapshot will not work.

Listing 2-4 shows how to create a database snapshot. Ensure you provide a unique, meaningful name to the database snapshot.

LISTING 2-4 Create a database snapshot

```
CREATE DATABASE WorldWideImporters_20160917
ON (
    NAME = WorldWideImporters_Data'
    FILENAME = 'R:\SQLData\WorldWideImporters_20160917.ss')
AS SNAPSHOT OF [WorldWideImporters];
```

 EXAM TIP

Watch out for any exam items that include database snapshots. If the underlying database files are unavailable you will not be able to revert the database snapshot.

Back up databases to Azure

There are a number of compelling reasons for backing up your database to the cloud, including triple redundancy, off-site location, and cost-effectiveness. SQL Server supports the following tools and features:

- Backup to URL
- Backup to Microsoft Azure tool
- Managed backup to Microsoft Azure

SQL Server 2012 Service Pack 1 Cumulative Update 2 introduced the capability to back up directly to (and restore from) Microsoft Azure Blob Storage. Both the Backup Task in SQL Server Management Studio and the Maintenance Plan Wizard support backups to Microsoft Azure Blob Storage.

Backing up databases to Microsoft Azure Blob Storage is great if your databases are hosted in Microsoft Azure. For on-premise database solutions, however, you need to take into account your database size, volume of modifications, and upload/download bandwidth.

To back up to Microsoft Azure Blob Storage with the BACKUP statement, use the TO URL clause as show in Listing 2-5.

LISTING 2-5 Backup to URL

```
-- Create storage account identity and access key
CREATE CREDENTIAL MyCredentialName
WITH IDENTITY = 'MyStorageAccountName',
SECRET = '<MyStorageAccountAccessKey>';
GO
-- Backup database to URL using storage account identity and access key
BACKUP DATABASE MyDB
TO URL = 'https://<MyStorageAccountName>.blob.core.windows.net/<MyStorageAccountContainerN
ame>/MyDB.bak'
WITH CREDENTIAL = 'MyCredentialName'
```

> **NEED MORE REVIEW? SQL SERVER BACKUP TO URL**
>
> To learn how to configure Microsoft Azure Blob Storage to support SQL Server backup operations to URL visit *https://docs.microsoft.com/en-us/sql/relational-databases/backup-restore/sql-server-backup-to-url*.

Introduced in SQL Server 2014, the SQL Server Managed Backup to Microsoft Azure feature automatically manages your backups to Microsoft Azure. This feature can be enabled at the instance or database level, through the [smart_admin].[sp_set_instance_backup] or [smart_admin].[sp_set_db_backup] system stored procedures respectively. The database engine then automatically performs full and log backups automatically. Backups are retained for up to 30 days.

Full backups are performed whenever any of the following are true:

- The last full backup is over a week old.

- The log has grown more than 1GB since the last full backup.

- Log chain is broken.

Log backups are performed whenever any of the following are true:

- More than two hours have expired since the last log backup.

- The log has grown in 5MB.

- The log backup is behind the full backup.

Listing 2-6 shows an example of how to configure SQL Server Managed Backup to Microsoft Azure at the instance level.

LISTING 2-6 SQL Server Managed Backup to Microsoft Azure at the instance level

```
USE [msdb];
GO
EXEC [smart_admin].[sp_set_instance_backup]
    @enable_backup=1
    ,@storage_url = 'https://mystorageaccount.blob.core.windows.net/'
    ,@retention_days=30
    ,@credential_name='MyCredential'
    ,@encryption_algorithm ='AES_256'
    ,@encryptor_type= 'ServerCertificate'
    ,@encryptor_name='MyBackupCertificate';
GO
```

Listing 2-7 shows an example of how to configure SQL Server Managed Backup to Microsoft Azure at the database level.

LISTING 2-7 SQL Server Managed Backup to Microsoft Azure at the instance level

```
USE [msdb];
GO
EXEC [smart_admin].[sp_set_db_backup]
    @database_name='MyDB'
    ,@enable_backup=1
    ,@storage_url = 'https://MyStorageAccount.blob.core.windows.net/'
    ,@retention_days=30
    ,@credential_name='MyCredential'
    ,@encryption_algorithm ='NO_ENCRYPTION';
GO
```

The Microsoft SQL Server Backup to Microsoft Azure Tool is an externally available tool that enables backup to Azure Blob Storage and encrypts and compresses SQL Server backups stored locally or in the cloud. It works with all versions and editions of SQL Server, even if they do not support compression and encryption.

Back up VLDBs

As your database grows in size, the backup times, and more importantly the restore times, increase because both the backup and restore duration is dependent on the speed of your I/O subsystems. There are a number of techniques that can be used to decrease the time taken:

- Potentially implement data compression on tables within the database to reduce the size of the database. In most cases PAGE compression is superior to ROW compression.

- Assess taking advantage of columnstore indexes, which may substantially reduce the size of the tables. With columnstore indexes the table size can be potentially substantially reduced, as an example, from 120GB to 4GB. Be aware that columnstore indexes are designed primarily for data warehouse workloads where queries scan large volumes of data. For an On-Line Transaction Processing (OLTP) database you might still be able to use columnstore indexes on large tables that are rarely, if ever, queried. Examples of tables that fit this profile include auditing and logging tables.

- Consider moving old data out of your very large database into an archive database. Old data is infrequently queried and should not live in your OLTP database forever.

- Take advantage of backup compression to reduce the size of the backup set.

- Back up your database to multiple backup devices. The database engine is able to consume up to 64 threads to concurrently back up the extents of your database to 64 backup devices, one thread per device. You also need to maximize the I/O throughput at the database's storage subsystem level.

Most of these techniques focus on reducing the size of your database, which in turn reduces the duration of your backup and restore operations. At some point in time these techniques are not sufficient because your database evolves into what is sometimes referred to as a very large database or VLDB.

A VLDB can be defined as a database whose restore or backup time SLAs cannot be easily met through faster networking/storage hardware resources, or by using any of the techniques discussed above. Additional consideration needs to be given to designing a backup strategy for such VLDBs.

For example, a 4TB database can easily take longer than one day to restore, due to the backup size, storage subsystem speed, networking infrastructure, backup compression, and the number and size of transaction log backups that also need to be to restored. (This is why you should periodically test the time taken by your restore procedure to ensure that your RTO can be met.)

Although VLDBs are not really that common in the field, expect the exam to have some questions about how to best backup and restore a VLDB. You will most likely be either asked to design a backup strategy for a VLDB or provide the series of restore steps that need to be performed to recover a VLDB in the shortest period of time.

The most common and easiest technique to reduce your backup (and restore) times for VLDBs is to take advantage of filegroups and re-architect your VLDB from a single primary file into multiple data files. Each secondary data file, or set of data files, would be contained in its own filegroup. Each file should ideally be located on a separate disk. That way if any single disk fails, the damage is contained to that file/filegroup. To recover from the disaster, restore just the damaged file/filegroup, as opposed to the entire database. This technique can substantially reduce the time it takes to recover from a disaster, depending on what has failed. It should also reduce the backup duration because you do not backup the same volume of data.

> **IMPORTANT CONFIGURING THE PRIMARY DATA FILE FOR A VLDB**
>
> When creating a VLDB it is best practice to have no data within the primary data file of the database. This primary data file only contains the schema and code modules of our database. This ensures that the primary data file can be restored as quickly as possible when needed in a disaster recovery scenario. A database is never available until its primary data files are restored.

One commonly used technique is to simply spread your VLDB across a number of files. You would then back up only one of the files in your VLDB nightly, and rotate between the files over subsequent nights.

Let's consider the following scenario of 4TB VLDB that has six separate data files as shown in Listing 2-8. The VLDB has a filegroup called [DATA] that consists of four 1TB secondary data files. This [DATA] filegroup is configured as the default filegroup. This helps ensure that there's no data in the [PRIMARY] file group. Notice how these six data files are located on separate drives to help ensure that we do not lose two 1 TB data files at once. (Let's assume that there is no need to perform file backups on the weekend because this organization only operates during weekdays.)

LISTING 2-8 Creating a VLDB

```
CREATE DATABASE [VLDB]
  ON [PRIMARY]
    (NAME = N'VLDB_System'' FILENAME = N'D:\SQLData\VLDB_System.mdf'' SIZE = 100MB)'
  FILEGROUP [DATA]
    (NAME = N'VLDB_Data1'' FILENAME = N'E:\SQLData\VLDB_Data1.ndf'' SIZE = 1TB)'
    (NAME = N'VLDB_Data2'' FILENAME = N'F:\SQLData\VLDB_Data2.ndf'' SIZE = 1TB)'
    (NAME = N'VLDB_Data3'' FILENAME = N'G:\SQLData\VLDB_Data3.ndf'' SIZE = 1TB)'
    (NAME = N'VLDB_Data4'' FILENAME = N'H:\SQLData\VLDB_Data4.ndf'' SIZE = 1TB)'
    (NAME = N'VLDB_Data5'' FILENAME = N'I:\SQLData\VLDB_Data5.ndf'' SIZE = 1TB)
  LOG ON
    (NAME = N'VLDB_log'' FILENAME = N'L:\SQLLog\VLDB_Log.ldf' ' SIZE = 100GB) ;
GO
ALTER DATABASE [VLDB] MODIFY FILEGROUP [DATA] DEFAULT;
```

The VLDB in this scenario could potentially use the following backup strategy:

- Back up the primary data file nightly.
- Back up the [VLDB_Data1] file on Monday.
- Back up the [VLDB_Data2] file on Tuesday.
- Back up the [VLDB_Data3] file on Wednesday.
- Back up the [VLDB_Data4] file on Thursday.
- Back up the [VLDB_Data5] file on Friday.
- Back up the transaction log every 15 minutes.

If a single data drive failed, it would be sufficient to replace the damaged disk, restore the failed data file, and replay the transaction log until the data file is synchronized with the rest of the database.

The problem with this approach is that all of the data would be spread across all of the files. If a single data file is lost in a disaster, nobody can access any of the data within the VLDB until the restore and recover have completed. So you have improved your backup duration, and your RPO potentially, but not necessarily your availability (or RTO).

SQL Server supports a feature called partial availability. With partial availability users can still access portions of the database even though certain filegroups are unavailable. For partial availability to work, the primary data file and transaction log files must always be available. This approach also works with partitioning where a single table is split into multiple partitions, and each partition is stored in a separate filegroup.

Consequently, a better technique is to locate your data more intelligently on the filegroups within the VLDB. This requires more domain knowledge about the database and how your organization uses the VLDB.

It is common for VLDBs to have very large tables that contain the following types of data:

- Archive/historical data
- Audit information
- Logging information
- Read-only data
- Reference data

These tables might take up the majority of the capacity within the database. This data might not be as important as the rest of the data and can consequently be restored last. Also, it might not need to be backed up as frequently. In these cases, place these tables onto their own separate filegroups. Again, back up these filegroups at a separate frequency from the rest of the database. Back up read-only filegroups only when they are modified.

An alternative technique in deciding what tables should be split into their own filegroups takes into account the relative importance of the tables in the database.

Consider an online shopping VLDB with hundreds of tables that have the following tables:

- [Orders]
- [OrderHistory]
- [Products]
- [Customers]

In the case of a disaster incident it is critical to get these tables restored as soon as possible. You want to minimize the downtime for customer shopping! The database could be restored in the following order:

1. Primary data file
2. Products
3. Customers
4. Orders (at this stage customers could begin placing new orders)
5. Order history
6. The rest of the database

At some point in time a database can be too large to fail. At that stage, you need to consider implementing the appropriate high availability technology, such as Availability Groups and/or Log Shipping. These high availability technologies maintain multiple, separate copies of the database, which protects against instance and storage failure

Manage transaction log backups

So far we have looked at how you perform database backups and the different backup operations supported. Remember, no database backup operation automatically manages the transaction log for you by truncating it. In most cases the transaction logs for all your databases are typically co-located on the same disk. You don't want the transaction log of an unimportant database filling up the disk and effectively crashing all your mission-critical databases as a result. Consequently it is important to manage the transaction log to both minimize the amount of data loss in the event of a disaster incident, and to ensure that the transaction log does not grow out of control and fill up the disk on which it is located.

In this section we will examine how you perform log backups and what to do in the case of an incident where your transaction log fills up. We will also look at some transaction log configuration options and how they will impact your disaster recovery strategy. But before we can look at how to perform log backups we need to look at the crucial concept of database recovery models, which control how much information is logged to the transaction log and potentially what amount of data you will lose in the case of a disaster occurring.

In the exam you should expect questions on what recovery models to use in given scenarios, how to deal with a full transaction log incidents and broken log chains. An exam question on tail-logs is virtually guaranteed, so make sure you understand what tail-logs, how to back them up and the recovery scenarios in which they are used.

Configure database recovery models

Understanding the different recovery models that are supported by SQL Server is critical because they directly impact your disaster recovery planning and how much data you can potentially lose in the case of a disaster. They also impact your high-availability solution design, capacity planning, and transaction log management.

SQL Server supports the following recovery models:

- **Full**   Under the FULL recovery model the database engine fully logs every operation in the transaction log for recoverability purposes. Transaction log backups have no dependency on the database's data files. Under normal operations on a correctly managed SQL Server instance, no data loss occurs. The full recovery model is typically used in production environments.

- **Bulk-Logged**   The BULK_LOGGED recovery model reduces the amount of logging information written to the transaction log during minimally logged operations by only recording the extents that were modified. Consequently, transaction log backups rely on the database's data files that were modified by the minimally logged operations being available during the backup operation. The bulk logged recovery model is not typically used in production environments.

- **Simple**   With the SIMPLE recovery model the database engine automatically reclaims the space used by operations in the transaction log. No transaction log backups are possible. The simple recovery model is typically used in non-production environments, such as development, user acceptance, and testing.

The default recovery model of a database is determined by the [model] database's recovery model at the time of the database's creation. The [model] database's recovery model is full by default. The [master], [msdb], and [tempdb] system databases use the simple recovery model by default. You can change the [msdb] system database recovery model to full if you want the benefits of transaction log backups.

With the FULL recovery model, the transaction log continues to grow in size until it either fills up the disk, or reaches the transaction log's maximum size limit. If this occurs, the database engine generates a 9002 error. Users are no longer able to modify any data within the database. That is why you need to back up the transaction log periodically as it has the effect of reclaiming space from the log. As an alternative, the transaction log can be truncated, but this is uncommon.

Use the full recovery model when any of the following apply:

- You want to recover all of the data up to the point in time when the database crashed.
- You need to recover to a specific point in time.
- You need to recover to a marked transaction.
- You need to be able to restore individual pages.

- Your database contains multiple filegroups and you want to take advantage of piece-meal recovery.
- You are going to implement any of the following high availability technologies:
  - Availability Groups
  - Database Mirroring
  - Log Shipping

The BULK_LOGGED recovery model minimally logs bulk operations such as BCP, BULK IN-SERT, INSERT ... SELECT, and SELECT INTO. It also applies to indexing operations such as CREAT INDEX, ALTER INDEX, and DROP INDEX. Otherwise the database operates exactly like it would under the FULL recovery model.

Minimal logging involves logging only the information that is required to recover the transaction without supporting point-in-time recovery to when the bulk operation executed. The database engine only logs the extents that were modified during the minimally logged operations as opposed to the entire operation. This results in substantially less logging and consequently a much faster bulk operation.

> **NEED MORE REVIEW?** **MINIMALLY LOGGED OPERATIONS**
>
> You can learn more about the benefits of minimal logging and the prerequisites for setting up minimal logging for a minimally logged bulk-import operation at *https://docs.microsoft. com/en-us/sql/relational-databases/import-export/prerequisites-for-minimal-logging-in-bulk-import.*

Importantly, data loss is possible until you next back up your transaction log. This is because the database engine does not back up the extents that were modified until the next log back-up. Figure 2-5 shows at a high-level how the log backup operation saves the modified extents to the log backup, by referencing the Bulk Change Map (BCM). The database engine uses the BCM as a bitmap to record which extents were modified by bulk operations.

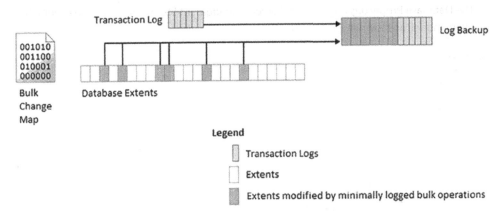

FIGURE 2-5 Log backups under bulk-logged recovery model

If you lose the data files that were modified by the bulk operation before you perform your next backup, you have lost all of the data that was modified since the bulk operation. That is why it is recommended to perform a backup after your bulk operation under the bulk-logged recovery model. A full, differential, or log backup is sufficient.

Use the BULK_LOGGED recovery model temporarily when any of the following apply:

- You want to perform a bulk operation with the best performance.
- You do not have sufficient transaction log space, or you want to use the least amount of transaction log space.

With the SIMPLE recovery model, the database engine automatically manages the transaction log by safely deleting operations that are no longer needed for recovery purposes. This mechanism does not guarantee that the transaction log will never fill up. The transaction log can still fill up 100 percent if there is a long running transaction for example. The main benefit for using the SIMPLE recovery model is that that there are no transaction logs to manage, and it is less likely that the transaction log is going to fill up.

Use the SIMPLE recovery model when any of the following apply:

- You are willing to lose all data modifications since the last full or differential database backup.
- The database is being used for non-production purposes, or as a read-only copy of a production database.
- You are relying on non-SQL Server based disaster recovery, such as through snapshotting technology that is typically available in virtualization or SAN technology.

Use the ALTER DATABASE statement to change a database's recovery model:

```
ALTER DATABASE { database_name  | CURRENT }
SET RECOVERY { FULL | BULK_LOGGED | SIMPLE }
```

The Database Properties page in SQL Server Management Studio allows you to change the recovery model, as shown in Figure 2-6.

FIGURE 2-6 Database properties page

You can switch the recovery model of any database at any time. When you switch to the simple recovery model, however, you break the log backup chain. We will look at log chains shortly in the section, "Understand log chains." Consequently, it is recommended that you perform a log backup before switching to the simple recovery model. Furthermore, when you switch from the simple recovery model it is recommended to perform a full or differential backup so as to initialize the log backup chain. A differential backup is typically smaller. Although you have switched recovery models, the database continues operating in the simple recovery model until you perform this initial backup operation.

If you want to determine what recovery model all your databases are using, you can query the [sys].[databases] system catalog as shown in Listing 2-9.

LISTING 2-9 Query the recovery model of all databases

```
USE master;
GO
SELECT name' recovery_model_desc
FROM sys.databases;
```

Under the FULL and BULK_LOGGED recovery models the database's transaction log will continue to grow until it fills up the disk drive it is located on. One of the primary responsibilities of the database administrator is to manage the transaction logs for their databases. This is typically done by backing up the log, and we will turn our attention there next.

Back up transaction logs

The primary technique of transaction log management is to periodically perform transaction log backups. A secondary technique is to simply truncate the transaction periodically, typically after a full database backup, although it is not commonly used as most organizations want a backup of the log for recoverability purposes.

Transaction log backups are not possible under the simple recovery model because the database engine automatically truncates the log.

Transaction log backups are also not possible in the full or bulk-logged recovery models until a full database backup has been performed. The database engine automatically truncates the log in this scenario because there is no point in retaining transaction log records until the first full database backup.

The BACKUP LOG statement has the following options:

- **NO_TRUNCATE**   This option does not truncate the transaction log at the end of the log backup operation. It also allows the database engine to attempt a log backup in situations where the database is damaged.

- **NORECOVERY**   This option backs up the tail-log and leaves the database in the RESTORING state. Tail-logs are discussed later on in this chapter. The NORECOVERY option is useful when you need to fail over to a secondary database in an Availability Group. It is also useful when you need to back up the tail-log before your RESTORE operations.

- **STANDBY**   This option backs up the tail of the log and leaves the database in a read-only and STANDBY state. This STANDBY state effectively creates a second transaction log that allows the database to be read, but also allows log backups to be restored. When the next log backup is applied, the second transaction log is rolled back so as to bring the database back into the NORECOVERY state.

Although these BACKUP LOG options are rarely used in the field they will most likely be tested in the exam. So make sure you know the difference between them and the when to use them. The exam might contain some recovery scenario where one of these BACKUP LOG options needs to be sued.

The STANDBY option is equivalent to the BACKUP LOG WITH NORECOVERY operation followed by a RESTORE WITH STANDBY operation.

> *NOTE* **NO_TRUNCATE BACKUP LOG OPTION**
>
> The NO_TRUNCATE option is equivalent to both the COPY_ONLY and CONTINUE_AFTER_ERROR options.

Use both the NO_TRUNCATE and NORECOVERY options to perform a best-effort log backup that does not truncate the log and changes the database into the RESTORING state in a single atomic operation.

Understand transaction log chains

We now turn our attention to transaction log chains, which are always tested in the exam. You must understand log chains to be able to answer recovery questions in the exam, especially for questions that require you to correctly sequence the correct answer choices.

A *log chain* is the continuous set of transaction log backups performed on a database after a full backup is performed. If a log chain is unbroken, the database can be recovered to the point in time when the disaster incident occurred. If the log chain is broken, you are not able to restore the database past the break in the log chain.

Consider the following scenario where the following backup strategy is used:

- A full backup is performed on Sunday at 23:00.
- A log backup is performed every hour from Monday till Saturday during business hours (08:00 – 18:00).

Assume the following sequence of events happens:

1. Sunday's full backup completes successfully.
2. All the log backups complete successfully.
3. The database crashes on Saturday at 20:00.
4. Tuesday's 15:00 transaction log backup is lost or corrupted.

In this case the log chain is broken and the database can only be restored till Tuesday at 14:00. Although all log backups after Tuesday at 14:00 are fine, they cannot be restored until the Tuesday 14:00 log backup is restored.

One way to mitigate against this kind of a scenario is to take a periodic differential backup. Assume that the above backup strategy also performed a differential backup from Monday to Saturday at 23:00.

In this case the database can be restored with no data loss by bypassing Tuesday's 15:00 log backup. It is simply the case of performing the following actions:

1. Restore Sunday's full backup.
2. Restore Monday's differential backup.
3. Restore all log backups from Tuesday through Saturday.

An alternative, and potentially quicker restore would involve the following actions:

1. Restore Sunday's full backup.
2. Restore Friday's differential backup.
3. Restore all log backups from Saturday.

Another way to mitigate against this kind of scenario is to mirror the log backup to another backup destination using the MIRROR TO clause discussed earlier. If one of the log backups is corrupted or lost, the mirrored one can be used.

This highlights the importance of ensuring that you have an unbroken log chain. It also highlights the importance of potentially designing multiple restore paths for your mission-critical database solutions.

EXAM TIP

Watch out for broken log chains in the exam. It's a great way for the exam to catch out exam takers who won't recognize a broken log chain and won't know the appropriate corrective action.

Perform tail-log backups

The *tail-log backup* captures all log records that have not yet been backed up. Unless you can perform a tail-log backup you incur data loss in the case of a disaster incident. With a tail-log backup, you are able to restore the database to the point in time when it failed.

That is why it is important to architect your databases to have redundancy at the transaction log. The easiest way is to provide redundancy at the disk or volume level. Hardware RAID 1 or Windows Server mirroring is sufficient.

In the case of a disaster incident, the first thing that you should always think about is whether the transaction log still exists, and whether a tail-log backup can be performed. This ensures that you minimize your data loss because all committed transactions are recoverable through the tail-log backup.

A tail-log backup is not required where you do not need to restore the database to the point in time of the disaster incident.

Consider the following experiment in Listing 2-10 that performs the following actions:

1. Creates a new database.
2. Creates a new table.
3. Inserts the first record into the table.
4. Performs a full database backup.
5. Inserts the second record into the table.
6. Performs a log backup.
7. Inserts the third record into the table.
8. Simulates a disaster by deleting the database's primary (MDF) data file.

LISTING 2-10 Orphaned log experiment

```
-- Set up experiment: Run selectively as and if required
/* You might have to enable xp_cmdshell by running the following:
EXEC sp_configure 'show advanced'' 1;
RECONFIGURE;
GO
EXEC sp_configure 'xp_cmdshell'' 1;
RECONFIGURE;
GO
-- Create directory for experiment
EXEC xp_cmdshell' 'md C:\Exam764Ch2\';
GO
*/
-- Create database
CREATE DATABASE TailLogExperimentDB
ON PRIMARY (NAME = N'TailLogExperimentDB_data'' FILENAME = N'C:\Exam764Ch2\
TailLogExperimentDB.mdf')
LOG ON (NAME = N'TailLogExperimentDB_log'' FILENAME = N'C:\Exam764Ch2\
TailLogExperimentDB.ldf')
GO
-- Create table
USE [TailLogExperimentDB]
GO
CREATE TABLE [MyTable] (Payload VARCHAR(1000));
GO
-- Insert first record
INSERT [MyTable] VALUES ('Before full backup');
GO
-- Perform full backup
BACKUP DATABASE [TailLogExperimentDB] TO DISK = 'C:\Exam764Ch2\TailLogExperimentDB_FULL.
bak' WITH INIT;
GO
-- Insert second record
INSERT [MyTable] VALUES ('Before log backup');
GO
-- Perform log backup
BACKUP LOG [TailLogExperimentDB] TO DISK = 'C:\Exam764Ch2\TailLogExperimentDB_LOG.bak'
WITH INIT;
GO
-- Insert third record
INSERT [MyTable] VALUES ('After log backup');
GO
-- Simulate disaster
SHUTDOWN;
/*
Perform the following actions:
    1. Use Windows Explorer to delete C:\Exam764Ch2\TailLogExperimentDB.mdf
    2. Use SQL Server Configuration Manager to start SQL Server
The [TailLogExperimentDB] database should now be damaged as you deleted the primary data
file.
*/
```

At this stage, you have a full and log backup that contains only the first two records that were inserted. The third record was inserted after the log backup. If you restore the database at this stage, you lose the third record. Consequently, you need to back up the orphaned transaction log.

Listing 2-11 shows the attempt to back up the orphaned transaction log.

LISTING 2-11 Attempted log backup

```
USE master;
SELECT name' state_desc FROM sys.databases WHERE name = 'TailLogExperimentDB';
GO
-- Try to back up the orphaned tail-log
BACKUP LOG [TailLogExperimentDB] TO DISK = 'C:\Exam764Ch2\TailLogExperimentDB_
OrphanedLog.bak' WITH INIT;
```

The database engine is not able to back up the log because it normally requires access to the database's MDF file, which contains the location of the database's LDF files in the system tables. The following error is generated:

```
Msg 945' Level 14' State 2' Line 56
Database 'TailLogExperimentDB' cannot be opened due to inaccessible files or
insufficient memory or disk space.  See the SQL Server errorlog for details.
Msg 3013' Level 16' State 1' Line 56
BACKUP LOG is terminating abnormally.
```

Listing 2-12 shows how to correctly back up the orphaned transaction log with the NO_TRUNCATE option.

LISTING 2-12 Orphaned log backup with NO_TRUNCATE option

```
-- Try to back up the orphaned tail-log again
BACKUP LOG [TailLogExperimentDB] TO DISK = 'C:\Exam764Ch2\TailLogExperimentDB_
OrphanedLog.bak' WITH NO_TRUNCATE;
```

The backup of the orphaned transaction log succeeds. You can now restore the database without any data loss. The next section will cover how to restore databases.

To clean up this experiment run the code in listing 2-13.

LISTING 2-13 Orphaned log experiment cleanup

```
-- Cleanup experiment: Run selectively as and if required
/*
EXEC xp_cmdshell 'rd /q C:\Exam764Ch2\';
GO
EXEC sp_configure 'xp_cmdshell'' 0;
RECONFIGURE;
GO
EXEC sp_configure 'show advanced'' 0;
RECONFIGURE;
GO
USE [master];
DROP DATABASE [TailLogExperimentDB];
*/
```

A tail-log backup is recommended in the following situations:

- If the database is online and you plan to perform a restore operation on the database. Start with a tail-log backup to avoid data loss. Don't forget that you might want to save all transactions, even though you might be restoring to an earlier point in time.

- If a database is offline and fails to start, and you plan to restore the database. Again, start with a tail-log backup to avoid data loss.

- If a database is damaged and you want to recover all the transaction in the orphaned transaction log a tail-lo backup should be considered.

IMPORTANT   **TAIL-LOG BACKUPS ON DAMAGED DATABASES**

Tail log backups on damaged databases only succeed if the log file is undamaged, the database state supports tail-log backups, and there are no bulk logged operations in the transaction log. If these criteria are not met, all committed transactions after the last successful log backup are lost.

EXAM TIP

In the exam, with any question dealing with disaster recovery, always be on the lookout for the orphaned tail-log and whether a tail-log backup can be performed to minimize the data loss.

Manage full transaction log incident

If your log backups are infrequent enough, or there is an unanticipated volume of data manipulation transactions, the database's transaction log might completely fill up. As an alternative, another database or some other external process might fill up a disk on which the transaction log is located and it will not be able to automatically grow. When the database cannot write to the transaction log because it is full it generates the 9002 error:

```
Msg 9002' Level 17' State 2' Line 91
The transaction log for database 'database_name' is full due to 'LOG_BACKUP'.
```

Because a database's transaction log can become full due to a myriad of reasons, it is important to determine the root cause of the error. Here are the common reasons for the 9002 error:

- There is no more free space in the transaction log and it has reached its maximum size limit.

- There is no more free space in the transaction log and it cannot grow because there is no more free space left on the disk.

- A long running transaction is preventing log truncation.

To determine what is preventing log truncation, execute the query shown in Listing 2-14 and examine the [log_reuse_wait_desc] column.

LISTING 2-14 Querying the database's transaction log reuse wait

```
USE master;
GO
SELECT [database_id], [name] as 'database_name', [state_desc], [recovery_model_desc],
[log_reuse_wait_desc]
FROM [sys].[databases];
```

Table 2-1 shows you how to interpret the [log_reuse_wait_desc] column.

TABLE 2-1 Description of LOG_REUSE_WAIT_DESC column for [sys].[databases]

log_reuse_wait	log_reuse_wait_desc	Description
0	NOTHING	There is one or more reusable virtual log files (VLFs).
1	CHECKPOINT	■ Checkpoint is preventing log truncation: ■ No checkpoint has occurred since the last log truncation. ■ The head of the log has not yet moved beyond a virtual log file (VLF).
2	LOG_BACKUP	Log backup is required to move the head of the log forward.
3	ACTIVE_BACKUP_OR_RESTORE	Database backup or a restore is in progress.
4	ACTIVE_TRANSACTION	Transaction is preventing log truncation: ■ A long-running transaction might exist at the start of the log backup. ■ A deferred transaction is running. A deferred transaction is an active transaction whose rollback is blocked because of some unavailable resource.
5	DATABASE_MIRRORING	Database mirroring is preventing log truncation: ■ Database mirroring is paused. ■ In high-performance mode the mirror database is significantly behind the principal database.
6	REPLICATION	Transactions relevant to replication publications have not been delivered to the distribution database.
7	DATABASE_SNAPSHOT_CREATION	A database snapshot is being created.
8	LOG_SCAN	A log scan is occurring.
9	AVAILABILITY_REPLICA	An Always On Availability Groups secondary replica is applying transaction log records of this database to a corresponding secondary database.
10		For internal use only.
11		For internal use only.
12		For internal use only.
13	OLDEST_PAGE	Indirect checkpoint is preventing log truncation. The oldest page in the database might be older than the checkpoint LSN.
14	OTHER_TRANSIENT	This value is currently not used.
15		
16	XTP_CHECKPOINT	An in-memory checkpoint is preventing log truncation.

To manage a full transaction log, the most common corrective actions include:

- **Adding a second transaction log to the database**   Although the database engine can only use one LDF file at a time, a database can have multiple LDF files. By creating a second empty log file you allow the database engine to start writing log records again.

- **Backing up the transaction log**   As discussed, whenever you back up the log, the database engine automatically truncates the log, freeing up space.

- **Freeing up disk space on the disk volume**   This allows the transaction log to grow in size if automatic growth is enabled.

- **Increasing the size of the disk volume**   It is common for SQL Server to be deployed in virtualized environments. In such environments, it is easy to increase the size of the virtual disks without incurring any outage.

- **Increasing the size of the log**   The database might have a size limit configured for the transaction log.

- **Killing a long running transaction**   A long running query can be holding up the truncation operation, which in turn causes the transaction to fill up. Use the KILL statement to end the process using its Server Process ID (SPID).

- **Moving the log to another disk that has sufficient capacity**   This involves detaching the database, moving the log files, and re-attaching the database. This might not be an option in scenarios where the database cannot be taken offline.

- **Truncating the transaction log**   This is not recommended because it breaks your log-chain. If you need to truncate the log, it is highly recommended that you immediately perform a full backup so as to re-initialize your log chain.

To kill a long running transaction query the [sys].[dm_tran_database_transactions] DMV to determine what transactions are currently executing in the database and how long they have been executing. As an alternative, execute the DBCC OPENTRAN command within the database. The DBCC OPENTRAN command displays information about the oldest active transaction within the transaction log of a database:

```
Transaction information for database 'WideWorldImporters'.
Oldest active transaction:
    SPID (server process ID): 69
    UID (user ID) : -1
    Name         : user_transaction
    LSN          : (34:12:7)
    Start time   : Sep 30 1984 12:13:21:666AM
    SID          : 0x0106000000000051500000820672ae6c43f9eb9788953c9e9030000
DBCC execution completed. If DBCC printed error messages' contact your system
administrator.
```

Use the KILL statement to kill the offending transaction. Listing 2-15 show an example of how to kill the server process ID (SPID) identified by the DBCC OPENTRAN command.

LISTING 2-15 KILL statement

```
KILL 69;
```

Be careful killing processes because they might be running important transactions. You cannot kill your own process. You should not kill system processes, including the following:

- AWAITING COMMAND
- CHECKPOINT SLEEP
- LAZY WRITER
- LOCK MONITOR
- SIGNAL HANDLER

In the exam you might get asked what corrective action to take when the transaction log become full in a specific scenario. Use the techniques in this section to work out the best corrective action in the exam.

Manage log with delayed durability

In the last couple of releases of SQL Server, Microsoft has added some functionality to the configuration and architecture of the transaction log. Consequently, these changes might be tested in the exam. Remember, they might not be tested directly, but will be part of the scenario, and as such will impact the answer choices.

With the release of SQL Server 2014, the database engine supports a feature called *delayed durability*. This feature potentially impacts the amount of data that is lost in the event of a disaster incident.

By default, when operations are recorded to the transaction log, they are initially written to the log cache (log buffers), which is located in memory. As part of the write ahead logging (WAL) protocol, the log cache is flushed to disk whenever one of the following occurs:

- A commit transaction record is written.
- The 60KB log block/buffer is filled.
- A CHECKPOINT operation is performed.
- The [sys].[sp_log_flush sysem] stored procedure is executed.

When delayed durability is enabled, the database engine no longer flushes the log buffers when the commit transaction occurs. It tries to wait until 60KB of records are written to the log buffer before flushing the buffer. This can improve performance where you have a transactional database solution that commits a large volume of small transactions.

Use the ALTER DATABASE statement to enable delayed durability:

```
ALTER DATABASE database_name
SET DELAYED_DURABILITY = DISABLED | ALLOWED | FORCED;
```

Setting delayed durability to FORCED forces all transactions to use delayed durability. Setting delayed durability to ALLOWED requires the developer to explicitly invoke delayed durability using the COMMIT TRANSACTION WITH (DELAYED_DURABILITY = ON) statement.

The next change made to the transaction log architecture is how it can use the latest generation of flash storage. We will now examine how SQL Server supports persistent memory for transaction logs.

Manage log with persistent memory

With the release of SQL Server 2016 Service Pack 1, the database engine officially supports non-volatile memory (NVDIMM) on Windows Server 2016. NVDIMM memory is also referred to as storage class memory (SCM) or persistent memory (PM). NVDIMM memory provides performance at memory speeds and survives a server crash or reboot. Table 2-2 shows the performance benefits of NVDIMM over traditionally used storage.

TABLE 2-2 Typical storage I/O response times

Storage Type	Response Time
Disk Drives (HDD)	4+ milliseconds (ms)
Solid State Drive (SSD)	<4 milliseconds (ms).
PCI NVMe SSD	microseconds (µs)
NVDIMM	nanoseconds (ns)

Due to current capacity limits of NVDIMM you cannot place the entire transaction log onto this SCM. Your transaction log size might easily exceed the maximum NVDIMM capacity. Also, it would not be cost effective for most customers.

Consequently, with the initial support for NVDIMM you can only place the transaction log's cache (or log buffers that live in memory) onto this new memory type. The main benefit is that the log cache contains multiple commit records. Normally the log cache is flushed as soon as a commit record is written. On high performance transactional databases this can become a bottleneck, with high WRITELOG waits. Figure 2-7 shows how the log buffer is stored in NVDIMM memory and contains multiple commit records.

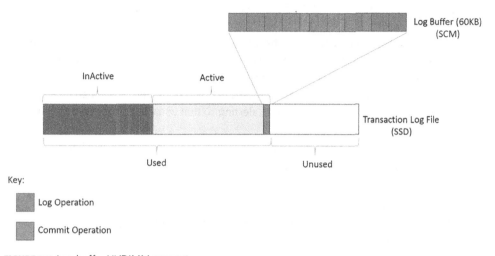

Key:

■ Log Operation

■ Commit Operation

FIGURE 2-7 Log buffer NVDIMM support

As the log records are fully durable as soon as they are copied into the log buffer there is no exposure to data loss, as in the case of delayed durability that was discussed in the previous section. Consequently, you do not need to back up the log more frequently to minimize potential data loss.

To take advantage of NVDIMM-N memory you need to perform the following tasks:

1. Install NVDIMM memory in your server.

2. Format the NVDIMM memory as a Direct Access (DAX) volume in Windows Server 2016.

3. Create a second 20MB transaction log for the database using the ALTER DATABASE statement:

```
ALTER DATABASE database_name
ADD LOG FILE (
NAME = logical_file_name'
FILENAME = os_file_name'
SIZE = 20 MB)
```

The database engine automatically detects that the second transaction log file is located on a DAX volume and creates a 20MB log file. This second log file on the DAX volume is always 20MB in size, irrespective of the size specified in the ALTER DATABASE statement. This might change in the future.

NVDIMM support for the log buffer is only available for SQL Server installed on physical machines. Virtualized SQL Server instances and failover clusters are not supported. Only secondary replicas are supported in Availability group architectures.

Configure backup automation

The final section of this skill will show you how to automate your backup strategy that we have discussed so far. One of SQL Server's strengths has always been how easy it is to schedule automation tasks and to be notified when a task succeeds or fails. We will first look at how to schedule scripts to automatically run before looking at the capabilities of maintenance plans. Finally, we will look at how you can configure alerting so that you will be notified if a scheduled job fails.

Backups can be scheduled to occur automatically in SQL Server through the SQL Server Agent. We will cover SQL Server Agent in more detail in Chapter 3, "Manage and monitor SQL Server instances."

The following steps show how to automate a full database backup through the SQL Server Agent. In this example, the backup of the [master] and [msdb] system databases are scheduled to be executed nightly at 02:00.

1. Open SQL Server Management Studio.

2. Expand the SQL Server Agent folder.

3. Right-click the Jobs folder, and select New Job.

4. In the New Job dialog box, on the General page, provide a Name and Description for the backup, as shown in Figure 2-8. It is best practice to configure the Owner as **sa**. You can create your own categories through the sp_add_category stored procedure located in the [msdb] system database.

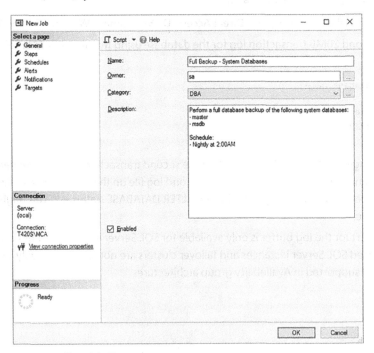

FIGURE 2-8 New Job: General page

5. Click the Steps page.

6. Click the New button to create a new step for the job.

7. In the New Job Step dialog box, on the General page, provide a name for the step and the BACKUP command that is performed to back up the [master] system database, as shown in Figure 2-9.

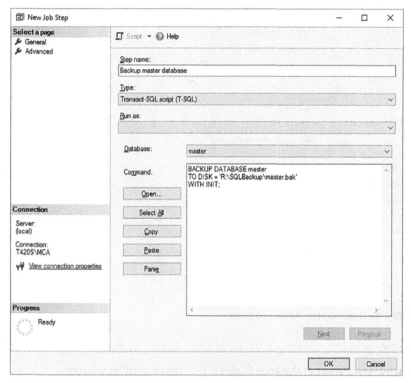

FIGURE 2-9 New Job Step: General page

8. Click the Parse button to ensure the T-SQL command is syntactically correct.

9. Click the OK button to close the Parse Command Text dialog box.

10. Click the Advanced page.

11. In the New Job Step dialog box, on the Advanced page, configure the job step to perform the next step on failure, as show in Figure 2-10. This ensures that the job attempts to back up the [msdb] database, even though the [master] database backup failed.

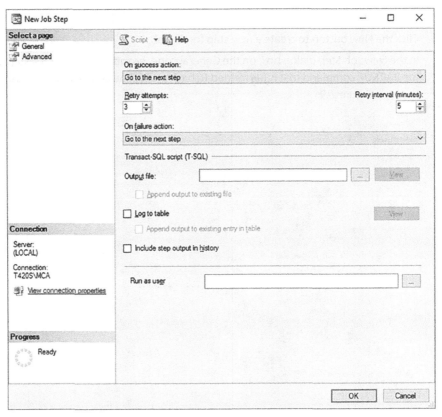

FIGURE 2-10 New Job Step: Advanced page

12. Click OK.

13. Click the New button as shown in Figure 2-11 to create another job step.

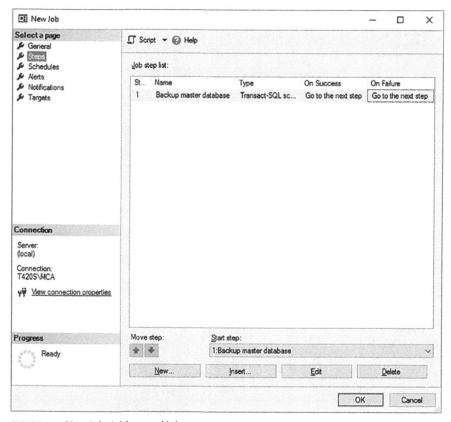

FIGURE 2-11 New Job: Add second job step

14. In the New Job Step dialog box, on the General page, provide a name for the step and the BACKUP command for the backup of the [msdb] system database, as shown in Figure 2-12.

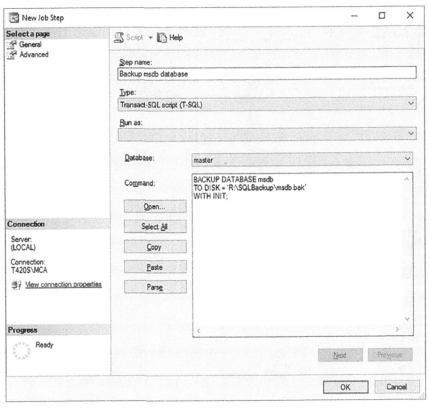

FIGURE 2-12 New Job Step: Add command for second job step

15. Click the OK button.

16. In the New Job Step dialog box, on the Advanced page, ensure the job steps are performed in the correct order, as show in Figure 2-13. Note how you can configure the job to perform any step in the job first.

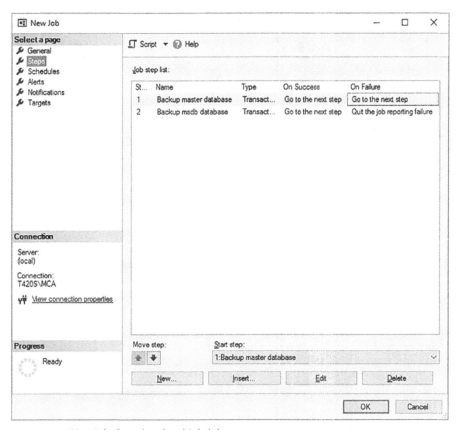

FIGURE 2-13 New Job: Completed multiple job steps

17. Click the Schedules page.

18. In the New Job Step dialog box, on the Schedules page, click the New button to sched-ule when you want the database backup to execute.

19. In the New Job Schedule dialog box, configure the name, frequency, and duration required, as shown in Figure 2-14.

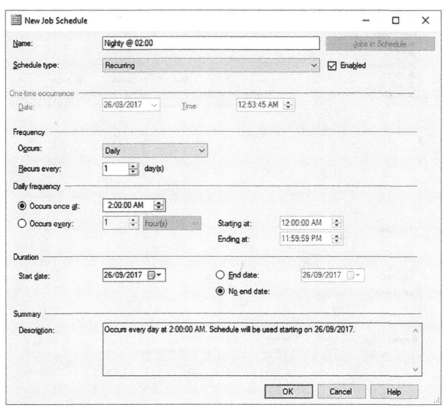

FIGURE 2-14 New Job Schedule dialog box

20. Click the OK button.

21. Confirm that the schedule has been saved correctly, as shown in Figure 2-15.

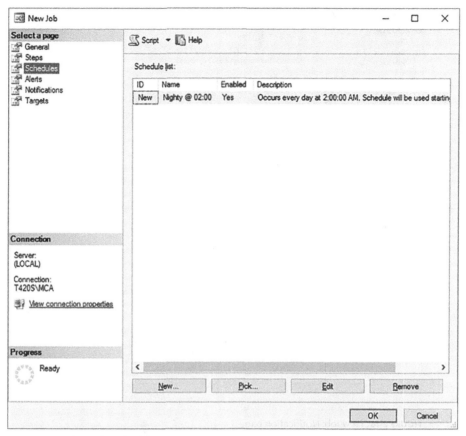

FIGURE 2-15 New Job's schedule

22. Click the Notifications page.

23. In the New Job Step dialog box, on the Notifications page, configure who needs to be notified if a job fails, succeeds, or completes, as shown in Figure 2-16. We will look at how you create operators in the "Create and manage operators" section in Chapter 3.

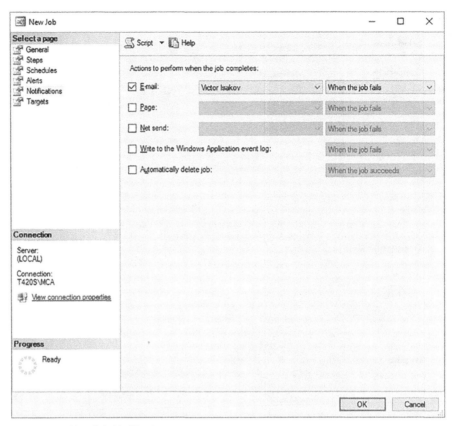

FIGURE 2-16 New Job: Notification page

24. Click the OK button to schedule the backup operation. The job is created in the Jobs folder of SQL Server Management Studio.

25. To document the scheduled job, right-click the job, select Script Job As, then CREATE TO, and finally New Query Editor Window.

Listing 2-16 shows the T-SQL script created for the scheduled backup job.

LISTING 2-16 Scheduling a backup through SQL Server Agent

```
USE [msdb  ]
GO
/****** Object:  Job [Full Backup - System Databases]    Script Date: 26/09/2017
11:56:45 PM ******/
BEGIN TRANSACTION
DECLARE @ReturnCode INT
SELECT @ReturnCode = 0
/****** Object:  JobCategory [DBA]    Script Date: 26/09/2017 11:56:45 PM ******/
IF NOT EXISTS (SELECT name FROM msdb.dbo.syscategories WHERE name=N'DBA' AND category_
class=1)
BEGIN
EXEC @ReturnCode = msdb.dbo.sp_add_category @class=N'JOB'' @type=N'LOCAL'' @name=N'DBA'
```

```
IF (@@ERROR <> 0 OR @ReturnCode <> 0) GOTO QuitWithRollback
END


DECLARE @jobId BINARY(16)
EXEC @ReturnCode =  msdb.dbo.sp_add_job @job_name=N'Full Backup - System Databases''
        @enabled=1'
        @notify_level_eventlog=0'
        @notify_level_email=2'
        @notify_level_netsend=0'
        @notify_level_page=0'
        @delete_level=0'
        @description=N'Perform a full database backup of the following system databases:
- master
- msdb

Schedule:
- Nightly at 2:00AM''
        @category_name=N'DBA''
        @owner_login_name=N'sa''
        @notify_email_operator_name=N'Victor Isakov'' @job_id = @jobId OUTPUT
IF (@@ERROR <> 0 OR @ReturnCode <> 0) GOTO QuitWithRollback
/****** Object:  Step [Backup master database]     Script Date: 26/09/2017 11:56:45 PM
******/
EXEC @ReturnCode = msdb.dbo.sp_add_jobstep @job_id=@jobId' @step_name=N'Backup master
database''
        @step_id=1'
        @cmdexec_success_code=0'
        @on_success_action=3'
        @on_success_step_id=0'
        @on_fail_action=3'
        @on_fail_step_id=0'
        @retry_attempts=3'
        @retry_interval=5'
        @os_run_priority=0' @subsystem=N'TSQL''
        @command=N'BACKUP DATABASE master
TO DISK = ''R:\SQLBackup\master.bak''
WITH INIT;''
        @database_name=N'master''
        @flags=0
IF (@@ERROR <> 0 OR @ReturnCode <> 0) GOTO QuitWithRollback
/****** Object:  Step [Backup msdb database]     Script Date: 26/09/2017 11:56:45 PM
******/
EXEC @ReturnCode = msdb.dbo.sp_add_jobstep @job_id=@jobId' @step_name=N'Backup msdb
database''
        @step_id=2'
        @cmdexec_success_code=0'
        @on_success_action=1'
        @on_success_step_id=0'
        @on_fail_action=2'
        @on_fail_step_id=0'
        @retry_attempts=0'
        @retry_interval=0'
        @os_run_priority=0' @subsystem=N'TSQL''
        @command=N'BACKUP DATABASE msdb
TO DISK = ''R:\SQLBackup\msdb.bak''
```

```
WITH INIT;''
        @database_name=N'master''
        @flags=0
IF (@@ERROR <> 0 OR @ReturnCode <> 0) GOTO QuitWithRollback
EXEC @ReturnCode = msdb.dbo.sp_update_job @job_id = @jobId' @start_step_id = 1
IF (@@ERROR <> 0 OR @ReturnCode <> 0) GOTO QuitWithRollback
EXEC @ReturnCode = msdb.dbo.sp_add_jobschedule @job_id=@jobId' @name=N'Nighty @ 02:00''
        @enabled=1'
        @freq_type=4'
        @freq_interval=1'
        @freq_subday_type=1'
        @freq_subday_interval=0'
        @freq_relative_interval=0'
        @freq_recurrence_factor=0'
        @active_start_date=20170926'
        @active_end_date=99991231'
        @active_start_time=20000'
        @active_end_time=235959'
        @schedule_uid=N'47e87563-0e09-4856-821d-eec181839d09'
IF (@@ERROR <> 0 OR @ReturnCode <> 0) GOTO QuitWithRollback
EXEC @ReturnCode = msdb.dbo.sp_add_jobserver @job_id = @jobId' @server_name = N'(local)'
IF (@@ERROR <> 0 OR @ReturnCode <> 0) GOTO QuitWithRollback
COMMIT TRANSACTION
GOTO EndSave
QuitWithRollback:
    IF (@@TRANCOUNT > 0) ROLLBACK TRANSACTION
EndSave:
```

In the exam you might get asked about the stored procedures highlighted in Listing 2-16 and their parameters. Make sure you are familiar with them for the exam.

This section showed you how to schedule Transact-SQL statements via SQL Server Agent jobs. If your SQL Server instance has a large number of databases this will be cumbersome to set up and difficult to manage. A better approach might be to take advantage of maintenance plans and we will look at their capabilities next.

Configure a maintenance plan

A more popular and easier technique to configure backup automation is to create a maintenance plan for your databases. The capabilities of maintenance plans change in subsequent releases of SQL Server. Even though you might have discounted their use in the past, make sure you are familiar with their capabilities in the latest version of SQL Server for the exam.

Use the Maintenance Plan Wizard to create a basic maintenance plan. You can then customize the maintenance plan further by opening up the maintenance plan in SQL Server Management Studio. We will go through such an exercise in this section.

Maintenance plans support the following tasks:

- **Back Up Database** This task allows you to specify the source databases, destination files or tapes, and overwrite options for a transaction log backup. It supports the following types of backups:

- Differential
- Full
- Transaction Log

- **Check Database Integrity**   This task performs internal consistency checks of the data and index pages within the database.
- **Clean Up History**   This task deletes historical data associated with Backup and Restore, SQL Server Agent, and maintenance plan operations. This task allows you to specify the type and age of the data to be deleted.
- **Execute SQL Server Agent Job**   This task allows you to select SQL Server Agent jobs to run as part of the maintenance plan.
- **Execute T-SQL Statement Task**   This task allows you to run any T-SQL script.
- **Maintenance Cleanup Task**   This task removes files left over from executing a maintenance plan.
- **Notify Operator Task**   This task sends an email to any SQL Server Agent operator.
- **Rebuild Index**   This task reorganizes data on the data and index pages by rebuilding indexes. This improves performance of index scans and seeks. This task also optimizes the distribution of data and free space on the index pages, allowing faster future growth.
- **Reorganize Index**   This task defragments and compacts clustered and non-clustered indexes on tables and views. This improves index-scanning performance.
- **Shrink Database**   This task reduces the disk space consumed by the database and the log files by removing empty data, index, and log pages.
- **Update Statistics**   This task ensures the query optimizer has up-to-date information about the distribution of data values in the tables. This allows the optimizer to make better judgments about data access strategies.

> *IMPORTANT* **DO NOT SHRINK DATABASES**
>
> Do not schedule the Shrink Database task in production environments because it substantially degrades the database's query performance. The database shrink operation results in heavily fragmented tables and indexes.

It is common to perform optimization tasks and integrity checks with your database backups. This helps ensure that your database backup contains no corruptions and that the database will run optimally straight away if it ever has to be restored. At the very least, configure the following maintenance tasks for all databases to minimize data loss and ensure optimal performance:

- Perform database backups to meet your RPO and RTO SLAs.
- Perform database consistency checks to detect and potentially fix database corruptions.

- Rebuild and reorganize indexes to ensure optimal query performance and efficient storage usage.

- Update statistics to ensure optimal query performance.

For simpler environments, it is common to create a single maintenance plan to perform all of these maintenance tasks. For more complex requirements, schedule multiple customer job steps.

The following steps demonstrate how to create a maintenance plan for all user databases that automatically performs a full database backup, consistency check, and index optimization tasks weekly on Sunday at 01:00:

1. Open SQL Server Management Studio.

2. Expand the Management folder.

3. Right-click the Maintenance Plans folder, and select the Maintenance Plan Wizard.

4. On the welcome screen, click the Next button, as show in Figure 2-17.

FIGURE 2-17 Maintenance Plan Wizard

5. In the Select Plan Properties screen, provide a name and description as shown in Figure 2-18.

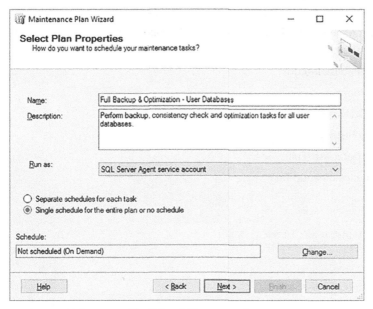

FIGURE 2-18 Maintenance Plan Wizard: Plan properties

6. Click the Change button to schedule your maintenance plan.

7. Define your desired schedule, as show in Figure 2-19, and click the OK button.

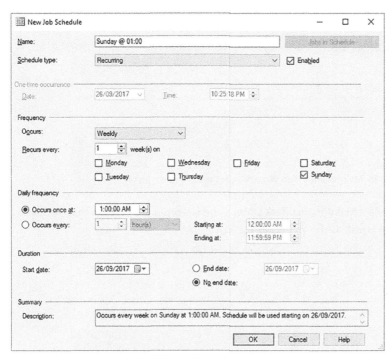

FIGURE 2-19 Maintenance Plan Wizard: Schedule

8. Click the Next button.

9. In the Select Maintenance Tasks screen, check the following options, as show in Figure 2-20:

   - Check Database Integrity

   - Rebuild Index

   - Update Statistics

   - Clean Up History

   - Back Up Database (Full)

   - Maintenance Cleanup Task

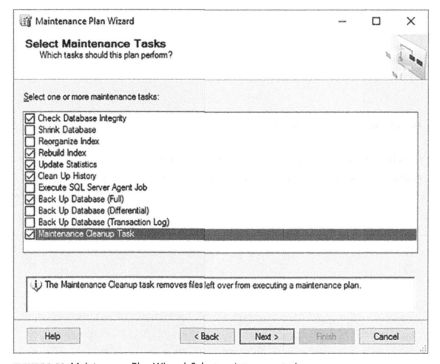

FIGURE 2-20 Maintenance Plan Wizard: Select maintenance tasks

10. In the Select Maintenance Task Order screen, reorder the tasks so that the Clean Up History task is last, as shown in Figure 2-21.

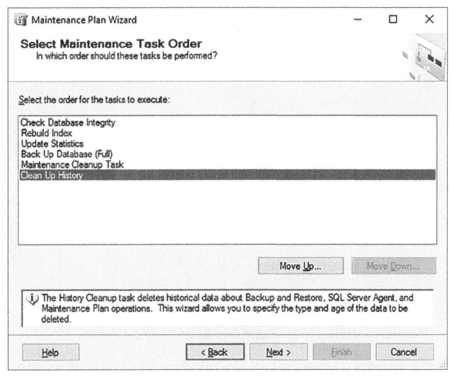

FIGURE 2-21 Maintenance Plan Wizard: Select maintenance task order

11. In the Define Database Check Integrity Task, select the Database drop-down list.

12. In the drop-down list, select All User Databases (Excluding master, model, msdb), as show in Figure 2-22.

13. Select the Ignore Databases When The State Is Not Online to ensure that there are no backup errors. Databases that are offline cannot be backed up.

14. Click the OK button.

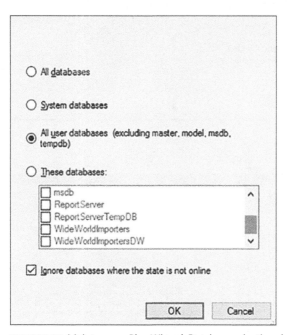

FIGURE 2-22 Maintenance Plan Wizard: Database selection drop-down list

15. In the Define Database Check Integrity Task, ensure the following options are checked, as shown in Figure 2-23:

   ■ Include Indexes

   ■ Physical Only

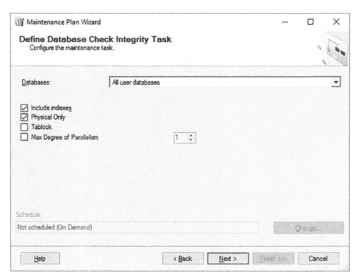

FIGURE 2-23 Maintenance Plan Wizard: Define database check integrity task

16. Click the Next button.

17. In the Define Rebuild Index Task, select All User Databases, and configure the following options, as shown in Figure 2-24:

- Configure a fillfactor of 100% by selecting 0% free space to ensure that all data pages are filled 100 percent.

- Use the [tempdb] system database for sorting operations.

- Perform an online index operation for all possible tables.

- Rebuild indexes offline for tables that do not support online index operations.

- Use a low priority for the index rebuild operations.

- If the index operation experiences blocking, abort the operation after five minutes.

18. Click the Next button.

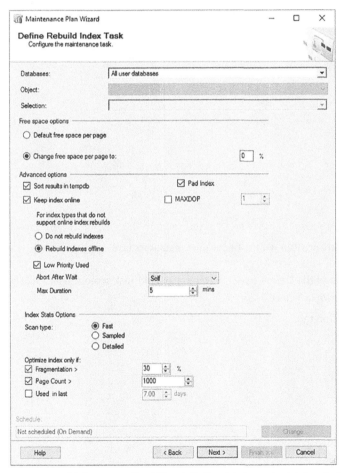

FIGURE 2-24 Maintenance Plan Wizard: Define database check integrity task

19. In the Define Update Statistics Task, select All User Databases, and configure the following options, as shown in Figure 2-25:
    - Update column statistics only. There is no need to update index statistics because the previous task performs that.

20. Click the Next button.

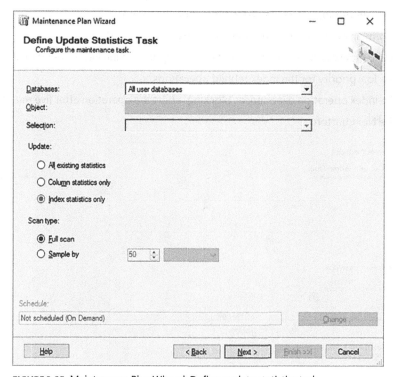

FIGURE 2-25 Maintenance Plan Wizard: Define update statistics task

21. In the General tab of the Define Back Up Database (Full) Task screen, select All User Databases, as shown in Figure 2-26.

22. Click the Destination tab.

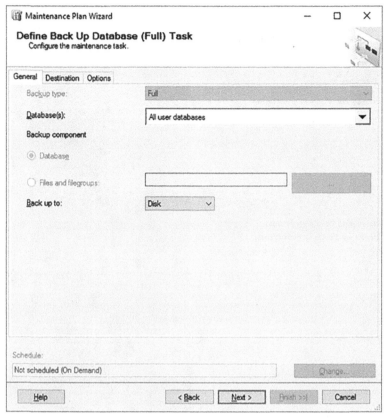

FIGURE 2-26 Maintenance Plan Wizard: General tab of define back up database (full) task

23. In the Destination tab of the Define Back Up Database (Full) Task screen, configure the destination folder and the following options, as shown in Figure 2-27.

- Select the Create A Sub-Directory For Each Database option. This option makes it easier to manage the database backups.

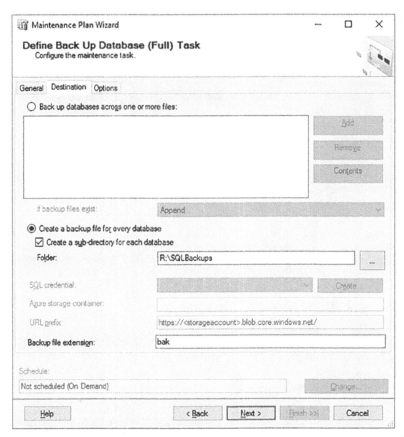

FIGURE 2-27 Maintenance Plan Wizard: Destination tab of define back up database (full) task

24. Click on the Options tab

25. In the Options tab of the Define Back Up Database (Full) Task screen, configure the following options, as shown in Figure 2-28.

- Enable backup compression.

- Perform checksum on the database. This helps check that the database contains no errors and can be restored.

- Verify the backup integrity. This helps check that the backup contains no errors and can be restored.

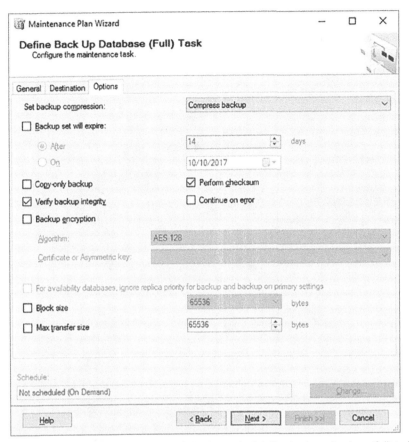

FIGURE 2-28 Maintenance Plan Wizard: Options tab of define back up database (full) task

26. In the Define Maintenance Cleanup Task, specify the backup location and configure the following cleanup options, as shown in Figure 2-29.

    ■ Include first-level options. This matches our configuration in the Define Backup Database Destination screen.

    ■ Delete backup files older than 5 weeks. This helps ensure that we do not run out of space in our backup store.

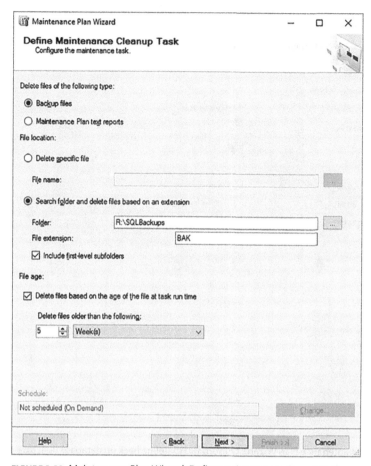

FIGURE 2-29 Maintenance Plan Wizard: Define maintenance cleanup task

27. Click the Next button.

28. In the Define History Cleanup Task, change the Remove Historical Data Older Than configuration option to 18 months, as shown in Figure 2-30.

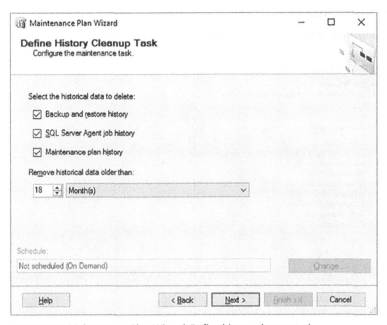

FIGURE 2-30 Maintenance Plan Wizard: Define history cleanup task

29. Click the Next button.

30. In the Select Report Options screen, change the report folder location, as shown in Figure 2-31. It is important to change it from the default directory, otherwise you will potentially generate thousands of small report files in SQL Server error log directory.

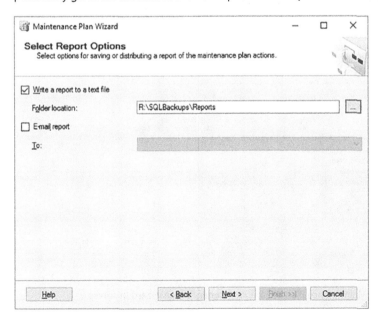

FIGURE 2-31 Maintenance Plan Wizard: Select report options

31. Click the Next button.

32. In the Complete The Wizard screen, review your configuration, as shown in Figure 2-32.

FIGURE 2-32 Maintenance Plan Wizard: Complete The wizard

33. Click the Finish button to create the maintenance plan.

34. In the Maintenance Plan Wizard Progress screen, ensure that all of the actions have run successfully, as shown in Figure 2-33.

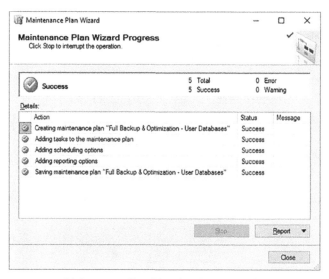

FIGURE 2-33 Maintenance Plan Wizard: Maintenance plan wizard progress

35. Click the Close button.

It is a common mistake not to configure alerting for when scheduled backup operations fail. If the SQL Server Agent crashes or is not restarted by a database administrator after a manual restart of SQL Server, no scheduled backup operations will execute. Without any alerting or notification this could lead to substantial data loss if a disaster occurs. We will examine how you can configure altering for failed backup operations next.

Configure alerting for failed backups

As we have seen, backups can be easily scheduled via a SQL Server Agent job, or a maintenance plan. Once a backup job is scheduled, however, you cannot assume that it will always execute successfully. At a minimum you need to configure some form of notification or alerting for failed backups. Ideally you should be notified of both failed and successful backups to ensure that backup operations are being completed successfully.

To configure alerting you need to perform the following high level steps:

1. Configure Database Mail.
2. Configure SQL Server Agent to use Database Mail.
3. Define operators.
4. Configure notifications when a job fails.

We will look at how you configure Database Mail in Chapter 3. In this section we will focus more on how to create an operator and configure alerting.

To configure an operator, perform the following steps:

1. Open SQL Server Management Studio.
2. Expand the SQL Server Agent folder.
3. Right-click the Operators folder, and select New Operator.
4. Configure the following properties for the operator, as shown in Figure 2-34.
   - Name
   - E-mail Name

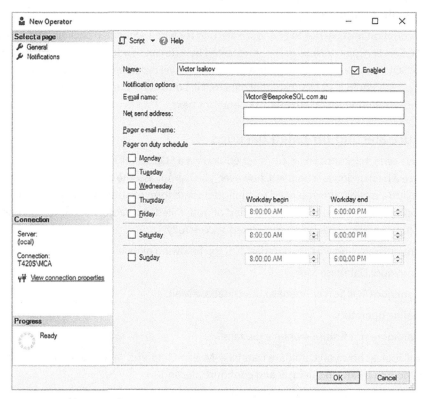

FIGURE 2-34 New operator

SQL Server Agent jobs easily allow you to be alerted when a job fails, succeeds, or completes. Be careful configuring jobs only to alert you when they fail. If the SQL Server Agent service is shutdown, or a job does not run for any reason, you will not be notified at all. As said earlier, it is better to configure important jobs to notify you when they complete either way.

As an example we will configure alerting for the "Full Backup – System Databases" SQL Server Agent job that we created earlier in this section. To configure alerting, perform the following steps:

1. Open SQL Server Management Studio.

2. Expand the Jobs folder.

3. Right-click the backup job that you want to configure an email notification for, and click Properties.

4. Click the Notifications page in the Job Properties dialog box.

5. Configure the operator that you want to be notified when the job completes, as shown in Figure 2-35.

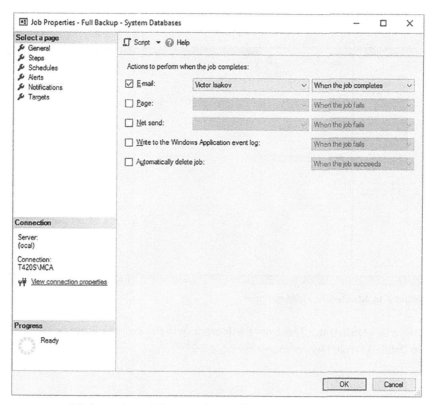

FIGURE 2-35 SQL Server Agent Job properties: Notification page

You can also configure notifications for maintenance plans. The Maintenance Plan Wizard does not provide that functionality in its setup beyond the ability to email the maintenance plan report. However, you can customize a maintenance plan to notify you if with a different email depending on whether a backup fails or succeeds.

In the following example we will customize the "Full Backup & Optimization – User Databases" maintenance plan we created earlier in this section. To configure a notification in an existing maintenance plan, perform the following steps:

1. Open SQL Server Management Studio.

2. Expand the Management folder.

3. Expand the Maintenance Plans folder.

4. Double-click the maintenance plan you want to configure. The maintenance plan is opened up in the Maintenance Plan Designer, as shown in Figure 2-36.

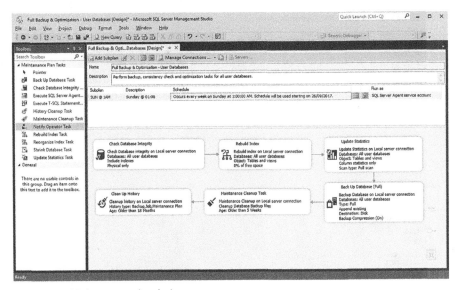

FIGURE 2-36 Maintenance plan designer

5. Drag a Notify Operator Task from the Toolbox onto the design surface below the Back Up Database (Full) task, as shown in Figure 2-37.

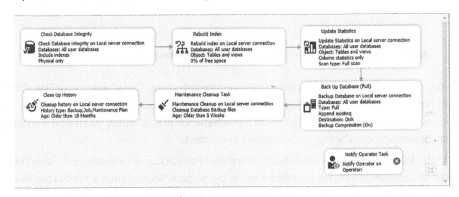

FIGURE 2-37 New notify operator task

6. Click on the name in the notify operator task and rename it to "Notify Operator of Success" as shown in Figure 2-38.

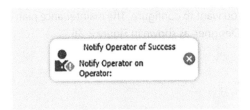

FIGURE 2-38 Renaming the notify operator task

7. Double-click the renamed Notify Operator of Success task, and configure the following properties, as shown in Figure 2-39.

   ■ Specify which operators are notified in the Operators To notify check box.

   ■ Provide an email subject in the Notification Message Subject text box to indicate the backups have completed successfully.

   ■ Provide an email body in the Notification Message Body text box to indicate the backups have completed successfully.

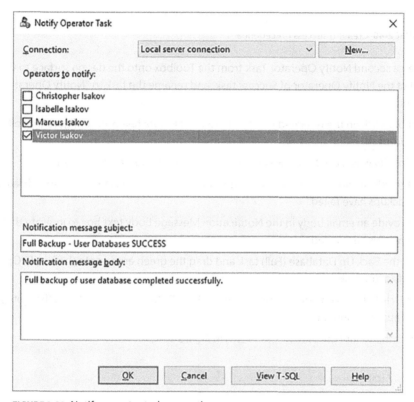

FIGURE 2-39 Notify operator task properties

8. Click the OK button.

9. Click the Back Up Database (Full) task, and drag the green arrow onto the Notify Operator of Success task, as shown in Figure 2-40. The green arrow indicates that the Notify Operator of Success task performs only if the Back Up Database (Full) task is executed successfully.

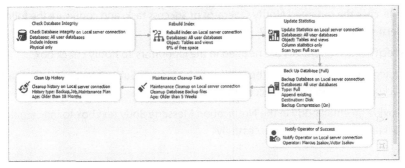

FIGURE 2-40 Creating success precedence

10. Drag a second Notify Operator Task from the Toolbox onto the design surface to the left of the Notify Operator of Success task, and rename the task to "Notify Operator Of Failure."

11. Double-click on the renamed Notify Operator of Failure task and configure the following properties:

    ■ Specify which operators are notified in the Operators To notify check box.

    ■ Provide an email subject in the Notification Message Subject text box to indicate that backups have failed.

    ■ Provide an email body in the Notification Message Body text box to indicate that the backups have failed.

12. Click the Back Up Database (Full) task and drag the green arrow onto the Notify Operator of Failure task.

13. Right-click the green arrow between the Back Up Database (Full) task and the Notify Operator of Failure task.

14. Select the Failure precedence, as shown in Figure 2-41.

FIGURE 2-41 Task precedence

15. Ensure that there is a red arrow between the Back Up Database (Full) task and the Notify Operator of Failure task, as shown in Figure 2-42. The red arrow indicates that the Notify Operator of Failure task only executes if the Back Up Database (Full) task fails.

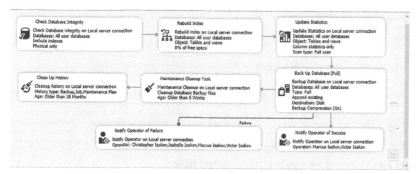

FIGURE 2-42 SQL Server Agent Job properties: Notification page

16. Close the maintenance plan in SQL Server Management Studio to save the changes.

Another alternative is to configure alerts for failed backups by taking advantage of SQL Server Agent alerts. SQL Server Agent has the capability of notifying operators whenever a SQL Server event alerts occurs. SQL Server event alerts are raised based on one of the following:

- An error number
- An error's severity level
- When the error message contains a particular string

The benefit of using alerts is that they can catch all backup errors, irrespective of how the backup statement was executed. For an alert to fire you need to know what error number is generated when a backup fails. The database engine maintains all the error messages in the [sys].[messages] table in the [master] system database. So you can query it to find the specific error you are interested in.

To configure an alert when a backup fails, perform the following steps:

1. Open SQL Server Management Studio.

2. Connect to your SQL Server instance.

3. Click the New Query button in the Standard tool bar to open a new query window.

4. Run the query, as shown in Figure 2-43 in the [master] database. The [sys].[messages] system table contains the error messages used by the database engine. You can use error number 3041 for your backup failure alert.

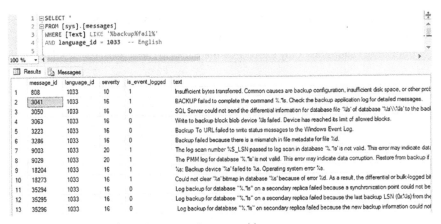

```
1  ⊟SELECT *
2  ⊟FROM [sys].[messages]
3    WHERE [Text] LIKE '%backup%fail%'
4    AND language_id = 1033  -- English
5
```

	message_id	language_id	severity	is_event_logged	text
1	808	1033	10	1	Insufficient bytes transferred. Common causes are backup configuration, insufficient disk space, or other prob
2	3041	1033	16	1	BACKUP failed to complete the command %. %ls. Check the backup application log for detailed messages.
3	3050	1033	16	0	SQL Server could not send the differential information for database file '%ls' of database '%ls\\%ls' to the bacl
4	3063	1033	16	0	Write to backup block blob device %ls failed. Device has reached its limit of allowed blocks.
5	3223	1033	16	0	Backup To URL failed to write status messages to the Windows Event Log.
6	3286	1033	16	0	Backup failed because there is a mismatch in file metadata for file %d.
7	9003	1033	20	1	The log scan number %S_LSN passed to log scan in database "%.*ls' is not valid. This error may indicate data
8	9029	1033	20	1	The PMM log for database "%.*ls' is not valid. This error may indicate data corruption. Restore from backup if
9	18204	1033	16	1	%ls: Backup device '%s' failed to %s. Operating system error %s.
10	18273	1033	16	1	Could not clear '%s' bitmap in database '%s' because of error %d. As a result, the differential or bulk-logged bit
11	35294	1033	16	0	Log backup for database "%.*ls" on a secondary replica failed because a synchronization point could not be
12	35295	1033	16	0	Log backup for database "%.*ls" on a secondary replica failed because the last backup LSN (0x%ls) from the
13	35296	1033	16	0	Log backup for database "%.*ls" on secondary replica failed because the new backup information could not

FIGURE 2-43 Querying the [sys].[messages] system table

5. Expand the Alerts folder.

6. Right-click the Alerts folder, and select New Alert.

7. In the General page of the New Alert dialog box, configure the following properties, as shown in Figure 2-44.

   - Provide a name for the alert in the Name text box.

   - Specify 3041 in the Error Number text box.

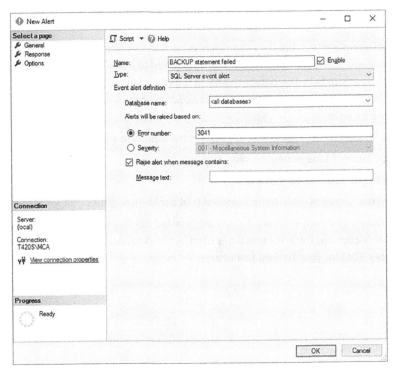

FIGURE 2-44 New Alert: General page

8. Click the Response page of the New Alert dialog box, and configure the following properties, as shown in Figure 2-45.

   - Select the Notify Operators check box.
   - Select the Email check box for all the operators you want the alert sent to.

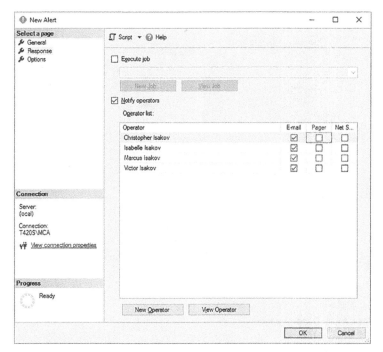

FIGURE 2-45 New Alert: Response page

9. Click the Options page of the New Alert dialog box and configure the following properties, as shown in Figure 2-46.

   - Select the Email check box for the Include Alert Error Text in options.
   - Configure the Delay Between Responses option for 5 minutes. This prevents too many emails being sent if an alerts fires multiple times within the 5 minute interval.

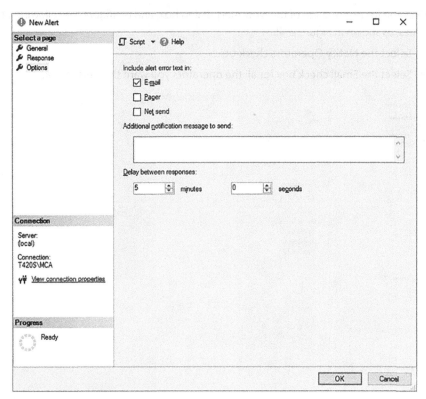

FIGURE 2-46 New Alert: General page

10. Click the OK button to create the alert.

Listing 2-17 shows how to create the same alert in T-SQL.

LISTING 2-17 Create [Backup Error] alert

```
USE [msdb]
GO
EXEC msdb.dbo.sp_add_alert @name=N'Backup Error''
        @message_id=3041'
        @severity=0'
        @enabled=1'
        @delay_between_responses=300'
        @include_event_description_in=1'
        @category_name=N'[Uncategorized]''
        @job_id=N'00000000-0000-0000-0000-000000000000'
```

Skill 2.2 Restore databases

When a disaster occurs, you need to decide which course of corrective action to take. This might involve restoring the database. In this case you might have multiple paths that you may take. It is important to take a path that restores the database in the quickest possible time with minimal or no data loss. Alternatively, you might choose the repair the database. We will look at how you repair databases in Skill 2.3.

In Skill 2.1 we looked at how to develop a backup strategy. The backup strategy that you use as a result of those skills and your experience will very much dictate what options you have available when a disaster occurs. This, in turn, dictates your restore strategy. So the skills in this section will closely match what was covered in Skill 2.1.

In this section we will look at the skills required to restore a database correctly and in a timely fashion. Be careful when restoring a database as you do not want to accidently delete data that is critical to your restore strategy, such as with the tail-log.

> **This section covers how to:**
>
> - Design a restore strategy
> - Restore a database
> - Revert a database snapshot
> - Perform piecemeal restores
> - Perform page recovery
> - Perform point-in-time recovery
> - Restore a filegroup
> - Develop a plan to automate and test restores

Design a restore strategy

It is important to design your restore strategy before performing any restore operations to ensure that you restore your database correctly, that you do not lose any data, and that you perform the restore within your RTO. The success of a restore strategy is dictated by such planning, as opposed to jumping in and potentially deleting the tail-log or other important data, evidence or information.

In the exam you might get a restore question that has a complex backup strategy, specific details as to what has gone wrong during a disaster and a business requirement to restore the crashed database. Always make sure you read the business requirements to ensure you understand whether you need to restore the database as quickly as possible, or with no data loss or with minimal data loss. You might then be as asked what order of restore statements will be required to meet your business objectives. Watch out for broken log chains!

There are multiple reasons why you need to initiate a restore procedure, including:

- Recover from a disaster incident.
- Recover from user error.
- Refresh a database in a non-production environment from a production database backup.
- Test your disaster recovery procedures.
- Set up a high-availability solution such as Log Shipping or Availability Groups.
- Perform an upgrade of a database between different versions of SQL Server.

In the case of a disaster incident, or user error, it is easy to panic and make mistakes. Consequently, to recover from a disaster incident, or user error, use the following procedure:

1. Do not panic.
2. Assess the situation. Start thinking about the people, processes, and recovery assets required.
3. Stop access to the database, if necessary.
4. Check to see if the tail-log exists.
5. Back up the tail-log, if it exists.
6. Assess the damage/corruption in the database.
7. Assess whether a restore strategy is required.
8. Assess whether point-in-time recovery is required.
9. Assess what backups exist.
10. Verify that the backups are current and valid.
11. Plan your restore strategy.
12. Initiate your restore process.

When planning your restore strategy, you need to ensure that all the required backups exist and are valid. You do not want to initiate a restore sequence of 10 log backups only to find that the ninth log backup is missing or corrupt.

Before you initiate a restore process, ensure that your backup devices have no errors and can be restored. The RESTORE statement has a number of options that allow you to investigate and check the backup media and backup set:

- **FILELISTONLY**   This statement returns a list of the database and log files contained in the backup set. This only lists the files without validating their contents.

- **HEADERONLY**   This statement returns the backup header information for all backup sets on a particular backup device. This lists the header information without further validation.

- **LABELONLY**   This statement returns information about the backup media identified by the given backup device. This lists the media information without further validation.

- **VERIFYONLY**   This statement verifies the backup, but it does not perform the re-store operation. It checks whether the backup set is complete and the entire backup is readable. The aim of the RESTORE VERIFYONLY operation is to be as close to an actual restore operation as practical. The RESTORE VERFIYONLY performs a number of checks that include:

  - Checking some header fields of database pages, such as the Page ID.

  - The backup set is complete and all volumes are readable.

  - The checksum is correct, if present.

  - There is sufficient space on the destination disks.

> **IMPORTANT**   **RESTORE VERIFYONLY**
>
> The RESTORE VERIFYONLY operation does not guarantee that the restore succeeds because it does not verify the structures of the data contained in the backup set.

Listing 2-18 shows an example of how to verify the backups.

LISTING 2-18 Verifying a backup set

```
RESTORE VERIFYONLY
FROM DISK = 'B:\SQLBackup\WordWideImporters_FULL.bak'
```

Don't forget that you might have multiple restore sequences for a database. These differ-ent restore sequences might have substantially different restore durations. Different restore sequences might also protect against backup set damage or corruption.

Let's assume you have an On-Line Transactional Processing (OLTP) database that is 400GB in size. The database is only used during weekdays between 09:00 and 17:00. The database has the following backup strategy:

- A full backup is performed every Sunday at 20:00.
    - The full backup is 250GB in size (due to compression).
    - The full backup takes under two hours to complete.
- A differential backup is performed every Monday, Tuesday, Wednesday, Thursday, and Friday at 23:00.
    - These differential backups take under one hour to complete.
    - These differential backups typically start off being 5GB in size, and grow to 9GB in size by Friday.
- Log backups are performed every hour from 09:00 to 18:00.
    - These log backups are on average 1GB in size, and take 15 minutes to complete.

If the database's data files crash on Friday at 10:30 you could use the following restore sequence:

1. Perform a tail-log backup.
2. Restore the full backup.
3. Restore Monday's 10 log backups.
4. Restore Tuesday's 10 log backups.
5. Restore Wednesday's 10 log backups.
6. Restore Thursday's 10 log backups.
7. Restore Friday's 9:00 and 10:00 backup.
8. Restore the tail log.

All the log restores would involve replaying 42GB of log backups. It would be quicker to use the following restore sequence:

1. Perform a tail-log backup.
2. Restore the full backup.
3. Restore Thursday's differential backup.
4. Restore Friday's 9:00 and 10:00 backup.
5. Restore the tail log.

Because this restore sequence would involve restoring an 8GB differential backup followed by 2GB worth of log backups, it would be much quicker.

If the differential backups grew by 15GB each day, Thursday's differential backup would be 60GB in size. In this case, it would probably be quicker to restore all 42 log backups.

> **IMPORTANT TESTING RESTORES**
>
> It is important for you to test restores in an environment similar to your production environment so that you can measure how long it takes to perform the various steps of your restore sequence.

Now let's assume that Thursday's differential failed due to a lack of disk space. In this case you would use the following restore sequence:

1. Perform a tail-log backup.
2. Restore the full backup.
3. Restore Wednesday's differential backup.
4. Restore Thursday's 10 log backups.
5. Restore Friday's 9:00 and 10:00 backup.
6. Restore the tail log.

Take advantage of both differential and log backups to give your disaster recovery plan both flexibility and resilience.

Restore a database

Restoring a database is not as complex as backing up a database because you are constrained by your backup strategy and your available backup sets. We covered the backup operations in detail in Skill 2.1 and you should not be surprised that the restore operations mirror them. SQL Server supports a number of different restore operations:

- Restore the entire database.
- Restore a part of a database (perform a partial restore).
- Restore a transaction log.
- Restore specific files of a database.
- Restore a specific filegroup of a database.
- Restore specific pages of a database.
- Revert a database snapshot.

We will cover all of these restore operations in this section and give examples of the syntax. The exam will be testing your knowledge of the syntax and the various options used to restore a database and its log.

The RESTORE statement is used to perform all restore operations. Use the following statement to restore a database:

```
RESTORE DATABASE { database_name | @database_name_var }
 [ FROM <backup_device> [ '...n ] ]
 [ WITH
   {
    [ RECOVERY | NORECOVERY | STANDBY =
        {standby_file_name | @standby_file_name_var }
      ]
   | '  <general_WITH_options> [ '...n ]
   | '  <replication_WITH_option>
   | '  <change_data_capture_WITH_option>
   | '  <FILESTREAM_WITH_option>
   | '  <service_broker_WITH options>
```

```
    | ' <point_in_time_WITH_options-RESTORE_DATABASE>
    } [ '...n ]
  ]
[;]
```

Use the following statement to restore a log:

```
--To Restore a Transaction Log:
RESTORE LOG { database_name | @database_name_var }
 [ <file_or_filegroup_or_pages> [ '...n ] ]
 [ FROM <backup_device> [ '...n ] ]
 [ WITH
   {
     [ RECOVERY | NORECOVERY | STANDBY =
       {standby_file_name | @standby_file_name_var }
       ]
     | ' <general_WITH_options> [ '...n ]
     | ' <replication_WITH_option>
     | ' <point_in_time_WITH_options-RESTORE_LOG>
   } [ '...n ]
 ]
[;]
```

As with the BACKUP statement, let's turn our attention to the various options supported by the RESTORE operation.

Use restore options

Now that we have covered the two RESTORE command we can turn to the options, as we did with the BACKUP command in Skill 2.1. The RESTORE statement has a number of WITH options, but not as many as the BACKUP statement. For the exam, make sure you understand what the following options do and when to use them:

- **MOVE** This option is used to relocate the database's set of files during the restore operation. It is commonly used when restoring a database to a different SQL Server instance that has a different storage layout.

- **NORECOVERY** This option specifies the restore operation to not roll back any uncommitted transactions. The database remains unavailable. Committed transactions are committed to the database. Uncommitted transactions are replayed/rolled forward. The database engine "assumes" that subsequent log restores commit these uncommitted transactions.

- **RECOVERY** This option specifies the restore operation to roll back any uncommitted transactions before making the database available for use. All committed transactions are included within the database. RECOVERY is the default behavior.

- **REPLACE** This option bypasses the database engine's internal safety check that helps you by automatically preventing you from overwriting existing database files. The safety checks include:

  - Overwriting existing files.

- Restoring over a database that is using the full or bulk-logged recovery model where a tail-log backup has not been taken, and the STOPAT option has not been specified.
- Restoring over an existing database with a backup of another database.

- **STANDBY** This option creates a second transaction log that allows the database to be read, but also allows subsequent log backups to be restored. This can be useful in recovery situations where you want to inspect the database between log restores. When the subsequent log is restored, the database engine rolls back all the operations from the second transaction log so that the database is back in the NORECOVERY mode when the STANDBY option is specified.

NOTE **RESTORING MULTIPLE LOG FILES**

When restoring multiple log files use the WITH NORECOVERY for all RESTORE statements in a multi-step restore sequence. You can execute a separate RESTORE DATABASE with the WITH RECOVERY operation at the end to make the database available to users.

EXAM TIP

Use the RECOVERY option on the very last restore operation that you plan to perform. After the database has been recovered and brought online, you are no longer able to perform additional restore operations.

Listing 2-19 shows an example of a restore sequence that restores the following from a share:

- Initial full backup, to a new location
- Differential backup
- Last three transaction log backups that occurred after the differential backup

Note the use of the recovery options throughout the code. Also note the sequence numbers use in the FILE option. This is what the exam might test you on.

LISTING 2-19 Restoring a database

```
USE [master];
GO
-- Restore full backup
RESTORE DATABASE [WorldWideImporters]
    FROM DISK = '\\SQLBACKUPS\SQLBackup\WordWideImporters\WordWideImporters_FULL.bak'
    WITH NORECOVERY'
    MOVE 'WorldWideImporters_Data' TO 'D:\SQLData\WorldWideImporters_Data.mdf''
    MOVE 'WorldWideImporters_Log' to 'L:\SQLLog\WorldWideImporters_Log.ldf';
GO
-- Restore differential backup
RESTORE DATABASE [WorldWideImporters]
    FROM DISK = '\\SQLBACKUPS\SQLBackup\WordWideImporters\WordWideImporters_DIFF.bak'
    WITH NORECOVERY;
GO
```

```
-- Restore last 3 log backups
RESTORE LOG [WorldWideImporters]
    FROM DISK = '\\SQLBACKUPS\SQLBackup\WordWideImporters\WordWideImporters_LOG.bak'
    WITH FILE = 11' NORECOVERY;
GO
RESTORE LOG [WorldWideImporters]
    FROM DISK = '\\SQLBACKUPS\SQLBackup\WordWideImporters\WordWideImporters_LOG.bak'
    WITH FILE = 12' NORECOVERY;
GO
RESTORE LOG [WorldWideImporters]
    FROM DISK = '\\SQLBACKUPS\SQLBackup\WordWideImporters\WordWideImporters_LOG.bak'
    WITH FILE = 13' NORECOVERY;
GO
-- Make database available
RESTORE DATABASE [WorldWideImporters]
    WITH RECOVERY;
GO
```

It would be equivalent to restore the last log backup using the WITH RECOVERY option instead, as show in Listing 2-20.

LISTING 2-20 Restoring last log backup

```
RESTORE LOG [WorldWideImporters]
FROM DISK = '\\SQLBACKUPS\SQLBackup\WordWideImporters\WordWideImporters_LOG.bak'
WITH FILE = 13' RECOVERY;
```

Revert a database snapshot

As discussed in earlier in the "Perform database snapshots" section, reverting a database snapshot is only possible if the database is undamaged and the database contains only the single database snapshot that you plan to revert. You need to drop all other database snapshots.

Reverting a database overwrites the data files, overwrites the old transaction log file, and rebuilds the transaction log. Therefore, it is recommended to perform a log backup before reverting a database. It is further recommended to perform a full backup after the revert operation completes to initialize the log chain again.

Listing 2-21 shows an example of how to revert a database snapshot.

LISTING 2-21 Revert a Database Snapshot

```
USE master;
GO
RESTORE DATABASE [WorldWideImporters]
FROM DATABASE_SNAPSHOT = 'WorldWideImporters_20160917';
```

Perform piecemeal restores

A *piecemeal restore* allows you to restore a database in stages, and can only be used for databases that have multiple filegroups. SQL Server Enterprise Edition supports online piecemeal restores, which means that as you restore and recovery filegroups within the database, you can make them available to users. This is a very important feature for VLDBs that have a small RTO as we saw in the "Back up VLDBs" section. Users can start using the database while you are still restoring other less important filegroups.

Restructure your database to use filegroups if you want to take advantage of this feature. Make sure you engage your business to determine the relative priority of the tables within the databases.

A piecemeal restore starts with an initial restore sequence called the *partial-restore sequence*. The partial-restore sequence must restore and recover the primary filegroup. During the partial-sequence sequence the database goes offline.

> **IMPORTANT** **MEMORY-OPTIMIZED FILEGROUP**
>
> For piecemeal restores the memory-optimized filegroup must be backed up and restored together with the primary filegroup.

Use the following statement to start a partial-restore sequence:

```
RESTORE DATABASE { database_name | @database_name_var }
    <files_or_filegroups> [ '...n ]
[ FROM <backup_device> [ '...n ] ]
    WITH
        PARTIAL' NORECOVERY
        [ ' <general_WITH_options> [ '...n ]
        | ' <point_in_time_WITH_options–RESTORE_DATABASE>
        ] [ '...n ]
[;]
```

After the partial-restore sequence, perform one or more *filegroup-restore sequences*. Each filegroup-restore sequence restores and recovers on or more filegroups. At the end of each filegroup-restore sequence, the restored filegroups are available to users. Prioritize the filegroups according to their importance to the users and how long they take to restore, until the entire database has been recovered and is online.

Piecemeal restores work with all recovery models, although there are limitations with the SIMPLE recovery model.

For a database that is using the full or bulk-logged recovery model, use the following steps to perform a piecemeal restore:

1. Perform the partial-restore sequence on the primary filegroup and any other important file groups.

2. Perform a filegroup-restore sequence on the remaining secondary file groups in order of their importance.

For a database that is using the simple recovery model, use the following steps to perform a piecemeal restore:

1. Perform the partial-restore sequence on the primary filegroup and all read/write secondary filegroups.

2. Perform a filegroup-restore sequence on the remaining read-only secondary file groups in order of their importance.

Assume you have a database named [OnlineStore] that is used by an online shopping website that has the following structure, as shown in Listing 2-22:

- A primary filegroup contains no user tables and is only 100MBs in size.

- A [Orders] secondary filegroup that has all the critical tables (like [Customers], [Products], [Orders], and [OrderDetails]) that enables customers to place orders. The [Sales] filegroup is 20GB in size.

- A [CompletedOrders] secondary filegroup that contains historical tables such as [CompletedOrders], [CompletedOrderDetails] that holds completed orders for the last two years. The [CompletedOrders] filegroup is 200GB in size.

- A [Data] default secondary filegroup that contains the remainder of the operational tables used in the database. The [Data] filegroup is 10GB in size.

- An [Archive] secondary filegroup that holds data that is older than two years. The [Archive] group is 1TB in size because it goes back 10 years.

LISTING 2-22 [OnlineStore] database definition

```
CREATE DATABASE [OnlineStore]
 ON  PRIMARY
( NAME = N'OnlineStore_Primary', FILENAME = N'D:\SQLData\OnlineStore_Primary.mdf'
, SIZE = 100MB),
 FILEGROUP [Archive]
( NAME = N'OnlineStore_Archive', FILENAME = N'E:\SQLData\OnlineStore_Archive.ndf'
, SIZE = 1TB),
 FILEGROUP [CompletedOrders]
( NAME = N'OnlineStore_CompletedOrders', FILENAME = N'F:\SQLData\OnlineStore_
CompletedOrders.ndf' , SIZE = 200GB),
 FILEGROUP [Data]
( NAME = N'OnlineStore_Data', FILENAME = N'G:\SQLData\OnlineStore_Data.ndf' , SIZE
= 10GB),
 FILEGROUP [Orders]
( NAME = N'OnlineStore_Orders', FILENAME = N'H:\SQLData\OnlineStore_Orders.ndf' ,
SIZE = 20GB)
 LOG ON
( NAME = N'OnlineStore_Log', FILENAME = N'L:\SQLLog\OnlineStore_Log.ldf' , SIZE =
1GB)
GO
ALTER DATABASE [OnlineStore]
MODIFY FILEGROUP [Data] DEFAULT;
```

Assume you have taken the following backups:

- Full backup

- Differential backup

- Log backup

Assume that the D, E, F, G, and H drives have all failed. Only the L drive that contains the transaction log has survived. You need to recover the database ASAP so that users can place orders.

Use the following steps to perform a piecemeal restore off the [OnlineStore] database:

1. Perform a tail-log backup, restore the primary file group, and bring the database online, as shown in Listing 2-23.

LISTING 2-23 Partial-restore sequence

```
-- Back up orphaned transaction log to minimize data loss
USE [master];
GO
BACKUP LOG [OnlineStore] TO DISK = 'B:\SQLBackup\OnlineStore_ORPHANEDLOG.bak' WITH
NO_TRUNCATE;
-- Start partial-restore sequence
USE [master]
GO
RESTORE DATABASE [OnlineStore]
FILEGROUP = 'PRIMARY' FROM DISK = 'B:\SQLBackup\OnlineStore_FULL.bak' WITH
NORECOVERY, PARTIAL;
GO
RESTORE DATABASE [OnlineStore]
FILEGROUP = 'PRIMARY' FROM DISK = 'B:\SQLBackup\OnlineStore_DIFF.bak' WITH
NORECOVERY;
GO
RESTORE DATABASE [OnlineStore]
FILEGROUP = 'PRIMARY' FROM DISK = 'B:\SQLBackup\OnlineStore_LOG.bak' WITH
NORECOVERY;
GO
RESTORE DATABASE [OnlineStore]
FILEGROUP = 'PRIMARY' FROM DISK = 'B:\SQLBackup\OnlineStore_ORPHANEDLOG.bak' WITH
NORECOVERY;
GO
RESTORE DATABASE [OnlineStore] WITH RECOVERY;
```

2. Restore and recover the [Orders] file group and bring it online, as shown in Listing 2-24.

LISTING 2-24 [Orders] filegroup-restore sequence

```
USE [master];
GO
-- Restore Orders filegroup and bring it online
RESTORE DATABASE [OnlineStore]
FILEGROUP = 'Orders' FROM DISK = 'B:\SQLBackup\OnlineStore_FULL.bak' WITH
NORECOVERY;
GO
RESTORE DATABASE [OnlineStore]
FILEGROUP = 'Orders' FROM DISK = 'B:\SQLBackup\OnlineStore_DIFF.bak' WITH
NORECOVERY;
GO
RESTORE DATABASE [OnlineStore]
FILEGROUP = 'Orders' FROM DISK = 'B:\SQLBackup\OnlineStore_LOG.bak' WITH
NORECOVERY;
```

```
GO
RESTORE DATABASE [OnlineStore]
FILEGROUP = 'Orders' FROM DISK = 'B:\SQLBackup\OnlineStore_ORPHANEDLOG.bak' WITH
NORECOVERY;
GO
RESTORE DATABASE [OnlineStore] WITH RECOVERY
```

3. Check to make sure that the [Orders] filegroup is online and that users can query the [Orders] table, as shown in Listing 2-25.

LISTING 2-25 Check partial availability of database files

```
USE [OnlineStore];
GO
-- Check to see if [Orders] filegroup is online
SELECT file_id, name, type_desc, state_desc
FROM sys.database_files
GO
-- Ensure users can query the critical tables
SELECT * FROM  [Orders]
```

Figure 2-47 shows the result set of the query that checks to see what filegroups are available within the database.

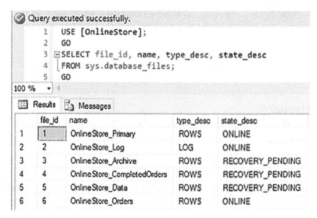

FIGURE 2-47 Testing partial availability

4. Restore and recover the [Data] and [CompletedOrders] filegroups, as shown in Listing 2-26

LISTING 2-26 [Data] and [CompletedOrders] filegroup-restore sequence

```
USE [master];
GO
RESTORE DATABASE [OnlineStore]
FILEGROUP = 'Data', FILEGROUP = 'CompletedOrders' FROM DISK = 'B:\SQLBackup\
OnlineStore_FULL.bak' WITH NORECOVERY;
```

```
GO
RESTORE DATABASE [OnlineStore]
FILEGROUP = 'Data', FILEGROUP = 'CompletedOrders' FROM DISK = 'B:\SQLBackup\
OnlineStore_DIFF.bak' WITH NORECOVERY;
GO
RESTORE DATABASE [OnlineStore]
FILEGROUP = 'Data', FILEGROUP = 'CompletedOrders' FROM DISK = 'B:\SQLBackup\
OnlineStore_LOG.bak' WITH NORECOVERY;
GO
RESTORE DATABASE [OnlineStore]
FILEGROUP = 'Data', FILEGROUP = 'CompletedOrders' FROM DISK = 'B:\SQLBackup\
OnlineStore_ORPHANEDLOG.bak' WITH NORECOVERY;
GO
RESTORE DATABASE [OnlineStore] WITH RECOVERY
GO
```

5. Restore and recover the final 1TB [Archive] filegroup, as shown in Listing 2-27.

LISTING 2-27 [Archive] filegroup-restore sequence

```
USE [master];
GO
RESTORE DATABASE [OnlineStore]
FILEGROUP = 'Archive' FROM DISK = 'B:\SQLBackup\OnlineStore_FULL.bak' WITH
NORECOVERY;
GO
RESTORE DATABASE [OnlineStore]
FILEGROUP = 'Archive' FROM DISK = 'B:\SQLBackup\OnlineStore_DIFF.bak' WITH
NORECOVERY;
GO
RESTORE DATABASE [OnlineStore]
FILEGROUP = 'Archive' FROM DISK = 'B:\SQLBackup\OnlineStore_LOG.bak' WITH
NORECOVERY;
GO
RESTORE DATABASE [OnlineStore]
FILEGROUP = 'Archive' FROM DISK = 'B:\SQLBackup\OnlineStore_ORPHANEDLOG.bak' WITH
NORECOVERY;
GO
RESTORE DATABASE [OnlineStore] WITH RECOVERY
GO
```

Alternatively, assume that only the E drive that contains the [CompletedOrders] has failed. The rest of the [OnlineSales] database is fine and accessible.

1. In this case recover and restore the [CompletedOrders] filegroup while the rest of the database is available, as shown in Listing 2-28. This is referred to as *partial availability*.

LISTING 2-28 [CompletedOrders] filegroup-restore sequence for a partially available database

```
USE [master];
GO
-- Take the [CompletedOrders] file offline
ALTER DATABASE
```

```
                    MODIFY FILE (name = OnlineStore_CompletedOrders' OFFLINE);
                    GO
                    -- Back up orphaned transaction log to minimize data loss
                    BACKUP LOG [OnlineStore] TO DISK = 'B:\SQLBackup\OnlineStore_ORPHANEDLOG.bak' WITH
                    NO_TRUNCATE;
                    GO
                    --
                    RESTORE DATABASE [OnlineStore]
                    FILEGROUP = 'CompletedOrders' FROM DISK = 'B:\SQLBackup\OnlineStore_FULL.bak' WITH
                    NORECOVERY;
                    GO
                    RESTORE DATABASE [OnlineStore]
                    FILEGROUP = 'CompletedOrders' FROM DISK = 'B:\SQLBackup\OnlineStore_DIFF.bak' WITH
                    NORECOVERY;
                    GO
                    RESTORE DATABASE [OnlineStore]
                    FILEGROUP = 'CompletedOrders' FROM DISK = 'B:\SQLBackup\OnlineStore_LOG.bak' WITH
                    NORECOVERY;
                    GO
                    RESTORE DATABASE [OnlineStore]
                    FILEGROUP = 'CompletedOrders' FROM DISK = 'B:\SQLBackup\OnlineStore_ORPHANEDLOG.
                    bak' WITH NORECOVERY;
                    GO
                    RESTORE DATABASE [OnlineStore] WITH RECOVERY
                    GO
```

As you can see from this section, performing a piecemeal restore is complicated and can involve substantial downtime. What happens if only a small number of pages in your database were corrupted? Ideally, you would not have to restore large data files, but could instead restore just the damaged pages. Fortunately, SQL Server supports the ability to restore just the damaged pages in a database and we will look at that next.

Perform page recovery

SQL Server has improved page corruption detection over earlier versions. All newly created databases by default use checksum page verification. Various database engine processes and features check to see that the checksum is correct. If a page's checksum is invalid that means that the page has been corrupted for some reason. The database engine keeps track of page corruptions in the [msdb] system database's [suspect_pages] table.

> **IMPORTANT**   **PAGE CORRUPTION DETECTION**
>
> The database engine can only detect corrupt pages in a database whose page verification has been set to CHECKSUM (or TORN_PAGE_DETECTION) and the page has been written after this option was set. Do not use TORN_PAGE_DETECTION because CHECKSUM is a superior method for page corruption detection. TORN_PAGE_DETECTION predates CHECKSUM, and is included for backward compatibility.

To obtain a list of the corrupted pages, you can query a number of sources, including:

- The [msdb] system database's [suspect_pages] table
- The database engine's ERRORLOG
- The output of a DBCC command

If your database only has a small number of isolated pages that are damaged, you can take advantage of the page restore process. It is quicker to restore a small number of pages than to restore an entire database.

Ideally you should determine what kind of a page has been damaged. If the damaged pages are in a nonclustered index for example, it could be substantially easier to drop the index and recreate it, than to initiate a page recovery process.

> **IMPORTANT**   **PAGE CORRUPTION ROOT CAUSE ANALYSIS**
>
> It is important to perform a root cause analysis on why your database is experiencing page corruption. Without understanding what has caused the page corruption, you risk it occurring again, with potentially greater damage. Page corruption could be indicative of impeding hardware failure.

Page restore only works for read/write files in databases that are using the full or bulk-logged recovery models. Page restore cannot be used for corruptions in the transaction log. Furthermore, page restore does not work for the following types of database pages:

- Database Boot Page (Page 1:9)
- File Boot Page (Page 0 of all data files)
- Full-text catalog
- Global Allocation Map (GAM)
- Page Free Space (PFS)
- Secondary Global Allocation Map (SGAM)

Use the following RESTORE statement to restore pages within the database:

```
--To Restore Specific Pages:
RESTORE DATABASE { database_name | @database_name_var }
   PAGE = 'file:page [ '...n ]'
 [ ' <file_or_filegroups> ] [ '...n ]
 [ FROM <backup_device> [ '...n ] ]
   WITH
       NORECOVERY
       [ ' <general_WITH_options> [ '...n ] ]
[;]
```

Page restore works with all editions of SQL Server. Only SQL Server Enterprise Edition supports online page restore. However, online page restore might not be possible in certain cases where critical pages have been damaged. With all other editions, excluding the Developer Edition, the database has to be offline.

Use the following process to perform a page restore:

1. Restore a full database with the PAGE restore option.

2. List all the Page IDs to be restored.

3. Restore any differential backups, if appropriate.

4. Restore the log chain after the full backup.

5. Perform a new log backup that includes the final LSN of the restored pages.

6. Restore this new log backup.

Listing 2-29 shows an example of a page restore process.

LISTING 2-29 Page restore

```
USE [msdb];
GO
-- Determine corrupted pages
SELECT database_id' file_id' page_id' event_type' error_count' last_update_date
FROM dbo.suspect_pages
WHERE database_id = DB_ID('WorldWideImporters');
GO
--   Restore 4 corrupt pages
USE [master];
GO
RESTORE DATABASE [WorldWideImporters] PAGE='1:300984' 1:300811' 1: 280113' 1:170916'
    FROM WideWorldImporters_Backup_Device
    WITH NORECOVERY;
GO
RESTORE LOG [WorldWideImporters]
    FROM WideWorldImporters_Log_Backup_Device
    WITH FILE = 1' NORECOVERY;
GO
RESTORE LOG [WorldWideImporters]
    FROM WideWorldImporters_Log_Backup_Device
    WITH FILE = 2' NORECOVERY;
    WITH NORECOVERY;
GO
BACKUP LOG [WorldWideImporters]
TO DISK='B:\SQLBackup\PageRecovery.bak';
GO
RESTORE LOG <database>
FROM DISK='B:\SQLBackup\PageRecovery.bak'
WITH RECOVERY;
GO
```

In the exam, if you get a question on performing page recovery, it will most likely test you on the specific order of steps that must be taken to restore pages and get them transactionally consistent with the rest of the database. So make sure you understand the order of the high-level steps discussed in this section.

Perform point-in-time recovery

In certain disaster incidents, there's no hardware failure or database corruption, but some sort of accidental user error. Perhaps a user accidentally deletes or truncates a table. In this case, you need to restore the database to a particular point in time.

With point-in-time recovery you need to know the precise time to which you want to restore the database. Importantly, any need to understand that any transactions that were committed after this point in time is lost.

That is why point-in-time recovery is not commonly used in the industry. If point-in-time recovery is required, it is more common to restore your database into a separate non-production database to the required point in time and then for the appropriate table(s) to be transferred to the production database.

The RESTORE statement supports point-in-time recovery. SQL Server supports recovery to these different types of point in times:

- **Date/Time** A specific date and time.
- **Log Sequence Number (LSN)** An internal numbering sequence used for each operation within the transaction log. This is used internally by the database engine and typically not used by database administrators.
- **Marked Transaction** An explicitly named explicit transaction.

Typically, a point-in-time recovery is performed from a log backup, but it can be used with database backups as well. Remember, a database backup contains a portion of the transaction log. Use the STOPAT clause for point-in-time-recovery.

The STOPAT clause supports the following variations when restoring from a database backup:

```
<point_in_time_WITH_options—RESTORE_DATABASE>::=
  | {
    STOPAT = { 'datetime'| @datetime_var }
  | STOPATMARK = 'lsn:lsn_number'
                  [ AFTER 'datetime']
  | STOPBEFOREMARK = 'lsn:lsn_number'
                  [ AFTER 'datetime']
```

The STOPAT clause supports the following variations when restoring from a log backup:

```
<point_in_time_WITH_options—RESTORE_LOG>::=
  | {
    STOPAT = { 'datetime'| @datetime_var }
  | STOPATMARK = { 'mark_name' | 'lsn:lsn_number' }
                  [ AFTER 'datetime']
  | STOPBEFOREMARK = { 'mark_name' | 'lsn:lsn_number' }
                  [ AFTER 'datetime']
  }
```

The STOPATMARK clause rolls the transaction log forward to the mark and includes the marked transaction. The STOPBEFOREMARK clause rolls the transaction log forward to the mark, but excludes the marked transaction.

Listing 2-30 restores a database to a particular point in time using the BACKUP LOG statement.

LISTING 2-30 Point-in-time recovery with a date/time

```
RESTORE LOG WideWorldImporters
   FROM WideWorldImporters_Log_Backup_Device
   WITH FILE=6' RECOVERY'
STOPAT = 'Sep 17' 2016 2:30 AM';
```

Sometimes you do not know precisely when a particular event happened. In this case, you can query the transaction log using undocumented commands and potentially work out when the particular event occurred. The database engine writes all database modifications serially to the transaction log, and timestamps all records using the Log Sequence Number (LSN).

The undocumented [fn_dblog] function can be used to query the database's transaction log. If you can work out what operation caused the incident, you determine the corresponding LSN. This LSN can be used to restore the transaction log to its point in time.

Consider the following experiment that performs the following high-level steps:

1. Inserts three records into a table.
2. Performs a database backup.
3. Inserts a record into a table.
4. Examines the transaction log's operations and their LSNs (Figure 2-48 shows the partial output).
   - Record the last LSN

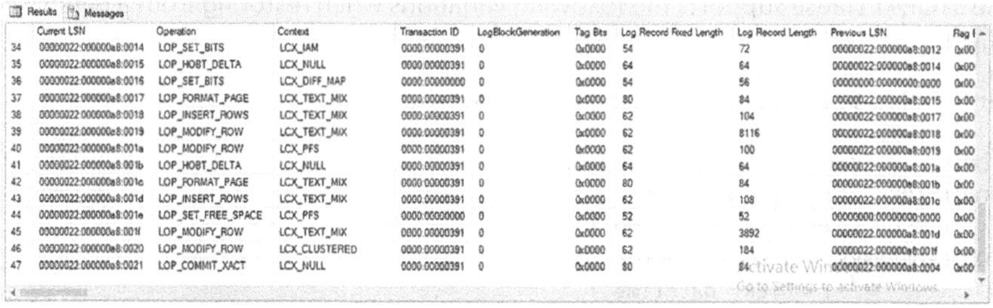

	Current LSN	Operation	Context	Transaction ID	LogBlockGeneration	Tag Bits	Log Record Fixed Length	Log Record Length	Previous LSN	Flag I
34	00000022:000000a8:0014	LOP_SET_BITS	LCX_IAM	0000:00000391	0	0x0000	54	72	00000022:000000a8:0012	0x00
35	00000022:000000a8:0015	LOP_HOBT_DELTA	LCX_NULL	0000:00000391	0	0x0000	64	64	00000022:000000a8:0014	0x00
36	00000022:000000a8:0016	LOP_SET_BITS	LCX_DIFF_MAP	0000:00000000	0	0x0000	54	56	00000000:00000000:0000	0x00
37	00000022:000000a8:0017	LOP_FORMAT_PAGE	LCX_TEXT_MIX	0000:00000391	0	0x0000	80	84	00000022:000000a8:0015	0x00
38	00000022:000000a8:0018	LOP_INSERT_ROWS	LCX_TEXT_MIX	0000:00000391	0	0x0000	62	104	00000022:000000a8:0017	0x00
39	00000022:000000a8:0019	LOP_MODIFY_ROW	LCX_TEXT_MIX	0000:00000391	0	0x0000	62	8116	00000022:000000a8:0018	0x00
40	00000022:000000a8:001a	LOP_MODIFY_ROW	LCX_PFS	0000:00000391	0	0x0000	62	100	00000022:000000a8:0019	0x00
41	00000022:000000a8:001b	LOP_HOBT_DELTA	LCX_NULL	0000:00000391	0	0x0000	64	64	00000022:000000a8:001a	0x00
42	00000022:000000a8:001c	LOP_FORMAT_PAGE	LCX_TEXT_MIX	0000:00000391	0	0x0000	80	84	00000022:000000a8:001b	0x00
43	00000022:000000a8:001d	LOP_INSERT_ROWS	LCX_TEXT_MIX	0000:00000391	0	0x0000	62	108	00000022:000000a8:001c	0x00
44	00000022:000000a8:001e	LOP_SET_FREE_SPACE	LCX_PFS	0000:00000000	0	0x0000	52	52	00000000:00000000:0000	0x00
45	00000022:000000a8:001f	LOP_MODIFY_ROW	LCX_TEXT_MIX	0000:00000391	0	0x0000	62	3892	00000022:000000a8:001d	0x00
46	00000022:000000a8:0020	LOP_MODIFY_ROW	LCX_CLUSTERED	0000:00000391	0	0x0000	62	184	00000022:000000a8:001f	0x00
47	00000022:000000a8:0021	LOP_COMMIT_XACT	LCX_NULL	0000:00000391	0	0x0000	80	84	00000022:000000a8:0004	0x00

FIGURE 2-48 Differential backup high-level internals

5. Simulates a mistake by updating all the records in the table.
6. Drops the database.
7. Restores the full backup.
8. Restores the log backup stopping at the LSN recorded at Step 4.
9. Confirms the database has been restored to before the mistake was simulated.

Listing 2-31 demonstrates how to restore to a particular LSN.

LISTING 2-31 Restoring a database to a LSN

```
-- Set up experiment
/* You might have to enable xp_cmdshell by running the following:
EXEC sp_configure 'show advanced'' 1;
RECONFIGURE;
GO
EXEC sp_configure 'xp_cmdshell'' 1;
RECONFIGURE;
GO
*/
USE [master];
EXEC xp_cmdshell 'md C:\Exam764Ch2\';
GO


-- Create database
CREATE DATABASE [RestoreToLSNExperimentDB]
ON  PRIMARY (
        NAME = N'RestoreToLSNExperiment_data''
        FILENAME = N'C:\Exam764Ch2\RestoreToLSNExperiment.mdf')
LOG ON (
        NAME = N'RestoreToLSNExperiment_log''
        FILENAME = N'C:\Exam764Ch2\RestoreToLSNExperiment.ldf')
GO
USE [RestoreToLSNExperimentDB]
GO
-- Create table
CREATE TABLE [MyTable] (Payload VARCHAR(1000))
GO
-- Step 1: Insert 3 records
INSERT [MyTable] VALUES ('Record 1')' ('Record 2')' ('Record 3')
GO
-- Step 2: Perform full backup
BACKUP DATABASE [RestoreToLSNExperimentDB]
TO DISK = 'C:\Exam764Ch2\RestoreToLSNExperimentDB_FULL.bak'
WITH INIT;
GO
-- Step 3: Insert 1 record
INSERT [MyTable] VALUES ('Record 4');
GO
SELECT * FROM [MyTable]
-- Step 4: Query the transaction log
SELECT * FROM fn_dblog(NULL'NULL);
-- Record the last LSN: 0x00000025:000000a9:0007
GO
-- Step 5: Accidentally update all 4 records (simulating a mistake)
UPDATE [MyTable] SET Payload = 'MISTAKE'
GO
SELECT * FROM [MyTable]
SELECT * FROM fn_dblog(NULL'NULL);
-- Perform log backup
BACKUP LOG [RestoreToLSNExperimentDB]
TO DISK = 'C:\Exam764Ch2\RestoreToLSN_LOG.bak'
WITH INIT;
GO
-- Step 6: Drop database
```

```
USE master;
DROP DATABASE [RestoreToLSNExperimentDB];
-- Step 7: Restore full backup
RESTORE DATABASE [RestoreToLSNExperimentDB]
FROM DISK = 'C:\Exam764Ch2\RestoreToLSNExperimentDB_FULL.bak'
WITH NORECOVERY;
-- Step 8: Restore lob backup at LSN recorded above
RESTORE LOG [RestoreToLSNExperimentDB]
FROM DISK = 'C:\Exam764Ch2\RestoreToLSNExperimentDB_LOG.bak'
WITH RECOVERY' STOPATMARK = 'lsn:0x00000025:000000a9:0007';
-- Step 9: Confirm restore doesn't include "mistake"
USE [RestoreToLSNExperimentDB];
SELECT * FROM [MyTable];
-- Cleanup experiment
/*
USE master;
DROP DATABASE [RestoreToLSNExperimentDB];
GO
EXEC xp_cmdshell 'rd /s /q C:\Exam764Ch2;
GO
EXEC sp_configure 'xp_cmdshell'' 0;
RECONFIGURE;
GO
EXEC sp_configure 'show advanced'' 0;
RECONFIGURE;
GO
*/
```

Using the date/time, or LSN as a recovery point can be imprecise because it requires you to know exactly what happened when. If you want to potentially roll back a significant modification, such as an end-of-day process, you might want to take advantage of marked transactions.

A *marked transaction* is an explicit marker that you can record in the transaction log to effectively create a recovery point.

Marked transactions can also be used to create a consistent recovery point across multiple databases. This is a common requirement for multi-database solutions such as Microsoft BizTalk, Microsoft SharePoint, or Microsoft Team Foundation Server (TFS).

Listing 2-32 shows you how to create a marked transaction.

LISTING 2-32 Create a transaction log mark

```
USE [WideWorldImporters];
GO
BEGIN TRANSACTION PriceIncrease
    WITH MARK 'PriceIncrease';
UPDATE [Warehouse].[StockItems]
    SET [RecommendedRetailPrice] = [RecommendedRetailPrice] * 1.25;
COMMIT TRANSACTION PriceIncrease;
GO
```

You can query the [msdb] database's [logmarkhistory] to see all marked transactions, as show in Listing 2-33.

LISTING 2-33 Query all marked transactions

```
SELECT [database_name]' [mark_name]' [description]' [user_name]' [lsn]' [mark_time]
FROM [msdb].[dbo].[logmarkhistory];
```

Listing 2-34 shows the RESTORE LOG statement that restores the database to the marked transaction created in Listing 2-33.

LISTING 2-34 Restore database to marked transaction

```
USE [WorldWideImporters];
GO
RESTORE LOG [WideWorldImporters]
FROM DISK = 'B:\SQLBackup\WideWorldImporters_LOG.bak'
WITH RECOVERY'
STOPATMARK = 'PriceIncrease';
GO
```

For the exam make sure you understand the use cases for when you would create and use the different marks in the transaction log. Make sure you also understand the difference between the STOPATMARK and STOPBEFOREMARK options and when to use them. So read the exam question carefully to know which one potentially represents the correct answer.

Restore a filegroup

In Skill 2.1 we looked at how you potentially configure VLDBs to use multiple files/filegroups and then design your backup strategy around them. In this section we will look at how you restore such VLDBs, depending on what has failed. Otherwise, there is no need to restore the entire database if only a single file or filegroup is damaged. It is sufficient to restore the file or filegroup and perform log recovery so that it is consistent with the rest of the database.

Separating your database into a number of files or filegroups allows you to reduce your RTO because there is less data to restore in the case of a single file or filegroup being damaged.

If you are restoring a read/write filegroup, perform the following steps:

1. Perform a tail-log backup, if necessary.
2. Restore the filegroup.
3. Restore any different backups, if necessary.
4. Restore the log-chain to bring the filegroup into sync with the rest of the files in the database.
5. Stop at a point in time if necessary.
6. Recover the filegroup and bring it online.

If you are restoring a read-only filegroup, it may be unnecessary to apply the log chain. If the file was marked as read-only after the backup, additional restore operations need to be applied.

All editions of SQL Server support offline file restore. With offline file restore the entire database is unavailable for the duration of the file restore operation.

SQL Server Enterprise Edition supports online file restore. With online file restore only the restoring file group is unavailable until it is restored and recovered.

Use the following syntax to restore a filegroup:

```
--To Restore Specific Files or Filegroups
RESTORE DATABASE { database_name | @database_name_var }
   <file_or_filegroup> [ '...n ]
 [ FROM <backup_device> [ '...n ] ]
   WITH
   {
      [ RECOVERY | NORECOVERY ]
      [ ' <general_WITH_options> [ '...n ] ]
   } [ '...n ]
[;]
```

Listing 2-35 shows an example of a file restore operation.

LISTING 2-35 Filegroup restore example

```
USE master;
GO
-- Restore filegroup
RESTORE DATABASE [WordWideImporters]
   FILEGROUP = 'WordWideImporters_OrderHistory''
   FROM WordWideImporters_Backup_OrderHistory_Device
   WITH NORECOVERY'
   REPLACE;
GO
-- Restore first log backup
RESTORE LOG [WordWideImporters]
   FROM WordWideImporters_Log_Device
   WITH FILE = 1' NORECOVERY;
GO
-- Restore second log backup and recover database
RESTORE LOG [WordWideImporters]
   FROM WordWideImporters_Log_Device
   WITH FILE = 2' RECOVERY;
GO
```

Develop a plan to automate and test restores

It is important to periodically test your restore strategy. This can be easily automated using PowerShell or T-SQL jobs scheduled through the SQL Server Agent.

You need to test your restore strategy for the following reasons:

- To test that your backups are restorable.
- To make sure that all stakeholders understand the restore process.
- To time the length that your restore process takes.

The backup and restore operations' duration are dependent on the following:

- The size of your database

- The size of your backup set
- The speed of your database's storage subsystem
- The speed of your backup destination's storage subsystem
- The speed of your network
- The speed and number of processor cores being used
- How compressible the data being backed up is

A restore operation is not necessarily symmetrical with a backup process. In other words, if a full backup takes 200 minutes, it might take 300 minutes to restore that same backup. Do not rely on the backup duration to predict your restore duration.

> **IMPORTANT** **TESTING RESTORES**
>
> It is important to time the duration of your restore process. Without knowing its duration, you cannot guarantee that you can meet your SLAs. Testing your restores periodically might reveal that you need to change your backup strategy because the existing one cannot meet your SLAs.

Skill 2.3 Manage database integrity

Although rare, it is possible for a database to become corrupted. Database corruption typically occurs as a result of hardware issues, but can also occur due to virtualization technologies. For a database administrator it is always important to identify the root cause of a database corruption to prevent its re-occurrence.

In this skill we will examine how you can identify database corruption before repairing a corrupt database. Microsoft always recommends restoring a database from a last known good backup over database repair techniques. That is why you should ensure that your backups are completing successfully and can be restored. Performing period database consistency checks helps ensure backups can be restored and this skill will show you how to perform these checks.

This section covers how to:
- Implement database consistency checks
- Identify database corruption
- Recover from database corruption

Implement database consistency checks

It is important to implement database consistency checks as part of your database management strategy. We saw how easy it was to implement that through maintenance plans in the earlier in the "Configure maintenance plan" section. It is critical to detect any database corruptions as early as possible as typically you have to stop users using a corrupt database. Use Database Console Command (DBCC) to perform your database consistency checks.

The following DBCC commands perform consistency checks on a database:

- **DBCC CHECKALLOC** Checks the consistency of disk space allocation structures with a database.
- **DBCC CHECKCATALOG** Checks the consistency of the system tables with a database.
- **DBCC CHECKDB** Checks the logical and physical integrity of all the objects of a database.
- **DBCC CHECKFILEGROUP** Checks the allocation and structural integrity of all tables and indexed views in a filegroup.
- **DBCC CHECKTABLE** Checks the allocation and structural integrity a table.

When you perform any of these DBCC commands, the database engine automatically creates a transactionally consistent internal database snapshot. DBCC operates on this database snapshot. The snapshot minimizes false errors and allows DBCC to run as an online operation that prevents blocking and concurrency problems.

DBCC is not able to create an internal database snapshot and uses table locks in certain situations, including when the database is located on:

- A disk formatted using the FAT file system
- A disk filesystem that does not support named streams, such as ReFS
- A disk filesystem that does not support alternate streams, such as ReFS

Use the DBCC CHECKDB command to implement your database consistency checks. Use the other DBCC CHECK commands when you want to fine-tune your database consistency check, such as in the case when you need to perform them against a VLDB.

The DBCC CHECKDB command has the following syntax.

```
DBCC CHECKDB
    [ ( database_name | database_id | 0
        [ ' NOINDEX
        | ' { REPAIR_ALLOW_DATA_LOSS | REPAIR_FAST | REPAIR_REBUILD } ]
    ) ]
    [ WITH
        {
            [ ALL_ERRORMSGS ]
            [ ' EXTENDED_LOGICAL_CHECKS ]
            [ ' NO_INFOMSGS ]
            [ ' TABLOCK ]
            [ ' ESTIMATEONLY ]
            [ ' { PHYSICAL_ONLY | DATA_PURITY } ]
            [ ' MAXDOP  = number_of_processors ]
        }
    ]
]
```

The DBCC CHECKDB operation performs the following operations:

■ DBCC CHECKALLOC

■ DBCC CHECKTABLE on every table within a database

■ DBCC CHECKCATALOG

■ Performs a consistency check on all indexed views within a database

■ Performs a consistency check on FILESTREAM data within a database

■ Performs a consistency check on the Service Broker data within a database

DBCC CHECKDB supports a number of different options:

■ **DATA_PURITY**   This option specifies that column values should be checked to ensure that they are valid for the domain and not out of range.

■ **ESTIMATEONLY**   This option causes DBCC not to perform any checks, but to estimate how much [tempdb] space is consumed instead.

■ **NO_INFOMSGS**   This option specifies that no information messages are reported. DBCC only reports errors.

■ **NOINDEX**   This option specifies that comprehensive checks should not be performed on nonclustered indexes.

■ **PHYSICAL_ONLY**   This option limits DBCC to checking the allocation consistency, physical structure of the pages, and record headers. It detects checksum and torn pages errors, which are typically indicative of a hardware problem with your memory or storage subsystem.

■ **TABLOCK**   This option specifies that the internal database snapshot should not be taken and that table lock be used instead. This can improve performance in certain cases. Use the TABLOCK when you know there is no user activity. The TABLOCK option causes the DBCC CHECKCATALOG and Service Broker checks not to run.

- **MAXDOP** This option controls the degree of parallelism that the DBCC operation uses. The DBCC operation typically dynamically adjusts the degree of parallelism during its execution.

A complete DBCC CHECKDB operation can take a substantial period of time on a large database in later versions of SQL Server. Microsoft has introduced more comprehensive logical checks; internal database structures are more complex and there is more functionality in the database engine.

Use the following techniques to reduce the overall time that DBCC takes:

- Use the NOINDEX option to direct the database engine to skip checking nonclustered indexes for user tables. This can substantially reduce the time taken in data warehouse use cases, where there might be a substantial number of nonclustered indexes. If a non-clustered index becomes corrupt you can drop and re-create it.

- Use the PHYSICAL_ONLY option to direct the database engine to skip all logical checks. This can substantially reduce the take that DBCC CHECKDB takes. It is the goal of Microsoft to make DBCC CHECKDB WITH PHYSICAL ONLY to run as quickly as a BACKUP to a nul device operation. In this instance the duration of the DBCC operation is totally dependent on your storage subsystem's performance.

- Take advantage of DBCC CHECKFILEGROUP to check a subset of the database's filegroups. Rotate these operations between all the filegroups in your database to ensure that there are no database consistency problems. Consider not running consistency checks against read-only filegroups that are consistent.

- Take advantage of DBCC CHECKTABLE and rotate the consistency checks across all the tables in the database across successive nights, similarly to DBCC CHECKFILEGROUP.

In the exam you might get asked a question on how to reduce the time taken by DBCC CHECKDB to complete for a VLDB in a given scenario. Use the guidance in the above bullet points to help you in the exam.

Be aware that DBCC is not linear in its execution. If, at any point in time the DBCC operation detects a potential corruption, it triggers extra checks that perform a deeper analysis and consistency check of the database.

Use the T-SQL query in Listing 2-36 to show the progress of a running DBCC operation.

LISTING 2-36 DBCC operation progress

```
SELECT session_id' db_name(database_id) as database_name'
          start_time' command' percent_complete' estimated_completion_time
FROM sys.dm_exec_requests
WHERE command LIKE 'dbcc%';
```

Listing 2-37 shows an example of a database consistency check that includes the extended logical checks, uses a table lock, and does not generate information messages:

LISTING 2-37 DBCC consistency check

```
DBCC CHECKDB ([AdventureWorksDW])
WITH EXTENDED_LOGICAL_CHECKS' TABLOCK' NO_INFOMSGS;
GO
```

Use SQL Server Agent or maintenance plans to schedule period database consistency checks. Keep track of how long the consistency checks take and whether they are increasing in duration as you might have to optimize their execution time using some of the techniques discussed in this section.

Although you might have schedule database integrity checks you might still experience a database corruption. It is important to identify and diagnose the database corruption before attempting recovery. We will look at how you do these next.

Identify database corruption

Scheduling regular database consistency checks through SQL Server Agent jobs or maintenance plans helps identify database corruption. Otherwise user applications potentially will receive a database corruption message if they try to access a corrupt portion of the database.

The database engine automatically logs database consistency errors in certain places:

- The database engine's ERRORLOG captures any DBCC CHECK operations. Additional information is written in the event of a database corruption.
- The Windows Application Log should also capture the same DBCC error.
- The [msdb] system database also tracks suspect pages in the [suspect_pages] table. The database engine records any suspect pages encountered during operations such as:
  - A query reading a page.
  - A DBCC CHECKDB operation.
  - A backup operation.

- The database engine creates a dump file in the LOG directory whenever a DBCC CHECKDB detects a consistency problem. The dump file uses the SQLDUMP*nnnn*.txt naming convention. The dump file contains the results of the DBCC CHECKDB operation and additional diagnostic output. This dump file is automatically sent to Microsoft via the Feature Usage data collection and Error Reporting feature of SQL Server.

You should periodically check these repositories so that you can identify any database corruption as soon as possible. This can be automated through SQL Server Agent jobs or external programs.

You should also schedule SQL Server Agent alerts on the following error messages:

- **823** This error message is generated whenever the Windows environment issues a cyclic redundancy check. It represents a disk error. It typically indicates that there is a problem with the storage subsystem, hardware, or driver that is in the I/O path.

- **824** This error message is generated when a logical consistency check fails after reading or writing a database page. It also typically indicates that there is a problem with the storage subsystem, hardware, or driver that is in the I/O path.

- **825** This error message is called the Read Retry error and is generated whenever the database engine has had to retry a read or write operation. The database engine retries the I/O operation up to four times before failing it.

- **832** This error message is generated when a page in memory has been corrupted. In other words, the checksum has changed since it was read from disk into memory. It is a rare error. It possibly indicates bad memory.

Table 2-3 shows the different error messages for these four different 8xx errors:

TABLE 2-3 SQL Server I/O Errors

Error Number	Message
823	The operating system returned error %ls to SQL Server during a %S_MSG at offset %#016l64x in file '%ls'. Additional messages in the SQL Server error log and system event log may provide more detail. This is a severe system-level error condition that threatens database integrity and must be corrected immediately. Complete a full database consistency check (DBCC CHECKDB). This error can be caused by many factors; for more information see SQL Server Books Online.
824	SQL Server detected a logical consistency-based I/O error: %ls. It occurred during a %S_MSG of page %S_PGID in database ID %d at offset %#016l64x in file '%ls'. Additional messages in the SQL Server error log or system event log may provide more detail. This is a severe error condition that threatens database integrity and must be corrected immediately. Complete a full database consistency check (DBCC CHECKDB). This error can be caused by many factors; for more information, see SQL Server Books Online.
825	A read of the file '%ls' at offset %#016l64x succeeded after failing %d time(s) with error: %ls. Additional messages in the SQL Server error log and system event log may provide more detail. This error condition threatens database integrity and must be corrected. Complete a full database consistency check (DBCC CHECKDB). This error can be caused by many factors; for more information, see SQL Server Books Online.
832	A page that should have been constant has changed (expected checksum: %08x, actual checksum: %08x, database %d, file '%ls', page %S_PGID). This usually indicates a memory failure or other hardware or operating system corruption.

> **IMPORTANT ROOT CAUSE ANALYSIS**
>
> It is important and critical to perform a root cause analysis on why your database has been corrupted. Without understanding what has caused the database corruption, you risk it occurring again, with potentially greater damage. Database corruption could be indicative of impeding hardware failure.

Once you have identified a database corruption incident you need to take corrective action. We will examine the options you have with recovering from database corruption next.

Recover from database corruption

When a DBCC operation runs and detects any corruption it describes the corruptions encountered and recommends a course of action and the minimum level of repair that is required. In subsequent versions of SQL Server Microsoft have attempted to make it easier to identify and dealt with database corruption. The output of the DBCC CHECKDB command tries to be as explicitly clear as it can be.

Figure 2-49 shows an example of a database corruption. Notice how the DBCC CHECKDB recommends the minimum repair commands that are required to fix the errors encountered.

```
DBCC CHECKDB(WideWorldImporters) WITH NO_INFOMSGS
100 %  ▾
  Messages
  Msg 8978, Level 16, State 1, Line 16
  Table error: Object ID 60, index ID 1, partition ID 281474980642816, alloc unit ID 281474980642816 (type In-row data). Page (1:133) is missing a reference
  Msg 8939, Level 16, State 98, Line 16
  Table error: Object ID 60, index ID 1, partition ID 281474980642816, alloc unit ID 281474980642816 (type In-row data), page (1:1248). Test (IS_OFF (BUF_IC
  Msg 8974, Level 16, State 1, Line 16
  Table error: Object ID 60, index ID 1, partition ID 281474980642816, alloc unit ID 281474980642816 (type In-row data). Page (1:1252) was not seen in the s
  Msg 8928, Level 16, State 1, Line 16
  Object ID 60, index ID 1, partition ID 281474980642816, alloc unit ID 281474980642816 (type In-row data): Page (1:1248) could not be processed.  See other
  CHECKDB found 0 allocation errors and 4 consistency errors in table 'sys.sysobjvalues' (object ID 60).
  CHECKDB found 0 allocation errors and 4 consistency errors in database 'WideWorldImporters'.
  repair_allow_data_loss is the minimum repair level for the errors found by DBCC CHECKDB (WideWorldImporters).
```

FIGURE 2-49 Backup example timeline

The first step in dealing with a database corruption incident is to obtain as much information as possible about what has been corrupted, before planning a course of action.

Use the OBJECT_NAME system function to identify the database object that has been corrupted. An Index ID value of 0 represents a heap. An Index ID value of 1 represents a clustered index. An index value greater than 1 represents a nonclustered index.

If the database corruption is contained to a nonclustered index, you may choose to simply drop and rebuild the nonclustered index.

Otherwise, Microsoft recommends that you should restore the database from a backup instead of performing a repair with one of the repair options. The repair options do not consider any constraints that may exist between the tables when performing their repair operations.

> **IMPORTANT** **DBCC REPAIR OPERATIONS**
>
> The primary purpose of DBCC's repair operations is to get a corrupted database into a non-corrupted state, not to protect your data. If that means DBCC has to get rid of your data, it does so. That is why Microsoft recommends that in the case of a database corruption your primary corruption recovery path should be to restore the database from the last good backup.

> **REAL WORLD** **DBCC CHECKCONSTRAINTS**
>
> Perform a DBCC CHECKCONSTRAINTS operation on any table that was repaired by the DBCC repair process. DBCC CHECKCONSTRAINTS checks the integrity of a specified constraint or all constraints on a specified table.

In some circumstances, and especially for databases that have been upgrade from an earlier version of SQL Server, the values stored in a column might not be valid for that column. Execute the DBCC CHECKDB with the DATA_PURITY option on all the databases that have been upgrade from an earlier version of SQL Server. This only ever needs to be performed once per database. Any detected errors have to be updated manually because the database engine cannot know what the valid value should be.

Most DBCC repair operations are fully logged in the transaction. Consequently, it is recommended that you perform repairs in a transaction by using the BEGIN TRAN statement. If a repair is completed successfully, you can commit this repair transaction.

Consider backing up your corrupt database at the database or file level before attempting any repair operations. You can use the backup to attempt a repair on another SQL Server instance.

Set the corrupted database to single user mode before performing any repair operations. You don't want users accessing a database that has corrupt data. Nor do you want them interfering with your repair attempts.

The REPAIR_REBUILD repair operation is generally considered safe to use. The REPAIR_REBUILD repair process guarantees that there is no possibility of data loss. The REPAIR_REBUILD repair typically involves small repairs, such as repairing missing rows in a nonclustered index, or more time consuming operation such as rebuilding an entire nonclustered index on a table.

Listing 2-38 shows an example of how to set a database to single user mode.

LISTING 2-38 Repairing a database using the REPAIR_REBUILD operation

```
USE [master];
-- Change database to single user mode
ALTER DATABASE [WideWorldImporters] SET SINGLE_USER WITH ROLLBACK IMMEDIATE;
GO
-- Perform safe repair
DBCC CHECKDB ([WideWorldImporters]) WITH REPAIR_REBUILD;
GO
```

The DBCC command can fail during its operation, in which case it generates an error message. The state value of the error message helps you to troubleshoot what went wrong. Use Table 2-4 to troubleshoot any DBCC execution errors.

TABLE 2-4 DBCC ERROR STATES

State	DESCRIPTION
0	Error number 8930 was raised. This indicates a corruption in metadata that terminated the DBCC command.
1	Error number 8967 was raised. There was an internal DBCC error.
2	A failure occurred during emergency mode database repair.
3	This indicates a corruption in metadata that terminated the DBCC command.
4	An assert or access violation was detected.
5	An unknown error occurred that terminated the DBCC command.

Perform an emergency repair

Perform an emergency repair using the REPAIR_ALLOW_DATA_LOSS option as an absolute last resort when you need to recover from a database corruption incident. Somebody has "goofed up" if you find yourself in this situation. Hopefully it was not you!

The goal of the REPAIR_ALLOW_DATA_LOSS option is to get the database into a transactionally consistent state. A REPAIR_ALLOW_DATA_LOSS repair most likely results in a loss of data. Compare the amount of data lost by using this emergency repair method versus how much data would be lost if you restored the database through your backups, which might be out of date, corrupt, or lost.

The emergency repair process cannot be rolled back. It is a one-way operation.

> **IMPORTANT FILE LEVEL BACKUP**
>
> Before performing a repair with the REPAIR_ALLOW_DATA_LOSS, it is highly recommended that you perform a file level backup of a database. Or even at the virtual machine level if you using a virtualized environment. Do not forget to include all files associated with the database, including any containers that are being used by FILESTREAM, full text indexes, and memory-optimized tables.

The REPAIR_ALLOW_DATA_LOSS repair operation differs in that it can use database pages that have been marked as inaccessible because of I/O or checksum errors. It performs the following operations:

- Forces recovery to run on the transaction log to salvage as much information as possible.
- Rebuilds the transaction log if it is corrupt. At this stage, you have lost your full ACID guarantee.
- Runs DBCC CHECKDB with the REPAIR_ALLOW_DATA_LOSS option on the database.
- If the DBCC CHECDB operation succeeds, set the database state to online.

The recovered database is now in a consistent state, but there is no guarantee of any data consistency.

If the emergency repair process fails, the database cannot be repaired by DBCC.

> **IMPORTANT DBCC CANNOT REPAIR ALL ERRORS**
>
> There is no guarantee that DBCC is able to fix all errors. In some cases, critical sections of a database have been corrupted, preventing DBCC from repairing the database. In other cases the repair logic would be too complicated, or the chance of a specific error is so rare that Microsoft has not implemented the repair logic in DBCC.

Listing 2-39 shows an example of an emergency repair process performed on a database.

LISTING 2-39 Repairing a database using the REPAIR_ALLOW_DATA_LOSS operation

```
USE [master];
GO
ALTER DATABASE [WideWorldImporters] SET EMERGENCY;
GO
ALTER DATABASE [WideWorldImporters] SET SINGLE_USER;
GO
DBCC CHECKDB ('WideWorldImporters'' REPAIR_ALLOW_DATA_LOSS)
WITH NO_INFOMSGS;
GO
```

EXAM TIP

For any database corruption questions in the exam make sure you first determine what database object has been corrupted. There might be no need to initiate a restore or perform an emergency database repair. If, for example, the corruption is on a nonclustered index, or an indexed view, it will be sufficient to simply drop and recreate the corrupted object.

Thought experiment

In this thought experiment, demonstrate your skills and knowledge of the topics covered in this chapter. You can find answers to this thought experiment in the next section.

You work as a database administrator for World Wide Importers. You need to design a backup strategy for their mission critical 4TB database that is used as an online store. The SQL Server instance is using a SAN that can read/write 1,000MB/sec.

The database structure is as follows:

- The primary data file is 1GB in size and does not contain any data.
- The [AuditHistory] table is 1.5TB in size and located on its own [FG_Audit] read-only filegroup.
- The [OrderHistory] table is 1.5TB in size and located on its own [FG_OrderHistory] read-only filegroup.
- The default [FG_Data] filegroup contains the rest of the tables used by the online store.

The database has the following characteristics:

- The [AuditHistory] and [OrderHistory] tables are updated at the end of the month when a process runs that moves the oldest month's worth of audit, and orders data into these tables.
- The online store website predominantly inserts new records.
- Page verify = NONE.

You are responsible for designing their backup strategy. Management has given you the following requirements:

- The RPO is 15 minutes for the tables used by the online website.
- The RTO is one hour.
- The backup storage usage should be minimized.
- The backup set needs to be retained for 18 months.

An important end-of-week business process runs on Saturday at 17:00 that takes five hours to complete. This process initially commits a marked transaction. It then updates a substantial amount of data into the database. A database snapshot is performed before the process starts.

1. Management wants you to create a backup strategy that meets their requirements. What backup strategy should you use?

   A. Use the following backup strategy:
   - Perform a full backup every Sunday.
   - Perform differential backups nightly.
   - Perform log backups every hour.

   B. Use the following backup strategy:
   - Perform a file backup of the primary filegroup daily.
   - Perform a file backup of the [FG_Data] filegroup daily.
   - Perform file backup of the [AuditHistory] and [FG_OrderHistory] at the end of the month after they are updated.
   - Perform log backups every 15 minutes.

   C. Use the following backup strategy:
   - Perform a filegroup backup of the primary filegroup daily.
   - Perform a filegroup backup of the [FG_Data] filegroup daily.
   - Perform filegroup backup of the [AuditHistory] and [FG_OrderHistory] filegroups at the end of the month after they are updated.
   - Perform differential backups every 15 minutes.

   D. Use the following backup strategy:
   - Perform a file backup of the primary filegroup daily.
   - Perform a file backup of the [FG_Data] filegroup daily.
   - Perform file backup of the [AuditHistory] and [FG_OrderHistory] filegroups daily.
   - Perform log backups every 15 minutes.

2. Management discovers that Saturday's process crashed and wants you to recovery the database to 17:00, before the process ran. Upon further investigation, you discover that the process crashed because the disk that stored the [FG_Data] filegroup failed at 17:15. Management wants you to restore the database as soon as possible. What recovery strategy should you use?

   A. Revert the database using the database snapshot

   B. Use the DBCC REPAIR_REBUILD command to repair the damaged portions of the database.

   C. Initiate a restore process from your backup set. Use the STOPAT restore option to stop at 17:00 on Saturday

   D. Discover the damaged pages. Perform a page recovery process

3. A scheduled DBCC CHECKDB on the database generates the following error:

```
Msg 8978, Level 16, State 1, Line 1
Table error: Object ID 6341281, index ID 5, partition ID 54039787910657209, alloc
unit ID 92740571204375891 (type In-row data). Page (1:3126) is missing a reference
from previous page (1:3972). Possible chain linkage problem.
Msg 8939, Level 16, State 98, Line 1
Table error: Object ID 6341281, index ID 5, partition ID 54039787910657209, alloc
unit ID 92740571204375891 (type In-row data), page (1:3256). Test (IS_OFF (BUF_
IOERR, pBUF->bstat)) failed. Values are 25611328 and -69.
Msg 8976, Level 16, State 1, Line 1
Table error: Object ID 6341281, index ID 5, partition ID 54039787910657209, alloc
unit ID 92740571204375891 (type In-row data). Page (1:3972) was not seen in the
scan although its parent (1:16777) and previous (1:5612) refer to it. Check any
previous errors.
```

Management wants you to repair the database corruption as quickly as possible. What database corruption recovery technique should you perform?

- **A.** Perform an emergency repair after setting the database to single user mode.

- **B.** Perform a tail-log backup. Restore the last full, differential backups. Restore the log chain including the tail-log.

- **C.** Restore the last full, differential backups. Restore the log chain and stop at the time of when the DBCC CHECKDB ran.

- **D.** Rebuild the damaged nonclustered index.

Thought experiment answers

This section contains the solution to the thought experiment. Each answer explains why the answer choice is correct.

1. **Correct answer:** B

   - **A. Incorrect:** You cannot meet your RPO with hourly log backups.

   - **B. Correct:** The RTO requirements are met with log backups every 15 minutes. Backup storage usage is minimized with month backups of the [AuditHistory] and [FG_OrderHistory] filegroups.

   - **C. Incorrect:** You cannot meet your RTO by performing differential backups every 15 minutes.

   - **D. Incorrect:** You cannot meet the requirement to minimize the backup storage usage by backing up the [AuditHistory] and [FG_OrderHistory] filegroups daily.

2. **Correct answer:** C

    A. **Incorrect:** You cannot revert a database where the underlying files have been lost.

    B. **Incorrect:** DBCC cannot repair database files that have been lost.

    C. **Correct:** A restore process with the STOPAT option recovers the database to Saturday at 17:00.

    D. **Incorrect:** Page recovery cannot be performed because the database file has been lost. Furthermore, the database does not have checksums on the pages so it cannot detect corruption.

3. **Correct answer:** D

    A. **Incorrect:** An emergency repair is not required. It is considered a last resort, plus it will take the database offline.

    B. **Incorrect:** Restoring a database does not recover the database in the shortest period of time.

    C. **Incorrect:** Restoring a database does not recover the database in the shortest period of time.

    D. **Correct:** An index ID of 5 indicates a nonclustered index was damaged.

Chapter summary

- The full recovery model captures all the modifications made to a database in its transaction log.
- The simple recovery model automatically truncates the database's transaction log when the transaction log records are no longer required for recovery purposes.
- The bulk-logged recovery model optimizes bulk modification in the database by only recording the extents that had been modified by the bulk operation.
- A full backup operation backup backs up the entire database.
- A differential backup operation backs up the extents that have been modified since the last full backup.
- A log backup operation backs up the transaction log, and then truncates it.
- A full backup is required before you can perform log backups.
- When switching from the full recovery model to the bulk-logged recovery model, and then back to the full recovery model, perform a log (or differential) backup to maintain your log chain.
- The NORECOVERY restore option allows further backups to be restored and keeps the database unavailable.
- The RECOVERY performs recovery on the database, rolling back all uncommitted transactions and makes the database available.

- Use the DBCC command to periodically check a database's consistency checks.

- Microsoft recommends restoring backups as a primary means of recovering from a database corruption.

- The DBCC repair operation with the REPAIR_REBUILD option does not lose any data within the database.

- The DBCC repair operation with the REPAIR_ALLOW_DATA_LOSS option results in data loss.

- Use the emergency repair mode as an absolutely last resort to recover from database corruption.

CHAPTER 3

Manage and monitor SQL Server instances

This chapter deals with a database administrator's core responsibilities, covering what you do every day, and managing and monitoring SQL Server instances you are responsible for. Unlike the other chapters in this book, this chapter is more operational than design and implementation focused. So, for the exam on this topic you should expect more questions on what tools to use, what objects to query, and what commands to run. You should also be prepared for what approaches and techniques to use to solve a specific issue or problem.

The chapter uses a "funnel approach," which is a process you can use to narrow down the cause of performance problems. Skill 3.1 starts at a broader scope where you can monitor what sessions are currently connected to the database engine, what queries they are running, what executing plans they are using, and how you can identify which sessions are causing blocking and consuming [tempdb] system resources. It also looks at how you can configure the data collector to collect SQL Server instance level telemetry for historical analysis and retrospective query tuning. Skill 3.2 drills down to the query level and shows how you can identify problematic queries by examining the procedure cache. It looks at an exciting new important feature called Query Store that collects query telemetry at the database level to help you troubleshoot query performance. The skill also looks at how you can use Extended Events and the server health feature in SQL Server to troubleshoot the database engine in real-time. In Skill 3.3 we drill further down to the index level and examine how to deal with fragmentations, missing indexes, and underutilized indexes. Finally, Skill 3.4 covers statistics, their importance to query performance, and how they should be managed. Skill 3.5 then turns to how you can monitor SQL Server instances. We will focus more on the capabilities of the SQL Server Agent here and look at how you can use Policy Based Management to help ensure that your SQL Server fleet conforms to your organization's standards and policies.

Skills in this chapter:
- Monitor database activity
- Monitor queries
- Manage indexes
- Manage statistics
- Monitor SQL Server instances

Skill 3.1: Monitor database activity

When users start complaining about performance problems, you need to quickly identify the current database activity in real time. Alternatively, you might be asked to troubleshoot why a particular scheduled task takes longer to run when compared to its normal execution duration. In this section we examine how to monitor database activity in real-time, and historically as well, such as how it performed last month compared to today..

Initially we will examine how to query what sessions are currently being executed, or waiting to be executed, and whether the query is causing any blocking or is the victim of blocking. This section also covers how to identify sessions that are consuming resources in the [tempdb] system database, because this is a common bottleneck in a lot of scenarios. Finally, we will examine how to setup the data collection capability in the database engine that captures and stores query telemetry for troubleshooting and analysis purposes.

For the exam, you will be expected to know the various dynamic management views (DMVs), tools, and commands that can be used to monitor activity in the database. Do not focus solely on them, however, since you might also be given the output of a command or DMV and be required to interpret the output to answer the question.

> **This section covers how to:**
>
> - Monitor current sessions
> - Identify sessions that cause blocking activity
> - Identify sessions that consume tempdb resources
> - Configure the data collector

Monitor current sessions

The SQL Server database engine provides a number of DMVs that allow you, in real-time, to determine what users are currently connected to the SQL Server instance, what queries they are running, the resource consumption of those queries, whether they are experiencing any contention, and what resources they are waiting on. In this section we will examine these DMVs and learn how to query them.

Figure 3-1 shows the main DMVs and their relationships so that you can query the currently executing connections, sessions, requests, and query executions. For the exam you should focus on the following information in these DMVs:

- **sys.dm_exec_connections** Provides detailed information about the connections made to the database engine. Detailed information includes the authentication used (Kerberos, NTLM or SQL), the network transport protocol (shared memory or TCP), and the client IP address.

- **sys.dm_exec_requests** Provides information about each request that is executing with the database engine. For more information visit *https://docs.microsoft.com/en-us/sql/relational-databases/system-dynamic-management-views/sys-dm-exec-requests-transact-sql*. For the exam the following columns are important:

  - **blocking_session_id** The SPID of the session that is blocking the request. If the session is not being blocked, a value of 0 will be returned.

  - **command** The type of command currently being executed. The more common commands include BACKUP DATABASE, BACKUP LOG, DELETE, DBCC, INSERT, SELECT or UPDATE.

  - **dop** The degree of parallelism used by the query. This is new to SQL Server 2016.

  - **last_wait_type** The last wait type experienced by the session.

  - **percent_complete** The percentage completed for the ALTER INDEX REORGANIZE, ALTER DATABASE AUTO_SHRINK, BACKUP DATABASE, DBCC CHECKDB, DBCC CHECKFILEGROUP, DBCC CHECKTABLE, DBCC INDEXDEFRAG, DBCC SHRINKDATABASE, DBCC SHRINKFILE, RECOVERY, RESTORE DATABASE, ROLLBACK and TDE ENCRYPTION commands.

  - **status** The status of the request. It can be either background, running, runnable, sleeping, or suspended.

  - **transaction_isolation_level** The isolation level used by the transaction space.

  - **wait_time** How long the session has been waiting in milliseconds, when blocked.

  - **wait_type** The type of wait for blocked sessions.

- **sys.dm_exec_sessions** Provides information about all active user connections and internal tasks, including the client (TDS) version, client program name, client login time, login user, current session setting, resource consumption, status, context visit, and a range of metrics. For more information visit: *https://docs.microsoft.com/en-us/sql/relational-databases/system-dynamic-management-views/sys-dm-exec-sessions-transact-sql*.

- **sys.dm_tran_session_transactions** Returns correlation information for sessions and their associated transactions. It differentiates between local and distributed transactions.

- **sys dm_exec_session_wait_stats** New to SQL Server 2016, this DMV returns information about all of the waits encountered by threads for each session. Use this view to diagnose performance issues for a specific session. We will discuss waits in more detail in the last section of this chapter.

- **sys.dm_os_waiting_tasks** Returns information about the wait queue of tasks that are waiting on resources. Pay attention to the following columns:

  - **blocking_session_id** The SPID of the session that is blocking the request. If the session is not being blocked, a value of NULL will be returned.

  - **resource_id** A detailed description of the resource that is being consumed.

  - **wait_type** The type of wait.

  - **wait_duration_ms** The total wait time in milliseconds for the wait type.

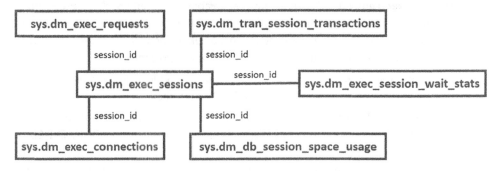

FIGURE 3-1 Executing session based DMVs

Listing 3-1 shows an example of a query that returns the currently connected sessions, the host used, the application in use, the network protocol used, the authentication protocol used, the amount of reads and writes performed, the time elapsed and the status.

LISTING 3-1 Querying current sessions

```
-- Query currently connected sessions with their stastics
SELECT c.session_id, c.net_transport, c.encrypt_option,
    c.auth_scheme, s.host_name, s.program_name,
    s.client_interface_name, s.login_name, s.nt_domain,
    s.nt_user_name, c.connect_time, s.login_time,
    s.reads, s.writes, s.logical_reads, s.status,
    s.cpu_time, s.total_scheduled_time, s.total_elapsed_time
FROM sys.dm_exec_connections AS c
JOIN sys.dm_exec_sessions AS s ON c.session_id = s.session_id;
GO
```

Although loathed by MVPs, the Activity Monitor in SQL Server Management Studio can be useful to quickly examine the sessions that are currently executing in your SQL Server instance. Figure 3-2 shows the Processes section. Note how you can see at a high level the processor utilization, the database disk I/O, the batch requests, and the number of waiting tasks. In this example, session 66's query is using parallelism, which can be seen through the CXPACKET wait. You can see via the Blocked By column on the far right that query's various internal threads are blocking the query.

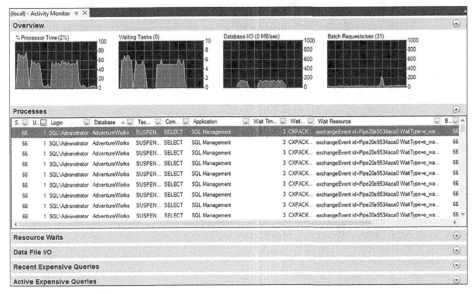

FIGURE 3-2 Activity Monitor

Identify sessions that cause blocking activity

Let's now move on to how to identify sessions that are causing blocking activity. Blocking is a common cause of poor performance in a database engine where multiple transactions are isolated from each other through locking. By identifying sessions that are causing blocking you will be able to kill the offending sessions, engage your developers to rewrite their code and reindex tables appropriately.

You saw in Figure 3-2 an example of a query whose threads are blocking itself through parallelism, so Activity Monitor can be used to filter sessions that are being blocked through the Blocked By column filter. The database engine offers a number of different techniques that you can use to identify sessions that cause blocking. The techniques include, but are not limited to:

- Using Activity Monitor
- Querying any of the following DMVs:
    - [sys].[dm_exec_requests]
    - [sys].[dm_os_waiting_tasks]
- Executing the [sp_who], or the undocumented [sp_who2] system stored procedures. These will most likely not be on the exam.
- Using the blocked processed report.
- Configuring and consuming the blocked process threshold reports in the database engine.

Listing 3-2 shows a number of examples of how to identify a session that is blocked. The technique you use depends upon what additional information you require: either the queries or the resources involved.

LISTING 3-2 Idle sessions with open transactions

```
-- Using the sys.dm_exec_requests
SELECT session_id, blocking_session_id, open_transaction_count, wait_time, wait_type,
    last_wait_type, wait_resource, transaction_isolation_level, lock_timeout
FROM sys.dm_exec_requests
WHERE blocking_session_id <> 0;
GO
-- Using the sys.dm_os_waiting_tasks
SELECT session_id, blocking_session_id, wait_duration_ms, wait_type, resource_
description
FROM sys.dm_os_waiting_tasks
WHERE blocking_session_id IS NOT NULL
```

Listing 3-3 shows an example of a query that finds idle sessions that have open transactions. Such sessions will potentially cause blocking.

LISTING 3-3 Idle sessions with open transactions

```
SELECT s.*
FROM sys.dm_exec_sessions AS s
WHERE EXISTS (
    SELECT *
    FROM sys.dm_tran_session_transactions AS t
    WHERE t.session_id = s.session_id
)
AND NOT EXISTS (
    SELECT *
    FROM sys.dm_exec_requests AS r
    WHERE r.session_id = s.session_id
);
```

Given this blocking discussion, we need to cover deadlocks and how they can be detected. You should expect a question on deadlocks in the exam. A deadlock can occur when two or more tasks permanently block each other. Each task has a lock on a resource that the other tasks are trying to lock. In this case the database engine will pick and kill off one of the tasks based on internal heuristics, which can be influenced, but not controlled. Again, there will be a number of techniques that you can use to detect deadlocks, including:

■ Use the 1204 or 1222 trace flags. These trace flags will write to the database error log whenever the deadlock monitor detects a deadlock. Using trace flags was the only option in ancient versions of SQL Server, so should no longer be used.

- Use the SQL Server Profiler to create a trace that records, replays, and displays deadlock events for analysis. The benefit of SQL Server Profiler over trace flags is that it captures a deadlock graph, which is much easier to work with because it is graphical. Figure 3-3 shows an example of a deadlock graph. Again, this technique is no longer typically used in SQL Server.

- Use Service Broker event notifications to capture deadlock graphs by creating a service and queue for the DEADLOCK_GRAPH trace event. You can potentially send an email to your development team whenever a deadlock occurs. It's a great way to get deadlocks resolved sooner rather than later, but again probably not the recommended technique in SQL Server 2016.

- Use extended events to create an extended event session to write deadlock events to some output. We will cover extended events in more details later on in Skill 3.2

- Query the default system_health session to retrieve deadlock graphs. Again, we will cover this in more detail in Skill 3.2

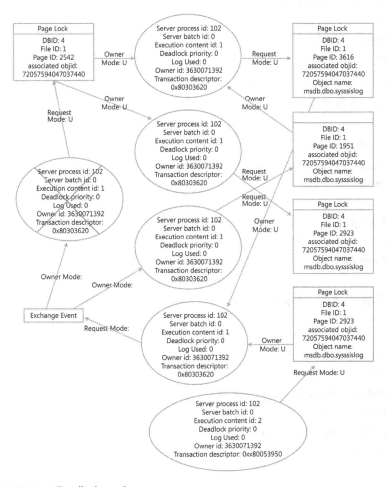

FIGURE 3-3 Deadlock graph

EXAM TIP

Make sure you can analyze deadlock graphs for the exam. The exam might give you an example of a deadlock graph where you will have to analyze the graph or recommend some corrective action.

Identify sessions that consume tempdb resources

The [tempdb] system database is a global resource used by the database engine for storing temporary objects, and is available to all users that are connected to the instance. Its configuration and maintenance is critical to good performance within SQL Server.

The [tempdb] system database stores user objects, internal objects, and version stores. User objects include global temporary tables and indexes, local temporary tables and indexes, system tables and indexes, table-valued functions output tables, table variables, user-defined tables, and indexes. Internal objects include sort runs, work files, and work tables. Work files are used by operations like hash joins. Work tables are commonly used by cursor operations, spool operations and temporary large object (LOB) storage. And the version store is used by the following operations in SQL Server:

- When the database is using ALLOW_SNAPSHOT_ISOLATION isolation level.
- When the database is using the READ_COMMITTED_SNAPSHOT isolation level.
- When DML triggers fired.
- When a Multiple Active Results Sets (MARS) session is enabled.
- During online indexing operations.

Due to the importance and potentially heavy usage of the [tempdb] system database Microsoft added some DMVs to enable you to better identify the resource consumption in the system database:

- **sys.dm_db_file_space_usage** Provides information about space usage of each file in the database. For the exam the following columns are important:
  - **allocated_extent_page_count** The total number of pages in theallocated extents in the file.
  - **internal_object_reserved_page_count** The total number of pages from the uniform extents allocated for internal objects in the file. Internal objects only apply to the [tempdb] system database.
  - **mixed_extent_page_count** The total number of allocated and unallocated pages in allocated mixed extents in the file.
  - **unallocated_extent_page_count** The total number of pages from the unallocated extents in the file.
  - **user_object_reserved_page_count** The total number of pages allocated from uniform extents for user objects in the database.

- **version_store_reserved_page_count**   The total number of pages from the uniform extents allocated to the version store, which always uses uniform extents.
- **sys.dm_db_session_space_usage**   Provides information about the number of pages allocated and deallocated by each session in a given database. This DMV only applies to the [tempdb] system database. Important columns include:
  - **internal_objects_alloc_page_count**   The count of pages reserved or allocated for internal objects by this session uniquely identified.
  - **internal_objects_dealloc_page_count**   The count of pages deallocated and no longer reserved for internal objects by this session.
  - **user_objects_alloc_page_count**   The count of pages reserved or allocated for user objects by this session.
  - **user_objects_dealloc_page_count**   The count of pages deallocated and no longer reserved for user objects by this session.
  - **user_objects_deferred_dealloc_page_count**   The count of pages that have been marked for deferred deallocation.
- **sys.dm_db_task_space_usage**   Provides information about the number of pages allocated and deallocated by each task in a given database. This DMV only applies to the [tempdb] system database. It contains the same [internal_objects_alloc_page_count], [internal_objects_dealloc_page_count], [user_objects_alloc_page_count] and [user_objects_dealloc_page_count] columns, as in the [sys].[dm_db_session_space_usage] DMV above.
- **sys.dm_tran_active_snapshot_database_transactions**   Provides information about all active transactions that generate or potentially access row versions. Use the following columns to see what transactions are consuming row versions:
  - **transaction_id**   The transaction unique identified.
  - **transaction_sequence_num**   The transaction sequence number (TSN).
  - **average_version_chain_traversed**   The average number of row versions in the version chains that are traversed.
  - **is_snapshot**   Whether snapshot isolation is being used.
  - **elapsed_time_seconds**   The time elapsed since the transaction acquired its TSN.
  - **first_snapshot_sequence_num**   The lowest TSN of the transactions that were active when a snapshot was taken.
  - **max_version_chain_traversed**   The maximum length of the version chain that is traversed to find a transactionally consistent version.
- **sys.dm_tran_version_store**   Provides information about all version records in the version store. Records that don't fit in the 8192 byte limit will consume both the [record_image_first_part] and [record_image_second_part] columns. Be careful with querying this DMV because it can be potentially wide and contain many rows.

Listing 3-4 show an example of a query that finds SPID, request_id, and query text of queries that have been allocated the most space resources in the [tempdb] system database.

LISTING 3-4 Queries allocated the most space in tempdb

```
SELECT r.session_id, r.request_id, t.text AS query,
    u.allocated AS task_internal_object_page_allocation_count,
    u.deallocated AS task_internal_object_page_deallocation_count
FROM (
    SELECT session_id, request_id,
        SUM(internal_objects_alloc_page_count) AS allocated,
        SUM (internal_objects_dealloc_page_count) AS deallocated
    FROM sys.dm_db_task_space_usage
    GROUP BY session_id, request_id) AS u
JOIN sys.dm_exec_requests AS r
ON u.session_id = r.session_id  AND u.request_id = r.request_id
CROSS APPLY sys.dm_exec_sql_text (r.sql_handle) as t
ORDER BY u.allocated DESC;
```

SQL Server has a number of [tempdb] system database related error messages that will be raised when there is insufficient disk space. Table 3-1 shows these [tempdb] system database related errors that might be useful to know for the exam.

TABLE 3-1 tempb related errors

Error	Context
1101 / 1105	Any session must allocate space
3958 / 3966	A transaction cannot find the required version record
3959	The version store is full. This error typically appears after a 1105 or 1101 error
3967	The version store is forced to shrink because [tempdb] system database is full

Configure the data collector

Introduced in SQL Server 2008, the data collector was a means of capturing server level metrics and query performance over time. It is not a real-time tool like Activity Monitor. It was designed for historical analysis, trend analysis, and troubleshooting/optimizing past events. It is not that commonly used in the industry because there are better solutions and Microsoft has stopped evolving its capabilities. Microsoft has invested more in technology like Query Store, which we cover in Skill 3.2.

There data collector architecture is made up of the following components:

- **Management data warehouse**   The MDW is a repository used by the data collector to store the metrics that are collected. The MDW can be hosted on the SQL Server where the data collector runs on a remote server. You can configure a single MDW on a dedicated server for your SQL Server fleet.

- **Data collector**   The data collector is made up of a number of scheduled SQL Server Agent jobs and SSIS packages that collect metrics through a number of DMOs, performance object counters, and SQL Trace events. The metrics it collects are stored in the MDW. It is extensible, so you customize what is collected. By default the data collector collects the following:

- **Disk Usage**   Collects metrics on the disk consumption of databases.
- **Query Statistics**   Collects execution statistics, query text, and query plans for queries.
- **Server Activity**   Collects server level metrics on the computer's various subsystem resource usage and waits.
- **Utility Information**   Only used if the SQL Server instance is managed by a utility control point (UCP).
- **Reports**   Returns information about the wait queue of tasks that are waiting on resources. Pay attention to the following columns:
  - **Disk Usage History**   Provides an overview of the disk space used for all the databases on the server and the growth trends for the data and log file for all databases.
  - **Query Statistics History**   Provides an overview of the query execution statistics for a given time range. You will be able to analyze the most expensive queries based on processor usage, duration, I/O consumption, physical reads, or logical writes. You can drill down to a specific query and see its query text, various execution statistics, its waits, and the potentially different query plans that are used.
  - **Server Activity History**   Provides an overview of the resource consumption and server activity. You will be able to drill down to a specific date range and see what the processor, memory, disk, and network usage was. You will also be able to examine the SQL Server waits.

Given the potential information that is collected by the data collectors and their extensibility, you will need to configure security appropriately within the data collector architecture. The data collector uses the role-based security model implemented by SQL Server Agent. The roles you can leverage are:

- **dc_admin**   Members of this role have full control of the data collection configuration and can set collector-level properties, add new collection sets, install new collection types, and perform all the operations of the dc_operator role.
- **dc_operator**   Members of this role can read and update data collection configuration. This includes starting or stopping a collection set, enumerating collection sets, changing the upload frequency for collection sets, and changing the collection frequency for collection items that are part of a collection set.
- **dc_proxy**   Members of this role have read access to a data collection configuration. They can also create SQL Server Agent job steps that use an existing proxy account, and execute SQL Server Agent jobs that they own. Members can view collection set configuration information, obtain internal encrypted information that can only be accessed by a signed stored procedure, and log collection-set run-time events.

To control access to the reports within MDW you can leverage the following roles:

- **mdw_admin**   Members of this role have full control over the MDW. They have permissions to read, write, update, and delete data from any table, modify the database schema, and perform administrative tasks on the MDW.

- **mdw_writer**   Members of this role can write and upload data to the MDW.

- **mdw_reader**   Members of this role can read data from the MDW.

Use the following steps to configure the MDW and enable the data collectors:

1. Connect to your SQL Server instance using SQL Server Management Studio, expand the Management folder, right-click on the Data Collection folder and select the Configure Management Data Warehouse task to start the wizard.

2. Click on Next in the Configure Management Data Warehouse Wizard.

3. Configure the MDW database and server that will be used to host the MDW, as shown in Figure 3-4, and click on Next.

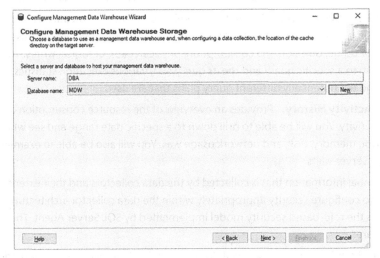

FIGURE 3-4 Configure Management Data Warehouse Storage

4. Configure the users that will be able to administer, read, and write to the MDW, as shown in Figure 3-5, and click on Next.

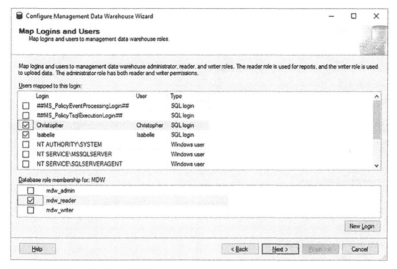

FIGURE 3-5 Map Logins and Users

5. Review the options you have selected and click on Finish.

6. Ensure the MDW has been created successfully and click on Close.

7. Back in SQL Server Management Studio right-click on the Data Collection folder and select the Configure Data Collection task to start the wizard.

8. In the Setup Data Collection Sets wizard page configure the MDW that you will be using and configure the following options as shown in Figure 3-6, and click on Next.

   ■ Specify the cache directory where collected data will be stored on the system, collecting the data before it is uploaded to the MDW. If the cache directory is not specified, the data collector attempts to use the Windows temp directory as controlled by system variables.

   ■ Enable the System Data Collection Sets.

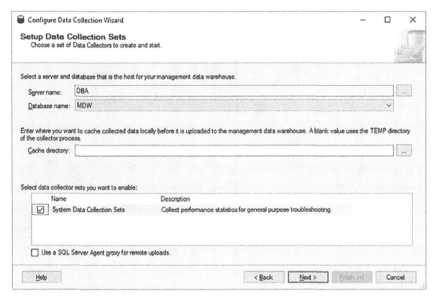

FIGURE 3-6 Setup Data Collection Sets

9. Review the options you have chosen and click on Finish.

10. Ensure the data collectors has been created successfully and click on Close.

Once enabled you can customize the data collector properties or create your own. Figure 3-7 shows an example of the Disk Usage data collector. Note the collection is not cached and is by default collected every 6 hours through a SQL Server Agent job. This data collector collects metrics about both the data and log files. The data is retained for 730 days. In this instance the data collector uses the DBCC SQLPEF(LOGSPACE) command to collect metrics about the databases' log files.

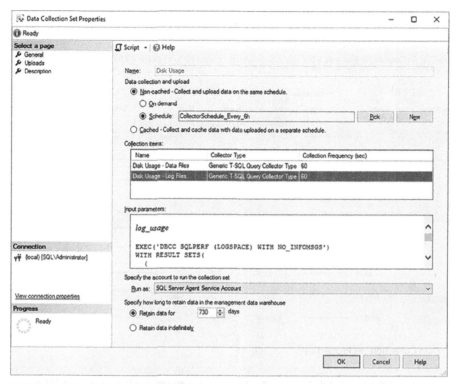

FIGURE 3-7 Data Collection Set Properties

You can now view the reports that the data collector generates by right-clicking on the Data Collection folder in SQL Server Management Studio and opening the various reports. Figure 3-8 shows the Disk Usage Collection Set report. For each database you will see the start size, current size, average growth per day, and a trend line for both the data and log files.

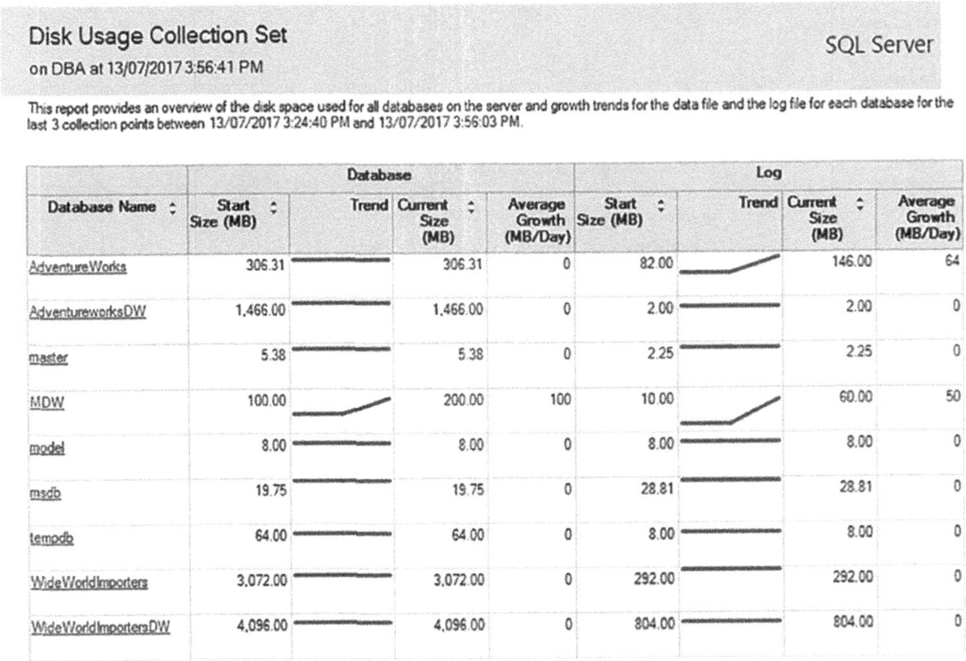

Disk Usage Collection Set
on DBA at 13/07/2017 3:56:41 PM

SQL Server

This report provides an overview of the disk space used for all databases on the server and growth trends for the data file and the log file for each database for the last 3 collection points between 13/07/2017 3:24:40 PM and 13/07/2017 3:56:03 PM.

Database Name ⇕	Database				Log			
	Start Size (MB) ⇕	Trend	Current Size (MB) ⇕	Average Growth (MB/Day)	Start Size (MB) ⇕	Trend	Current Size (MB) ⇕	Average Growth (MB/Day)
AdventureWorks	306.31		306.31	0	82.00		146.00	64
AdventureworksDW	1,466.00		1,466.00	0	2.00		2.00	0
master	5.38		5.38	0	2.25		2.25	0
MDW	100.00		200.00	100	10.00		60.00	50
model	8.00		8.00	0	8.00		8.00	0
msdb	19.75		19.75	0	28.81		28.81	0
tempdb	64.00		64.00	0	8.00		8.00	0
WideWorldImporters	3,072.00		3,072.00	0	292.00		292.00	0
WideWorldImportersDW	4,096.00		4,096.00	0	804.00		804.00	0

FIGURE 3-8 Data Collection Set Properties

Figure 3-9 shows the Query Statistics History report. You can see the top 10 queries by either CPU, Duration Total I/O, Physical Reads or Logical Writes in a bar chart for a specified time line. Clicking on query will drill down to the Query Details report.

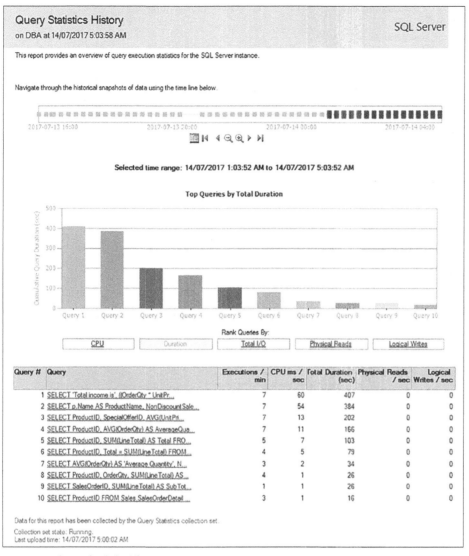

The figure shows a report titled:

Query Statistics History
on DBA at 14/07/2017 5:03:58 AM — SQL Server

This report provides an overview of query execution statistics for the SQL Server instance.

Navigate through the historical snapshots of data using the time line below.

Time line axis labels: 2017-07-13 16:00 | 2017-07-13 20:00 | 2017-07-14 00:00 | 2017-07-14 04:00

Selected time range: 14/07/2017 1:03:52 AM to 14/07/2017 5:03:52 AM

Top Queries by Total Duration

Rank Queries By: CPU | Duration | Total I/O | Physical Reads | Logical Writes

Query #	Query	Executions / min	CPU ms / sec	Total Duration (sec)	Physical Reads / sec	Logical Writes / sec
1	SELECT 'Total income is', ((OrderQty * UnitPr...	7	60	407	0	0
2	SELECT p.Name AS ProductName, NonDiscountSale...	7	54	384	0	0
3	SELECT ProductID, SpecialOfferID, AVG(UnitPri...	7	13	202	0	0
4	SELECT ProductID, AVG(OrderQty) AS AverageQua...	7	11	166	0	0
5	SELECT ProductID, SUM(LineTotal) AS Total FRO...	5	7	103	0	0
6	SELECT ProductID, Total = SUM(LineTotal) FROM...	4	5	79	0	0
7	SELECT AVG(OrderQty) AS 'Average Quantity', N...	3	2	34	0	0
8	SELECT ProductID, OrderQty, SUM(LineTotal) AS ...	4	1	26	0	0
9	SELECT SalesOrderID, SUM(LineTotal) AS SubTot...	1	1	26	0	0
10	SELECT ProductID FROM Sales.SalesOrderDetail ...	3	1	16	0	0

Data for this report has been collected by the Query Statistics collection set.
Collection set state: Running.
Last upload time: 14/07/2017 5:00:02 AM

FIGURE 3-9 Query Statistics History report

Figure 3-10 shows the Query Detail History report. All of the different query plans are shown at the bottom of the figure for analysis. You can further drill down into the individual query plans.

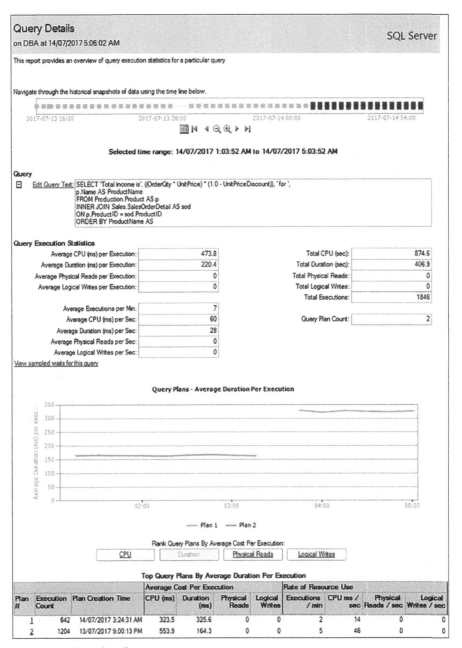

FIGURE 3-10 Query Details report

Skill 3.2 Monitor queries

In this section we examine the query level, showing how to troubleshoot queries historically and in real time. For detailed query troubleshooting you need to examine query execution plans. This skill, however, concentrates more on how to identify problematic query plans for more detailed analysis.

Let's start with Query Store, which captures query telemetry for historical and semi-realtime analysis. Introduced in SQL Server 2016, Query Store will definitely be on the exam. For true real-time analysis you will need to leverage extended events and the procedure cache. So let's look at what capabilities those features bring to help you monitor queries.

Extended events are not that commonly used by database administrators in the industry, so make sure you understand their capability, their options and their syntax for the exam.

> **This section covers how to:**
> - Manage the Query Store
> - Configure Extended Events and trace events
> - Identify problematic execution plans
> - Troubleshoot server health using Extended Events

Manage the Query Store

Query Store is an exciting new technology introduced in SQL Server 2016 that will greatly aid you in managing query performance. Once enabled at the database level, the Query Store starts collecting telemetry and metrics about all queries that are executed within the database. Metrics collected about a query include the query plan, logical I/O, degree of parallelism used, elapsed time, and CPU time.

Query Store was designed with the following use cases in mind:

- To help troubleshoot query performance over time. Because Query Store is potentially capturing all of the queries and their performance profile over a period of time it is easier to detect whether a query execution is consuming more CPU, consuming more I/O, or taking longer to run compared to its execution in the past.

- For mitigating the risks of query regressions caused by upgrading SQL Server. After upgrading to the latest version of SQL Server you can enable the Query Store for a database before changing the database compatibility level. After a period of time you chang the database compatibility level to the latest version. Query Store will now be able to detect and show you any queries whose performance has regressed.

- To help you easily force the execution plan for a query. One of Microsoft's primary goals with Query Store is to easily enable the database administrator to force the execution plan through SQL Server Management Studio for a given query by selecting the the optimal execution plan in the graphical interface. With the release of SQL Server 2017,

Microsoft has taken this capability further with the database engine being able to automatically force execution plans for regressed queries at the database level.

■ To perform A/B testing by using Query Store to track query performance before and after any changes that are deployed in a controlled fashion. You will be able to directly compare differences in execution plans via SQL Server Management Studio.

Figure 3-11 shows the high level architecture of Query Store. When a Transact-SQL query is executed, metrics about both the compilation and execution are written to Query Store's memory buffers. To minimize the impact on performance, these memory buffers are flushed asynchronously to a set of disk-based tables. You control the frequency of this asynchronous write-back via the DATA_FLUSH_INTERVAL_SECONDS configuration option. As each user database has its own persisted Query Store it will survive SQL Server restarts and the database being restored on another SQL Server instance.

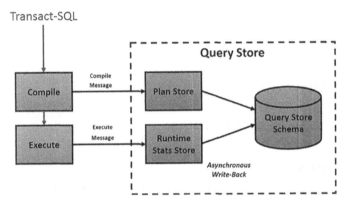

FIGURE 3-11 Query store architecture

Query Store is enabled at the database level. When enabling Query Store for a given database you have the following configuration options:

■ **Operation mode** The OPERATION_MODE option controls whether the Query Store can be written to (READ_WRITE) or if it is in read-only mode (READ_ONLY). Don't forget that you can potentially change this option on a scheduled basis, such as in the example where you only want to capture query performance during business hours.

■ **Data flush interval** The DATA_FLUCH_INTERVAL_SECONDS option controls how frequently the telemetry captured by Query Store in its memory buffers is flushed to the database. The default is 900 (15 minutes).

■ **Statistics collection interval** The INTERVAL_LENGTH_MINUTES option controls the window over which the aggregate statistical information is calculated. The default value is 60.

■ **Maximum size** The MAX_STORAGE_SIZE_MB configures the maximum size that will be taken up by Query Store. When Query Store hits this maximum size it will switch from read-write mode to read-only mode. The default is 100MBs.

- **Query store capture mode** The QUERY_CAPTURE_MODE option controls what information is captured by Query Store. The valid options are:
  - **ALL** Capture all queries.
  - **AUTO** Capture only relevant queries. Infrequent queries and queries with insignificant compilation and execution durations will be ignored.
  - **NONE** Don't capture any queries.
- **Size based cleanup mode** The SIZE_BASED_CLEANUP_MODE controls whether Query Store will automatically start cleaning out old data when the MAX_STORAGE_SIZE_MB is approached. The default of AUTO initiates this automatic cleanup.
- **Stale query threshold** The STALE_QUERY_THRESHOLD_DAYS option controls the number of days Query Store retains data. The default value is 30 days.

Figure 3-12 shows the Query Store configuration options as shown by SQL Server Management Studio. Note the pie charts at the bottom that show how much storage space Query Store is currently consuming.

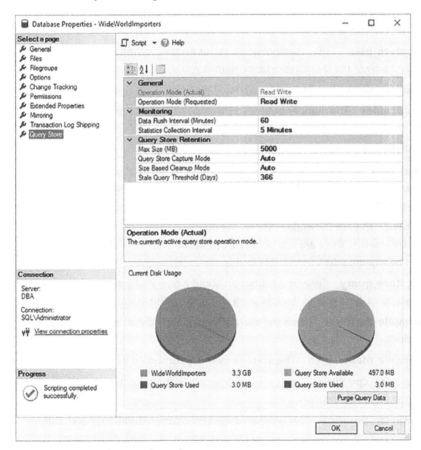

FIGURE 3-12 Query Store configuration

Listing 3-5 shows the same Query Store options as shown in Figure 3-12? being configured using Transact-SQL:

LISTING 3-5 Configuring Query Store

```
ALTER DATABASE [WideWorldImporters]
    SET QUERY_STORE (OPERATION_MODE = READ_WRITE,
    CLEANUP_POLICY = (STALE_QUERY_THRESHOLD_DAYS = 366),
    DATA_FLUSH_INTERVAL_SECONDS = 3600,
    INTERVAL_LENGTH_MINUTES = 5,
    MAX_STORAGE_SIZE_MB = 5000);
GO
```

Once enabled, Query Store will start collecting telemetry and metrics to a set of tables. Figure 3-13 shows this schema used by Query Store. The schema diagram also shows the columns that need to be used to join related tables together. In SQL Server 2016 Query Store is made up of the following system catalog views:

- **sys.query_context_settings** Collects information about the query execution affecting context settings, such as the date format, language used, and other SET options (ANSI_NULLS, ARITH_ABORT, DATEFIRST, QUOTED_IDENTIFIERS, and others).

- **sys.query_store_plan** Collects information about each execution plan associated with a query. Some of the more important columns you should focus on include:

  - **avg_compile_duration** The average compilation time.

  - **count_compiles** The number of times a plan was compiled. A focus on higher counts.

  - **is_parallel_plan** Whether the plan is parallel or not.

  - **is_trivial_plan** Whether the plan is trivial or not. With a trivial plan the database engine bails out at stage 0 of the query optimizer. Such plans can be ignored or even deleted out of the Query Store.

  - **query_plan** This is a showplan XML for the query plan. You can analyze the query plan to see whether there are any potential optimizations, such as better indexes, that can be implemented.

- **sys.query_store_query** Collects information about a query's aggregated runtime execution statistics. Be aware of the following columns for the exam:

  - **avg_compile_duration** This is the average compilation duration. Watch out for large values.

  - **avg_compile_memory_kb** The average memory consumed by compilation.

  - **avg_optimize_cpu_time** This is the average compilation duration. Large values might indicate complex plans.

  - **avg_optimize_duration** This is the average optimization duration. Watch out for large values.

- **count_compiles** A compilation count. Again, watch out for large values that indicate queries that are frequently run and consequently might be important to examine.

- **max_compile_memory_kb** The maximum memory consumption during compilation. Look for substantial variance from [avg_compile_memory_kb] value.

- **sys.query_store_query_text** This collects the Transact-SQL text of the query and its associated SQL handle.

- **sys.query_store_runtime_stats** This collects a rich set of runtime execution statistics for a query's execution. You can perform complex analysis of query performance over time with these metrics. Don't forget that the aggregations are based on the INTERVAL_LENGTH_MINUTES configuration options discussed above. Watch out for these metrics:

  - **CLR time** The [avg_clr_time], [last_clr_time], [min_clr_time], [max_clr_time], and [stdev_clr_time] columns capture aggregates for the query's time spent executing in the SQLCLR runtime.

  - **CPU time** The [avg_cpu_time], [last_cpu_time], [min_cpu_time], [max_cpu_time], and [stdev_cpu_time] columns capture aggregates for the query's time spent executing on a processor. The CPU time can be greater than the duration if the query used multiple threads to execute on multiple schedulers.

  - **Degree of parallelism** The [avg_dop], [last_dop], [min_dop], [max_dop], and [stdev_dop] columns capture aggregates for the degree of parallelism used during query execution.

  - **Duration** The [avg_duration], [last_duration], [min_duration], [max_duration], and [stdev_duration] columns capture aggregates for the query's duration.

  - **Log bytes used** The [avg_log_bytes_used], [last_log_bytes_used], [min_log_bytes_used], [max_log_bytes_used], and [stdev_log_bytes_used] columns capture aggregates for the number of bytes used in the transaction log.

  - **Logical I/O** The [avg_logical_io_reads], [last_logical_io_reads], [min_logical_io_reads], [max_logical_io_reads], and [stdev_logical_io_reads] columns capture aggregates for the number of logical reads. The [avg_logical_io_writes], [last_logical_io_writes], [min_logical_io_writes], [max_logical_io_writes], and [stdev_logical_io_writes] columns capture aggregates for the number of logical writes.

  - **Memory Grant** The [avg_query_max_used_memory], [last_query_max_used_memory], [min_query_max_used_memory], [max_query_max_used_memory], and [stdev_query_max_used_memory] columns capture aggregates for the degree of parallelism used during query execution.

  - **Physical I/O** The [avg_physical_io_reads], [last_physical_io_reads], [min_physical_io_reads], [max_physical_io_reads], and [stdev_physical_io_reads] columns capture aggregates for the number of physical I/O reads. Note there are no metrics captured for physical I/O writes.

- **Row Count** The [avg_rowcount], [last_rowcount], [min_rowcount], [max_rowcount], and [stdev_rowcount] columns capture aggregates for the degree of parallelism used during query execution.

- **sys.query_store_runtime_stats_interval** This collects the start and end time for each interval over which runtime execution statistics for a query have been collected. It is similar to the time dimension table in a data warehouse context.

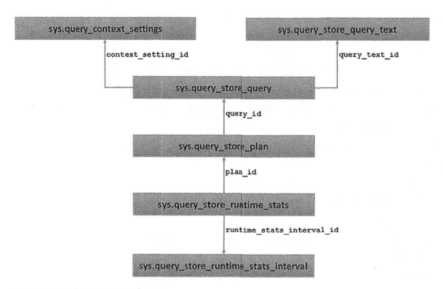

FIGURE 3-13 Query store schema

NOTE **SYS.QUERY_STORE_WAIT_STATS**

SQL Server 2017 has added the [sys].[query_store_wait_stats] system catalog view to Query Store. It collects important wait information about query execution. For more information visit: *https://docs.microsoft.com/en-us/sql/relational-databases/system-catalog-views/sys-query-store-wait-stats-transact-sql.*

Once Query Store has been configured you can analyze query performance through SQL Server Management Studio. Figure 3-14 shows an example of a query that has two different execution plans. Notice how you have buttons underneath the plan summary pane in the top left of the dialog box that allow you to force and unforce a plan for the query.

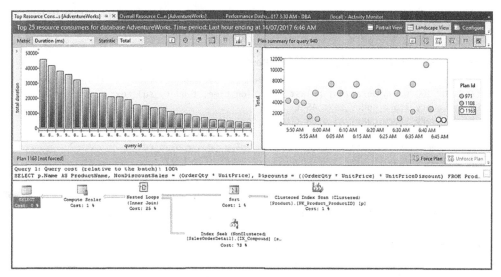

FIGURE 3-14 Top resource consuming queries report

Figure 3-15 shows an example of how you can now compare two different execution plans for a given query captured by Query Store. Notice how the area within the pink boundary shows identical sections between the two plan shapes. On the right hand side of the dialog box the properties for the two plans are shown side by side. An inequality graphic highlights the execution plan properties that are different between the two plans.

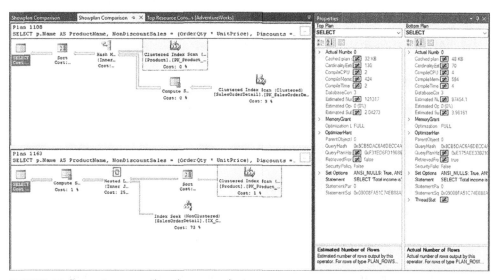

FIGURE 3-15 Query store execution plan comparison

Alternatively you can write your own queries to analyze the rich information collected by Query Store. Listing 3-6 shows an example of the Query Store being queried directly.

LISTING 3-6 Analyzing and managing the query store

```
-- Determine the top 100 queries with the longest average duration for the last week
SELECT TOP 100 r.avg_duration, r.last_execution_time, t.query_sql_text
FROM sys.query_store_query_text AS t
JOIN sys.query_store_query AS q ON t.query_text_id = q.query_text_id
JOIN sys.query_store_plan AS p ON q.query_id = p.query_id
JOIN sys.query_store_runtime_stats AS r ON p.plan_id = r.plan_id
WHERE r.last_execution_time > DATEADD(day, -7, GETUTCDATE())
ORDER BY r.avg_duration DESC;
GO
```

Listing 3-7 shows a number of examples of the Query Store being managed.

LISTING 3-7 Analyzing and managing the query store

```
-- Delete ad-hoc queries (single use plans) older than 24 hours
DECLARE @query_id INT;
DECLARE adhoc_queries_cursor CURSOR FOR
    SELECT q.query_id
    FROM sys.query_store_query_text AS t
    JOIN sys.query_store_query AS q ON q.query_text_id = t.query_text_id
    JOIN sys.query_store_plan AS p ON p.query_id = q.query_id
    JOIN sys.query_store_runtime_stats AS r ON r.plan_id = p.plan_id
    GROUP BY q.query_id
    HAVING SUM(r.count_executions) < 2
    AND MAX(r.last_execution_time) < DATEADD (hour, -24, GETUTCDATE())
    ORDER BY q.query_id;
OPEN adhoc_queries_cursor;
FETCH NEXT FROM adhoc_queries_cursor INTO @query_id;
WHILE (@@FETCH_STATUS = 0) BEGIN
    EXEC sp_query_store_remove_query @query_id
    FETCH NEXT FROM adhoc_queries_cursor INTO @query_id
END
CLOSE adhoc_queries_cursor;
DEALLOCATE adhoc_queries_cursor;
GO
-- Force a query to use a specific plan
EXEC sp_query_store_force_plan @query_id = 66, @plan_id = 69;
GO
-- Unforce a query to use a specific plan
EXEC sp_query_store_unforce_plan @query_id = 66, @plan_id = 69;
GO
```

EXAM TIP

For the exam make sure you understand when to force plans and how to force them in Query Store. Listing 3-7 showed how to use the [sp_query_store_force_plan] and [sp_query_store_force_plan] system stored procedures to force and unforced a plan. Figure 3-14 showed the equivalent buttons available in SQL Server Management Studio.

Configure Extended Events and trace events

Extended Events were introduced in SQL Server 2008 as a light weight performance monitoring system that was designed from the very start to use as few performance resources as possible. Extended Events were designed to supersede the capabilities of SQL Server Profiler and SQL Trace, both of which were dated and could impact the performance of the database engine.

Although you are welcome to create a number of Extended Event sessions, they are designed to be turned on when there is a requirement to troubleshoot a specific incident or problem. Extended Event use cases include:

- Detailed troubleshooting of the database engine, such as in the case for excessive CPU utilization, out-of-memory and memory pressure scenarios.
- Identifying which queries are responsible for specific events such as pages splits or particular waits.
- Capturing deadlocks.
- Correlating request activity with the Windows ETW logs.

Extended Events use an asynchronous model so as to minimize the impact on SQL Server performance. The metrics capture is separate from the filtering and processing. Another capability not available in SQL Server Profiler and and SQL Tace is the ability to filter events by sampling and aggregating the data as it is captured. Extended Events can be integrated with the event tracing for Windows (ETW) framework.

Figure 3-16 shows the Extended Events architecture at a high level. This architecture is made up of the following components:

- **Package**   Packages represent a container for Extended Events objects. The package can consist of actions, events, maps, predicates, targets and types. There are 3 types of packages:
  - **package0**   Extended Events system objects. This is the default package.
  - **sqlos**   SQL Server Operating System (SQLOS) related objects.
  - **sqlserver**   SQL Server related objects
- **Event**   Events are monitoring points that fire when a point is reached in the database engine's code base. When an event fires it contains useful state information that can be used for tracing purposes or triggering actions. All events have a versioned schema which defines their payload. Events have a categorization model, similar to ETW, as defined by the following properties.
  - **Channel**   A channel identifies the target audience for an event. Four channels are supported. The Admin channel is designed for administration and support. The Operational channel is for analyzing and diagnosing a problem or occurrence. The Analytic channel is used for high-volume events used in performance investigations. The Debug channel is used for ETW developer debugging events.

- **Keyword** Keywords are application-specific categorization that make it easier to specify and retrieve specific events. In SQL Server, Extended Eventkeywords map closely to the grouping of events in a SQL Trace definition.

- **Predicate** Predicates define the Boolean conditions for when an event needs to be fired. Predicates can be defined against either the event data columns or global attributes. Predicates can use basic arithmetic operations and comparison functions supported by Extended Events and support short-circuiting. Predicates can also store data in a local scope that can be subsequently used for creating additional predicates that return true a number of minutes have expired or an event fires a number of times.

- **Action** Actions give you the ability to primarily collect additional information for an event. Actions are executed after a predicate is evaluated and only if the event is going to fire. They can introduce overhead because they execute synchronously using the same threads used by the events. Listing 3-8 shows you how you can determine what actions are supported by the version of SQL Server you are using.

LISTING 3-8 Extended event actions

```
SELECT p.name AS package_name, o.name AS action_name, o.description
FROM sys.dm_xe_packages AS p
JOIN sys.dm_xe_objects AS o ON p.guid = o.package_guid
WHERE (p.capabilities IS NULL OR p.capabilities & 1 = 0) -- Exclude private packages
AND (o.capabilities IS NULL OR o.capabilities & 1 = 0) -- Exclude private objects
AND o.object_type = 'action'
ORDER BY package_name, action_name;
```

- **Targets** Targets consume event data after the event fires. Use targets to store the event data, analyse and aggregate it, or start a task. Extended Events supports the following targets:

  - **Event bucketing** A bucketizer and histogram target that generates aggregated data. It can be asynchronous or synchronous.

  - **Event file** This is an asynchronous file destination.

  - **Event pairing** This is an asynchronous target where you want to detect when an expected event does not fire. For example, you might want to detect orphaned transactions. In this instance look for the database_transaction_begin events without a corresponding database_transaction_end events.

  - **Event Tracing for Windows** A synchronous target to the Windows ETW feature.

  - **Ring buffer** An asynchronous FIFO memory buffer.

  - **Synchronous event counter** A synchronous target that counts the number of occurences of each event in a n event session. It is useful when you want to get a high level summary of events without introducing the full overhead of fully collecting events.

- **Maps** Enumerators that convert integer values from an internal map into readable text values.

- **Types** Data dictionary of data types used by Extended Events.

The Extended Events engine itself is made up a number of components. The Extended Event engine's key processes are the buffer, which uses a memory buffer to store events. As these buffers fill up they are sent to a target by the session. The dispatcher represents a thread pool of workers. Each Windows process can have one or more modules (Win32 process or Win32 module). Each of these Windows process modules can in turn contain one or more Extended Events packages.

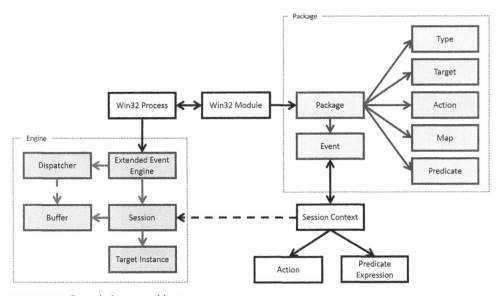

FIGURE 3-16 Extended event architecture

SQL Server supports the capability of creating an Extended Event sessions in SQL Server Management Studio. Let's look at an example of creating an Extended Event session that will track page splits:

1. Connect to your SQL Server instance using SQL Server Management Studio, expand the Management folder, expand the Extended Events folder, right-click on the Sessions folder, and select New Session. Let's not use a wizard for a change.

2. In the General page of the New Session dialog box give the Extended Event session a name, as shown in Figure 3-17. Note, you can configure the following properties:

   - Start the event session at server startup
   - Start the event session immediately after session creations
   - Watch live data on the screen as it is captured
   - Track how events are related to one another

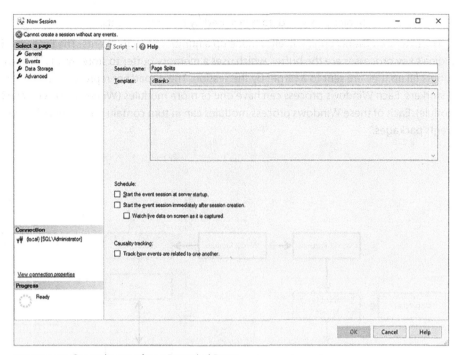

FIGURE 3-17 General page of new Extended Event

3. In the Events page of the New Session type in **split** in the event library search box to help you find the appropriate extended event for page splits.

4. Select the page_split extended event and add it to the selected events.

5. Click on the Configure button to configure the advanced options.

6. In the Global Fields (Actions) section scroll down until you find sql_text to collect the SQL text when an event fires, as shown in Figure 3-18.

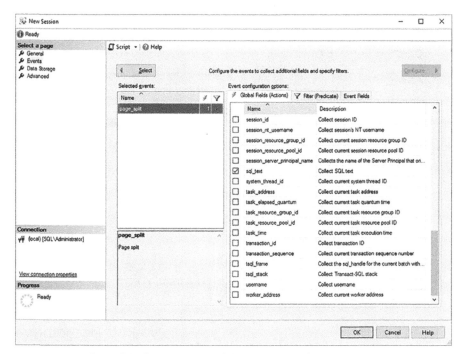

FIGURE 3-18 Actions tab in the Events page of the new Extended Event

7. In the Filter (Predicate) section we create a filter on the database_id so that we only fire
    events for page splits in a specific database, as shown in Figure 3-19. You will have to use
    the DB_ID system function to determine the appropriate database_id.

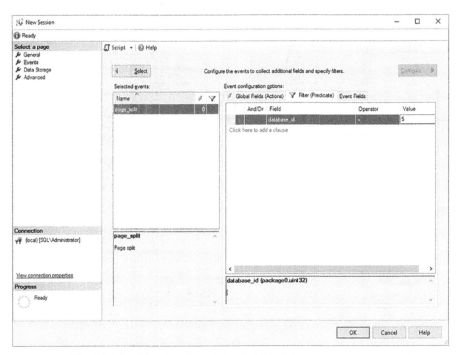

FIGURE 3-19 Filter tab in Events page of new Extended Event

8. In the Data Storage page of the New Session dialog box add the event counter and ring buffer targets, as shown in Figure 3-20. Note you can configure the following properties for the ring_buffer target:

    ■ The number of events to keep. The default of 0 means unlimited.

    ■ The maximum buffer memory size. Again, 0 means unlimited. It is recommended to put a limit on this in most cases.

    ■ Whether you want to keep a specified number of events, per type, when the buffer is full.

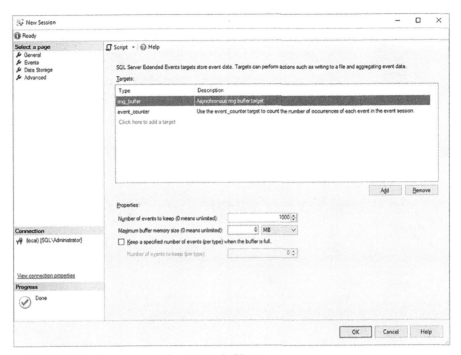

FIGURE 3-20 Data Storage page of new Extended Event

9. In the Advanced page of the New Session dialog, as shown in Figure 3-21, configure the following properties:

   ▪ The Event retention mode options are: Single Event Loss, Multiple Event Loss or No Event Loss.

   ▪ To determine whether the maximum dispatch latency is unlimited or constrained to a number of seconds.

   ▪ A maximum memory size in MB.

   ▪ A maximum event size in MB.

   ▪ Whether you want to partition the memory by NUMA node or CPU.

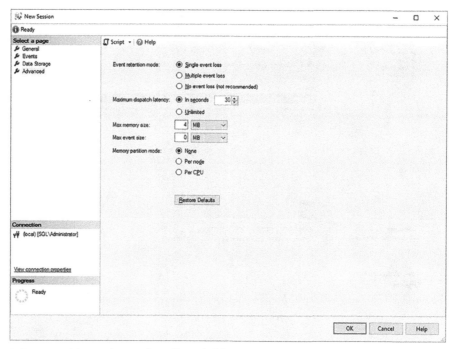

FIGURE 3-21 Advanced page of new Extended Event

10. Click on OK to create the Extended Event session.

11. Right-click on the Extended Event in SQL Server Management Studio and start the session.

Listing 3-9 shows the Transact-SQL script used to create the page split Extended Event in Figure 3-21.

LISTING 3-9 Extended event creation

```
CREATE EVENT SESSION [Page Splits] ON SERVER
ADD EVENT sqlserver.page_split(
    ACTION(sqlserver.sql_text)
    WHERE ([database_id]=(5)))
ADD TARGET package0.event_counter,
ADD TARGET package0.ring_buffer
WITH (MAX_MEMORY=4096 KB, EVENT_RETENTION_MODE=ALLOW_SINGLE_EVENT_LOSS,
MAX_DISPATCH_LATENCY=30 SECONDS, MAX_EVENT_SIZE=0 KB,MEMORY_PARTITION_MODE=NONE,
TRACK_CAUSALITY=OFF,STARTUP_STATE=OFF)
GO
```

SQL Server Management Studio has a basic Extended Event viewer as shown in Figure 3-22. Be careful when using it on a busy system that has a large volume of Extended Events because it can adversely impact performance.

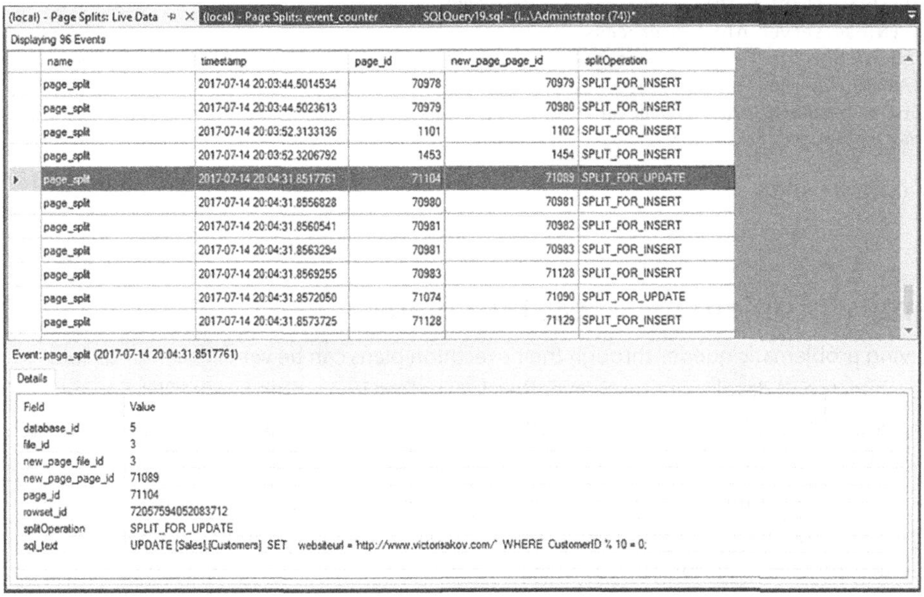

FIGURE 3-22 Extended event architecture

Listing 3-10 shows the Transact-SQL script used to create the page split Extended Event in Figure 3-22.

LISTING 3-10 Extended event creation

```
CREATE EVENT SESSION [Page Splits] ON SERVER
ADD EVENT sqlserver.page_split(
    ACTION(sqlserver.sql_text)
    WHERE ([database_id]=(5)))
ADD TARGET package0.event_counter,
ADD TARGET package0.ring_buffer
WITH (MAX_MEMORY=4096 KB, EVENT_RETENTION_MODE=ALLOW_SINGLE_EVENT_LOSS,
MAX_DISPATCH_LATENCY=30 SECONDS, MAX_EVENT_SIZE=0 KB,MEMORY_PARTITION_MODE=NONE,
TRACK_CAUSALITY=OFF,STARTUP_STATE=OFF)
GO
```

Listing 3-11 shows how you can use Extended Event to capture blocked process reports, as discussed earlier in Skill 3.1.

LISTING 3-11 Extended event creation

```
USE master;
exec sp_configure 'show advanced options',1;
GO
RECONFIGURE;
GO
EXEC sp_configure 'blocked process threshold',5;
GO
RECONFIGURE;
GO
```

```
CREATE EVENT SESSION [BlockedProcesses] ON SERVER
ADD EVENT sqlserver.blocked_process_report(
ACTION(sqlserver.client_app_name,sqlserver.client_hostname,sqlserver.database_name))
ADD TARGET package0.event_file(
    SET filename=N'C:\ExtendedEvents\BlockedProcesses.xel',
    max_rollover_files=(10)
)
WITH (STARTUP_STATE=ON)
GO
```

Identify problematic execution plans

Resolving problematic queries through their execution plans can be very challenging. Solution architects and developers are forever developing "the impossible query." SQL Server has a number of tools and mechanisms that you can use to help identify problematic queries through your execution plans, and we will turn our attention to that in this section.

Don't forget the other technologies that we have covered that can be used to identify problematic execution plans. You can configure Extended Event sessions for queries that take too long, use expensive operators such as hash joins, spill to the [tempdb] system database and so forth. Another easier technique is to enable Query Store and let it capture telemetry, which you can analyze in its rich graphical interface. You can also leverage the Performance Dashboard introduced in SQL Server Management Studio 17.2.

In this section, however, we will focus on the DMVs that the database engine maintains that are related to execution plans and their execution. Figure 3-22 shows the schema of these DMVs:

- **sys.dm_exec_cached_plans** This provides information about cached query plans. The more important information that is returned includes:

  - **cacheobjtype** The type of cached object. Cached objects can be either a CLR compiled function, CLR compiled procedure, compiled plan, compiled plan stub, extended procedure, or parse tree.

  - **objtype** The type of object. Objects can be either a ad-hoc query, default, check constraint, prepared statement, rule, stored procedure, system table, trigger, user table, or view.

  - **size_in_bytes** The size of the query plan.

  - **usecounts** The number of times the cached object has been used.

- **sys.dm_exec_query_plan** This returns the showplan in XML format format for the [plan_handle] passed to this DMF. The plan handle needs to be cached or currently executing.

- **sys.dm_exec_query_stats** It returns aggregate performance statistics for cached query plans, with one row per query statement within the cached plan. This DMV returns a massive set of metrics, even more than what we saw for the Query Store's [sys].[query_store_runtime_stats] system table. There have been a substantial number of new columns added in SQL Server 20126. Visit: *https://docs.microsoft.com/en-us/sql/relational-databases/system-dynamic-management-views/sys-dm-exec-query-stats-transact-sql* for the complete set of metrics.

- **sys.dm_exec_sql_text** This returns the Transact-SQL query based on the [sql_handle] passed to this DMF.
- **sys.dm_plan_attributes** This returns the attributes associated with the plan based on the [sql_handle] passed to this DMF. For a complete list of the attributes visit: *https://docs.microsoft.com/en-us/sql/relational-databases/system-dynamic-management-views/sys-dm-exec-plan-attributes-transact-sql*.

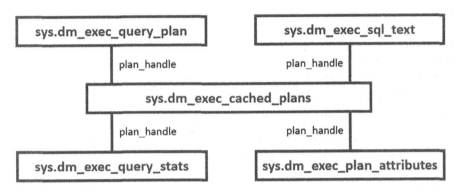

FIGURE 3-23 Extended event architecture

With this schema and the rich set of metrics that are collected you can formulate queries to help you identify problematic queries. Don't forget that these DMVs only store cached query plans. Furthermore, they are not persisted and will not survive a SQL Server instance restart.

Identifying problematic query plans depends on what you want to achieve. You can, for example, query the [sys].[dm_exec_query_stats] and look at queries that have excessive memory grants, large degrees of parallelism, excessive worker time, excessive logical or that use too many threads. Alternatively you can query the [sys].[dm_exec_cached_plans] and look for expensive operations like hash joins, where query execution has spilled to the [tempdb] system database or implicit conversions.

Listing 3-12 shows an example of how you can analyze the cached plans to determine the post expensive queries by their average execution time.

LISTING 3-12 Most expensive cached plans by average execution time

```
SELECT TOP(100) OBJECT_NAME(t.objectid, t.dbid) AS object_name,
    s.total_elapsed_time / s.execution_count AS average_duration,
    s.execution_count,
    s.last_execution_time,
    total_worker_time,
    SUBSTRING (t.[text],
        (s.statement_start_offset/2)+1,
```

```
            (( CASE statement_end_offset
            WHEN -1 THEN DATALENGTH(t.[text])
            ELSE s.statement_end_offset
            END - s.statement_start_offset)/2)+1
        ) AS statement,
        [text] as query,
        query_plan
FROM sys.dm_exec_query_stats AS s
CROSS APPLY sys.dm_exec_sql_text(s.sql_handle) AS t
CROSS APPLY sys.dm_exec_query_plan(s.plan_handle) AS p
ORDER BY average_duration DESC;
GO
```

Listing 3-13 shows an example of how you can find cached plans that have the missing index warning.

LISTING 3-13 Cached plans with missing indexes

```
;WITH XMLNAMESPACES(DEFAULT N'http://schemas.microsoft.com/sqlserver/2004/07/showplan')
SELECT p.usecounts, p.refcounts, p.objtype, p.cacheobjtype,
    db_name(t.dbid) as database_name, t.text as query, q.query_plan
FROM sys.dm_exec_cached_plans AS p
    CROSS APPLY sys.dm_exec_sql_text(p.plan_handle) AS t
    CROSS APPLY sys.dm_exec_query_plan(p.plan_handle) AS q
WHERE q.query_plan.exist(N'/ShowPlanXML/BatchSequence/Batch/Statements/StmtSimple/
QueryPlan/MissingIndexes/MissingIndexGroup') <> 0
ORDER BY p.usecounts DESC
```

Listing 3-14 shows an example of how you can find cached plans that have implicit warnings, which can substantially impact performance.

LISTING 3-14 Cached plans with implicit warnings

```
;WITH XMLNAMESPACES(DEFAULT N'http://schemas.microsoft.com/sqlserver/2004/07/showplan')
SELECT
    operators.value('@ConvertIssue', 'nvarchar(250)') as convert_issue,
    operators.value('@Expression', 'nvarchar(250)') AS convert_expression,
    t.text AS query, p.query_plan
FROM sys.dm_exec_query_stats s
CROSS APPLY sys.dm_exec_query_plan(s.plan_handle) p
CROSS APPLY query_plan.nodes('//Warnings/PlanAffectingConvert') rel(operators)
CROSS APPLY sys.dm_exec_sql_text(s.plan_handle) AS t
ORDER BY p.usecounts DESC
```

> ***NEED MORE REVIEW?*** **LIVE QUERY STATISTICS**
>
> SQL Server Management Studio now allows you to view the live execution plan of an active query as long as you are connected to SQL Server 2014 or a higher instance. To understand this capability of viewing query execution plans in real-time and prepare for the exam be sure to visit: *https://docs.microsoft.com/en-us/sql/relational-databases/performance/live-query-statistics.*

Troubleshoot server health using Extended Events

Every instance of SQL Server has a default Extended Event session created called system_health. This extended event session starts automatically when the data engine runs and should run without any noticeable performance effects. It was designed to collect system telemetry that can help you troubleshoot incidents and performance issues. Although you can stop or even delete it, this is not recommended because it is so useful for troubleshooting the database engine. Most database administrators don't even know it exists. Leverage it!

The system_health Extended Event session uses a ring buffer target to store the data, and collects information that includes the following:

- Any deadlocks that are detected.
- The sql_text and session_id for any sessions that raise an error with a severity level >=20.
- The sql_text and session_id for any sessions that raise a memory-related error (17803, 701, 802, 8645, 8651, 8657 and 8902).
- A record of any non-yielding scheduler (error 17883).
- The callstack, sql_text, and session_id for any sessions that have waited on latches, or other interesting resources for more than 15 seconds.
- The callstack, sql_text, and session_id for any sessions that have waited on locks for more than 30 seconds.
- The callstack, sql_text, and session_id for any sessions that have waited for a long time for preemptive waits.
- The ring_buffer events for the memory broker, scheduler monitor, memory node OOM, security, and connectivity.
- System component results from sp_server_diagnostics.
- Instance health collected by scheduler_monitor_system_health_ring_buffer_recorded.
- Connectivity errors using connectivity_ring_buffer_recorded.
- Security errors using security_error_ring_buffer_recorded.
- CLR allocation failures.
- The callstack and session_id for CLR allocation and virtual allocation failures.

Listing 3-15 shows an example of how you can leverage the system_health extended event session to detect deadlocks.

LISTING 3-15 Detecting deadlock in the server_health session

```
SELECT x.value('@timestamp', 'datetime') as deadlock_datetime,
    x.query('.') AS deadlock_payload
FROM (
    SELECT CAST(target_data AS XML) AS Target_Data
    FROM sys.dm_xe_session_targets AS t
    JOIN sys.dm_xe_sessions AS s ON s.address = t.event_session_address
    WHERE s.name = N'system_health' AND t.target_name = N'ring_buffer'
) AS XML_Data
```

```
CROSS APPLY
Target_Data.nodes('RingBufferTarget/event[@name="xml_deadlock_report"]') AS
XEventData(x);
```

Skill 3.3 Manage indexes

Indexes in databases are primarily used to improve performance, so you need to ensure that they have been optimally implemented. Indexes can potentially degrade performance if you have too many of them in an online-transaction processing (OLTP) environment. The database engine, however, has a number of DMVs that you can leverage to help you identify fragmented, missing and underutilized indexes

Let's first look at how you can detect the degree of fragmentation in an index and what corrective action can be taken. We will then look at how to identify missing and underutilized indexes. Finally, we will examine how to maintain columnstore indexes.

For the exam you should focus on how to detect fragmentation, analyse the degree of fragmentation and how to determine the appropriate corrective action. Another area you should focus on is how to detect and remove fragmentation for columnstore indexes, because SQL Server 2016 has introduced new capability in this space.

> **This section covers how to:**
> - Identify and repair index fragmentation
> - Identify and create missing indexes
> - Identify and drop underutilized indexes
> - Manage existing columnstore indexes

Identify and repair index fragmentation

Index fragmentation can potentially be the root cause for poor query performance in your databases. Consequently, it is important to identify heavily fragmented tables/indexes and repair the fragmentation using the correct techniques. Although for simpler environments, it might be sufficient to simply rebuild all indexes and tables on a nightly basis, for larger and more complex environments a more nuanced solution is typically required. Rebuilding indexes on large tables unnecessarily can take a long time and needlessly reduce your flash storage's life span. Furthermore, rebuilding indexes can cause blocking, which might in turn impact performance. In such cases it makes sense to reorganize the index.

Determining the level of fragmentation for a given table or index will help you determine the correct remediation strategy. Query the following DMV to determine the degree of fragmentation in a table or index:

```
sys.dm_db_index_physical_stats (
    { database_id | NULL | 0 | DEFAULT },
    { object_id | NULL | 0 | DEFAULT },
    { index_id | NULL | 0 | -1 | DEFAULT },
    { partition_number | NULL | 0 | DEFAULT },
    { mode | NULL | DEFAULT }
)
```

When querying the [sys].[dm_db_index_physical_stats] you need to choose the appropriate scanning mode, what will be returned, and how it operates. The DMV supports the following scanning modes:

- **LIMITED**   The LIMITED mode scans the level above the leaf level of an index and is consequently fast. It can, however, only return the logical fragmentation and the page count because it never scanned the leaf-level pages of the index. For a heap the page free space (PFS) and index allocation map (IAM) pages are examined, and the data pages of a heap scanned. This is the default scan mode.

- **SAMPLED**   The SAMPLED mode works differently, depending on the size of the table. A LIMITED mode scan is initially performed. If the leaf-level contains less than 100,000 pages, all leaf-level pages are scanned to calculate additional fragmentation. For the larger tables only 1% of the table is scanned by reading every 100th page.

- **DETAILED**   The DETAILED mode scans all pages and returns all statistics. It effectively calculates the fragmentation through a LIMITED mode scan and also calculates all remaining statistics by having to read every page at every level of the index. It is the most expensive and time consuming scanning mode.

In most cases a LIMITED scan is sufficient. But it is also worth your while to use the more detailed levels to get a more complete picture of the fragmentation state within your tables. When analyzing the output of [sys].[dm_db_index_physical_stats], examine the following columns:

- **avg_fragment_size_in_pages**   The average number of pages in one fragment of an index.

- **avg_fragmentation_in_percent**   The percent of fragmentation, or out-of-order pages/extents. Ideally this value should be as close as possible to 0. This value is key to understanding what remediation action you should perform for a fragmented index. Fragmentation for a heap or index is defined differently:

  - **Extent fragmentation**   The percentage of out-of-order extents in the leaf pages of a heap.

  - **Logical fragmentation**   The percentage of out-of-order pages in the leaf pages of an index.

- **avg_page_space_used_in_percent**   The average percentage of available data storage space used across all pages of the index or table. For optimal performance you should use as close as possible 100% of the page.

- **forwarded_record_count** The number of records in a heap that have forward pointers to another data location. Remember that is is only applicable to heaps, but can have a significant impact on performance.
- **fragment_count** The number of physically consecutive leaf pages, or fragments, in the index.
- **page_count** The total number of index or data pages. This can be useful to see the size of the index or table before and after any reindexing operations. You can also use it to determine whether an index or tables is too small to worry about reindexing.

Once you have identified fragmentation of your table or index you have the following possible corrective actions:

- **Drop and recreate the index** Use the DROP INDEX and CREATE INDEX statements to drop and create the index. This technique is typically not used due to the index being taken offline and resources used. If the index creation is interrupted, the index creation will fail. You can also disable an index instead of dropping it, because that will not drop the metadata associated with the index.
- **Index rebuild** The ALTER INDEX REBUILD rebuilds the index as either an online or offline operation. Online index rebuilds are only available in SQL Server Enterprise Edition. Rebuilding a clustered index does not rebuild the dependent nonclustered indexes unless you specify the ALL option. You should not use the DBCC INDEXREBUILD statement because it is deprecated.
- **Index reorganize** The ALTER INDEX REORGANIZE statement physically reorders the leaf-level pages of the index to match the logical, left to right, order. Reorganizing an index is always performed as an online operation. The operation does not hold locks long term and, therefore, does not block queries or updates that might be running. It can also be safely killed off. Reorganizing indexes is available in all SQL Server editions. You should not use the DBCC INDEXDEFRAG statement because it is deprecated.
- **Table rebuild** The ALTER TABLE REBUILD statement can be used to rebuild a heap. You no longer have to create and drop a clustered index to rebuild a heap.

> ***NEED MORE REVIEW?*** **ALTER INDEX STATEMENT**
>
> The ALTER INDEX statement supports a myriad of options. To help prepare for the exam visit: *https://docs.microsoft.com/en-us/sql/t-sql/statements/alter-index-transact-sql.* Watch out for options that might only apply to SQL Server 2017.

Rebuilding or reorganizing small indexes often does not reduce fragmentation, especially as the pages of small indexes can be stored on mixed extents. Otherwise, the correct remediation action depends on the type and degree of fragmentation. Although this is completely arbitrary, Table 3-2 shows what the industry seems to use as a guideline of what to do in the case of logical fragmentation:

TABLE 3-2 Index fragmentation thresholds

avg_fragmentation_in_percent	Remediation action
0	No action required
BETWEEN 5% AND 30%	ALTER INDEX REORGANIZE
> 30%	ALTER INDEX REBUILD

EXAM TIP

In the exam, make sure you understand the underlying table and indexing schema when dealing with fragmentation. An exam question might, for example, show the output of the [sys].[dm_db_index_physical_stats] DMV where the [forwarded_record_count] might be high. In this case you would need to rebuild the heap using the ALTER TABLE REBUILD statement. Alternatively, the [avg_page_space_used_in_percent] might be low for a table that has no logical fragmentation. It too would require an index rebuild.

Identify and create missing indexes

Indexes have the biggest impact on performance. A database with poor or no indexing will perform poorly even on a SQL Server instance with lots of processor and memory resources that uses flash storage. Fortunately SQL Server has the capability to help you identify potential missing indexes in your databases. Be careful with blindly following its recommendations, however, because sometimes the indexes that it recommends can be too wide.

Earlier, in Skill 3.2 we saw how you can query the cached query plans to determine potential missing indexes. The problem with that technique is that it only queries the cached query plans. And queries that are not cached will not have their potential missing indexes identified.

The database engine maintains the following DMVs to help you determine what useful indexes potentially exist. These DMVs are updated whenever a query is optimized by the query optimizer and it determines that a useful index did not exist. These DMVs do not make recommendations for spatial indexes.

- **sys.dm_db_missing_index_columns** This dynamic management function (DMF) returns information table columns that are missing an index. The [column_usage] column returns how the column is used:
  - **EQUALITY** This column is part of an equality predicate.
  - **INEQUALITY** This column is part of an inequality predicate.
  - **INCLUDE** This column is not part of a predicate. It is used for another reason such as to cover the query.
- **sys.dm_db_missing_index_details** This DMV returns detailed information about potential missing indexes. For each [index_handle] for a given [object_id] in a [database_id] the following information is returned:

- **equality_columns** A comma-separated list of columns that are part of equality predicates.

- **included_columns** A comma-separated list of columns that cover the query.

- **inequality_columns** A comma-separated list of columns that are part of inequality predicates.

- **sys.dm_db_missing_index_group_stats** This DMV returns summary information about groups of missing indexes. Use the following columns to help you determine a potential missing index's usefulness:

  - **avg_total_user_cost** Returns the average query cost of the user queries that can be reduced by the index in the group. There is an equivalent [avg_total_system_cost] column for system queries.

  - **avg_user_impact** Returns the average drop in query cost, expressed as a percentage, that user queries can potentially experience if this missing index group is implemented. There is an equivalent [avg_system_impact] column for system queries.

  - **last_user_scan** Date/time of last scan by a user query that the recommended index in the group could have been used. There is an equivalent [last_system_scan] column for system queries.

  - **last_user_seek** Date/time of last seek by a user query that the recommended index in the group could have been used. There is an equivalent [last_system_seek] column for system queries.

  - **unique_compiles** Number of compilations and recompilations from different queries that would benefit from this missing index group.

  - **user_scans** Number of scans caused by user queries that the recommended index in the group could have been used. There is an equivalent [system_scans] column for system queries.

  - **user_seeks** Number of seeks caused by user queries that the recommended index in the group could have been used. There is an equivalent [system_seeks] column for system queries.

- **sys.dm_db_missing_index_groups** This DMV's result set shows what missing indexes are contained in a specific missing index group.

Listing 3-16 shows an example of a query that identifies missing indexes. Remember not to implement the recommendations blindly, since they can be wrong.

LISTING 3-16 Identifying missing indexes

```
SELECT g.*, statement AS table_name, column_id, column_name, column_usage
FROM sys.dm_db_missing_index_details AS d
CROSS APPLY sys.dm_db_missing_index_columns (d.index_handle)
INNER JOIN sys.dm_db_missing_index_groups AS g ON g.index_handle = d.index_handle
ORDER BY g.index_group_handle, g.index_handle, column_id;
GO
```

Once you have identified a missing index you can use the CREATE INDEX statement to create it.

> **NEED MORE REVIEW?**   **CREATING INDEXES**
>
> There is a myriad of options available when creating indexes. The exam will expect you to know when to create clustered indexes versus nonclustered indexes, filtered indexes, partitioned indexes, included columns, and various indexing options such as FILLFACTOR and PAD_INDEX. For more information in the CREATE INDEX statement visit: *https://docs. microsoft.com/en-us/sql/t-sql/statements/create-index-transact-sql*.

Identify and drop underutilized indexes

It's not uncommon for solution architects and developers to implement indexes that are not used by the database engine. Alternatively, the data within you databases, or user query patterns, have changed such that existing indexes are no longer optimal and will not be used. Remember that you don't want to create too many indexes for an OLTP environment because too many indexes might potentially slow down DML operations.

On top of the DMVs we have examined so far in Skill 3.3 the database engine also maintains a set of DMVs that keep track of the index usage and operational statistics. The index usage DMV can be used to determine whether there are any indexes that do not have any lookup, scan, or seek operations. Such indexes become potential candidates to be dropped or disabled. Remember that DMVs are not persisted between SQL Server restarts, so you need to give the database engine enough time to collect a meaningful set of index usage telemetry.

Use the following DMV and catalog view to help you determine what indexes are underutilized:

- **sys.dm_db_index_usage_stats**   This DMV returns summary information about how many times queries have used an index. Use the following columns to help you decide whether there are any potential unused indexes:
  - **last_user_lookup**   Date/time of last bookmark lookup performed by a user query. There is an equivalent [last_system_lookup] column for system queries.
  - **last_user_scan**   Date/time of last scan performed by a user query. There is an equivalent [last_system_scan] column for system queries.
  - **last_user_seek**   Date/time of last seek performed by a user query. There is an equivalent [last_system_seek] column for system queries.
  - **last_user_update**   Date/time of last modification by a user query. There is an equivalent [last_system_update] column for system queries.
  - **user_lookups**   Number of bookmark lookups performed by user queries. There is an equivalent [system_lookups] column for system queries.
  - **user_scans**   Number of index scans performed by user queries. There is an equivalent [system_scans] column for system queries.

- **user_seeks** Number of index seeks perfomed by user queries. There is an equivalent [system_seeks] column for system queries.

- **user_updates** Number of modifications performed by user queries. Each separate INSERT, DELETE and UPDATE operation constitutes a modification operation. There is an equivalent [system_updates] column for system queries.

- **sys.indexes** This per database system catalog view returns the name, type and various properties of the indexes within a database. Use the [object_id] and [index_id] columns to join [sys].[indexes] to [sys].[dm_db_index_usage_stats].

Listing 3-17 shows an example of a query that identifies underutilized indexes. Note how it includes the last access time from the various operations. Examine the [user_updates] to see if the index has been ever updated.

LISTING 3-17 Identifying underutilized indexes

```
SELECT DB_NAME(s.database_id) AS 'datase_name', OBJECT_NAME(s.object_id) AS 'table_
name',
    i.name AS 'index_name',
    s.user_seeks, s.user_scans, s.user_lookups, s.user_updates,
    s.last_user_seek, s.last_user_scan, s.last_user_lookup, s.last_user_update
FROM sys.dm_db_index_usage_stats AS s
JOIN sys.indexes AS i ON s.index_id = i.index_id
AND s.object_id = i.object_id
WHERE s.database_id = DB_ID()
AND s.user_seeks = 0 AND s.user_scans = 0 AND s.user_lookups = 0;
GO
```

Listing 3-18 shows a more nuanced example that identifies nonclustered indexes that have more modifications than seeks, scans, and lookups combined.

LISTING 3-18 Identifying underutilized indexes

```
SELECT DB_NAME(s.database_id) AS 'datase_name', OBJECT_NAME(s.object_id) AS 'table_
name',
    i.name AS 'index_name',
    s.user_seeks, s.user_scans, s.user_lookups, s.user_updates,
    s.last_user_seek, s.last_user_scan, s.last_user_lookup, s.last_user_update
FROM sys.dm_db_index_usage_stats AS s
JOIN sys.indexes AS i ON s.index_id = i.index_id
AND s.object_id = i.object_id
WHERE s.database_id = DB_ID()
AND s.user_updates > (s.user_seeks + s.user_scans + s.user_lookups)
AND s.index_id > 1;
```

> ***NEED MORE REVIEW?*** **SYS.DM_DB_INDEX_OPERATIONAL_STATS**
>
> The [sys].[dm_db_index_operational_stats] DMV returns I/O, latching, locking, compression, and access method metrics on the index. It's worth reviewing it for the exam: *https://docs. microsoft.com/en-us/sql/relational-databases/system-dynamic-management-views/sys-dm-db-index-operational-stats-transact-sql.*

Use the DROP INDEX statement to drop any indexes that you have concluded are definitely not required. If you suspect that an index might be required and don't want to drop it because the definition will be lost, you can use the ALTER INDEX DISABLE statement to disable the index. Disabling an index removes the underlying B-tree, but retains the metadata for the index. If users start to complain about poor performance after you disable an index, you can simply rebuild the index to bring it back to life.

Don't forget to take into account that certain indexes might not be used that often, but they might be used by critical business-related processes that run infrequently such as end of financial year reports, end-of-day batch processes, and so forth. You should not blindly drop indexes that have a low usage count without consulting the business first.

Manage existing columnstore indexes

Both clustered and nonclustered columnstore indexes can become fragmented like any other indexes in the database engine. Given how the primary use case of columnstore indexes is for large scans by analytic queries, you do not want them to become too fragmented. With SQL Server 2016 Microsoft has substantially improved how you manage fragmentation within columnstore indexes.

A columnstore index is considered fragmented when it has multiple delta rowgroups, deleted rows, or rowgroups that have not been optimally compressed. Whether rowgroups have been optimally compressed will depend on your data modification pattern.

Deleted rows in particular can slow down analytic queries because the database engine must filter out the deleted rows by internally executing an anti-semijoin against the delete-bit-map before the query results can be returned. To determine this level of fragmentation in the columnstore indexes, query the [sys].[dm_db_column_store_row_group_physical_stats] DMV as shown in Listing 3-19. Microsoft recommends you take corrective action when the fragmentation is greater than 20%. The query will also show you the what rowgroups are open via the [state_desc] column.

LISTING 3-19 Identifying fragmentation in columnstore indexes

```
SELECT i.object_id,
    OBJECT_NAME(i.object_id) AS table_name,
    i.name AS index_name,
    i.index_id,
    i.type_desc,
    100*(ISNULL(deleted_rows,0))/total_rows AS 'Fragmentation',
    s.*
FROM sys.indexes AS i
JOIN sys.dm_db_column_store_row_group_physical_stats AS s
ON i.object_id = s.object_id AND i.index_id = s.index_id
ORDER BY fragmentation DESC;
```

To remove the fragmentation, use the ALTER INDEX REORGANIZE statement to force all of the rowgroups into the columnstore. This operation will combine the rowgroups into fewer rowgroups and remove the rows that have been deleted from the columnstore. The columnstore reorganize statement supports the LOB_COMPACTION option similar to rowstore indexes.

When you rebuild a columnstore index the operation acquires an exclusive lock during the rebuild process, and consequently the data will be unavailable for the duration of the rebuild. Starting with SQL Server 2016, rebuilding the columnstore index is typically not required because the new reorganize operation performs the essentials of a rebuild operation in the background, but as an online operation.

When reorganizing a columnstore index SQL Server 2016 now supports the COMPRESS_ALL_ROW_GROUPS option. This option provides a way to force all rowgroups into the columnstore, regardless of their size and state (CLOSED or OPEN). This is why it is not necessary to rebuild the columnstore index to empty the delta rowgroups. This new feature, together with the other remove and merge defragmentation features, make the reorganization operation superior to the rebuild operation.

Listing 3-20 shows an example of a columnstore index being reorganized. All of the rowgroups will be reorganized.

LISTING 3-20 Reorganizing columnstore index

```
USE AdventureworksDW
GO
ALTER INDEX IndFactResellerSalesXL_CCI ON dbo.FactResellerSalesXL_CCI
REORGANIZE WITH (LOB_COMPACTION = ON, COMPRESS_ALL_ROW_GROUPS = ON);
```

If you want to change the data compression used by your columnstore index from COLUMNSTORE to COLUMNSTORE_ARCHIVE, or vice versa, you will need to use the ALTER INDEX REBUILD or ALTER TABLE REBUILD statement. Again, these are offline operations. Listing 3-21 shows an example of a the columnstore indexes being rebuilt with different data compression types.

LISTING 3-21 Rebuilding columnstore index

```
USE AdventureworksDW
GO
ALTER INDEX IndFactResellerSalesXL_CCI ON dbo.FactResellerSalesXL_CCI
REBUILD WITH (DATA_COMPRESSION = COLUMNSTORE_ARCHIVE);
/*
-- Let's assume the [IndFactResellerSalesXL_CCI] table was partitioned
-- Rebuild only 1 partition
ALTER TABLE IndFactResellerSalesXL_CCI
REBUILD PARTITION = 1 WITH (DATA_COMPRESSION =  COLUMNSTORE_ARCHIVE);
GO
-- Rebuild all partitions but with different data compression
ALTER TABLE [ColumnstoreTable]
REBUILD PARTITION = ALL WITH (
    DATA_COMPRESSION = COLUMNSTORE ON PARTITIONS (5,6,7,8,9,10,11,12),
    DATA_COMPRESSION = COLUMNSTORE_ARCHIVE ON PARTITIONS (1,2,3,4)
);
*/
```

Skill 3.4 Manage statistics

The database engine does a reasonable job of automatically managing statistics, especially starting with SQL Server 2016. You might need to fine tune statistics maintenance for larger or more volatile scenarios. This section focuses primarily on how to update statistics because it can have such an impact on cardinality estimation and therefore query performance.

We will initially look at how to query the statistics' metadata to help you determine whether the statistics are out-of-date statistics or contributing towards poor query performance. We will then look at the various options you have of automatic statistics maintenance at the database level. Finally, we will look at some techniques, and new capabilities in SQL Server 2016, to manage statistics for very large tables.

The exam might ask you what commands to run to identify whether statistics need to be updated. It might also ask you what statistics update strategy to use for the given scenario. Focus in particular on the different techniques for larger tables.

> **This section covers how to:**
> - Identify and correct outdated statistics
> - Implement Auto Update Statistics
> - Implement statistics for large tables

Identify and correct outdated statistics

Outdated statistics can substantially degrade query and potentially server performance. Consequently, it is important to identify and correct outdated statistics. Historically there have been many ways of determining whether statistics are outdated, but you should favor querying the new DMVs over querying system tables and executing DBCC commands.

Query the [sys].[dm_db_stats_properties] DMF to determine when statistics were last updated. You will have to use the [sys].[dm_db_incremental_stats_properties] DMF for partitioned tables. Both of these DMFs will return the date and time when the statistics were last updated, the corresponding row count, rows sampled, number of steps in the histogram used by statistics, and the modification counter for the leading statistics column.

Be careful of relying on the date and time when the statistics object was last updated. You can compare the number of rows in the in the statistics objects to the number of rows in the table or index to see if there is a large discrepancy.

List 3-22 shows an example of a query that returns the statistics for all user tables within a database, there properties, when they have been last updated, and how many days have passed since they were last updated.

LISTING 3-22 Querying statistics metadata for all user tables

```
SELECT s.name AS statistic_name, s.auto_created, s.user_created,
    s.no_recompute, s.is_incremental, s.is_temporary, s.has_filter,
    p.last_updated, DATEDIFF(day,p.last_updated, SYSDATETIME()) AS days_past,
    h.name AS schema_name, o.name AS table_name, c.name AS column_name,
    p.rows, p.rows_sampled, p.steps, p.modification_counter
FROM sys.stats AS s
JOIN sys.stats_columns i
ON s.stats_id = i.stats_id AND s.object_id = i.object_id
JOIN sys.columns c
ON c.object_id = i.object_id AND c.column_id = i.column_id
JOIN sys.objects o
ON s.object_id = o.object_id
JOIN sys.schemas h
ON o.schema_id = h.schema_id
OUTER APPLY sys.dm_db_stats_properties (s.object_id,s.stats_id) AS p
WHERE OBJECTPROPERTY(o.object_id, N'IsMSShipped') = 0
ORDER BY days_past DESC;
```

If you are interested in a specific set of statistics you can also use the DBCC SHOW_STA-TISTICS command. This can be done via a query or through SQL Server Management Studio. Figure 3-24 shows the output of the command in SQL Server Management Studio. You can see an overlap in its output with the [sys].[dm_db_incremental_stats_properties] DMF, plus the additional information about the histogram used.

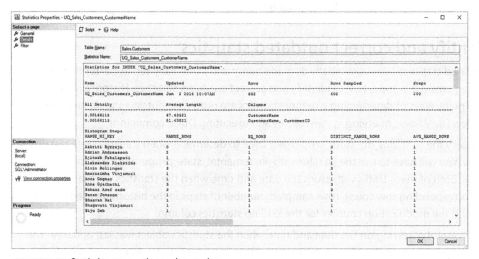

FIGURE 3-24 Statistics properties and metadata

NEED MORE REVIEW? **DBCC SHOW_STATISTICS**

The DBCC SHOW_STATISTICS command has a number of execution options that return different details information about the statistics on a table's index or column. To learn more about the command visit: *https://docs.microsoft.com/en-us/sql/t-sql/database-console-commands/dbcc-show-statistics-transact-sql*.

Once you have confirmed that your statistics are out of date, you have a number of options as to how you can correct the problem:

- **Update statistics** Execute the UPDATE STATISTICS statement on the table or indexed view as appropriate. The statement has the following options:
  - **ALL | COLUMNS | INDEX** Update all existing statistics, only statistics created on one or more columns, or only statistics created for indexes.
  - **FULLSCAN** Compute statistics by scanning all rows in the table or indexed view. The sampling of statistics using FULLSCAN can run in parallel since SQL Server 2005.
  - **INCREMENTAL** Introduced in SQL Server 2014, statistics are recreated as per partition statistics.
  - **NORECOMPUTE** Disable the automatic statistics update option for the specified statistics.
  - **RESAMPLE** Update statistics based on the most recent sample rate. The RESAMPLE option supports the ON PARTITIONS, which forces the leaf-level statistics in the partitions specified to be recomputed and merged into the global statistics. This option was introduced in SQL Server 2014.
  - **SAMPLE number { PERCENT | ROWS }** Specifies the approximate percentage or number of rows in the table or indexed view to be sampled when statistics are updated. This option is useful for special use cases where the default sampling is not optimal. Typically the query optimizer uses sampling and determines a statistically significant sample size to enable it to create high-quality query plans. Starting with SQL Server 2016 this sampling of statistics is done in parallel.
- **Rebuild index** When you rebuild an index, the database engine also updates the statistics for that index.
- **Update Statistics Task** Create a maintenance task that uses the Update Statistics Task, as shown in Figure 3-25.

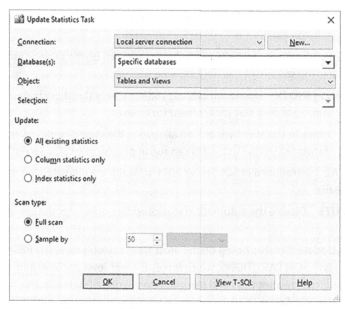

FIGURE 3-25 Update Statistics Tasks

- **sp_updatestats** The [sp_updatestats] stored against all user-defined and internal tables in the current database. The stored procedure supports the RESAMPLE option. It only updates statistics that require updating, based on the [modification_counter] column in the [sys].[dm_db_stats_properties] system catalog view.

- **Rebuild Index Task** Create a maintenance task that uses the Rebuild Index Task, as shown in Figure 3-26.

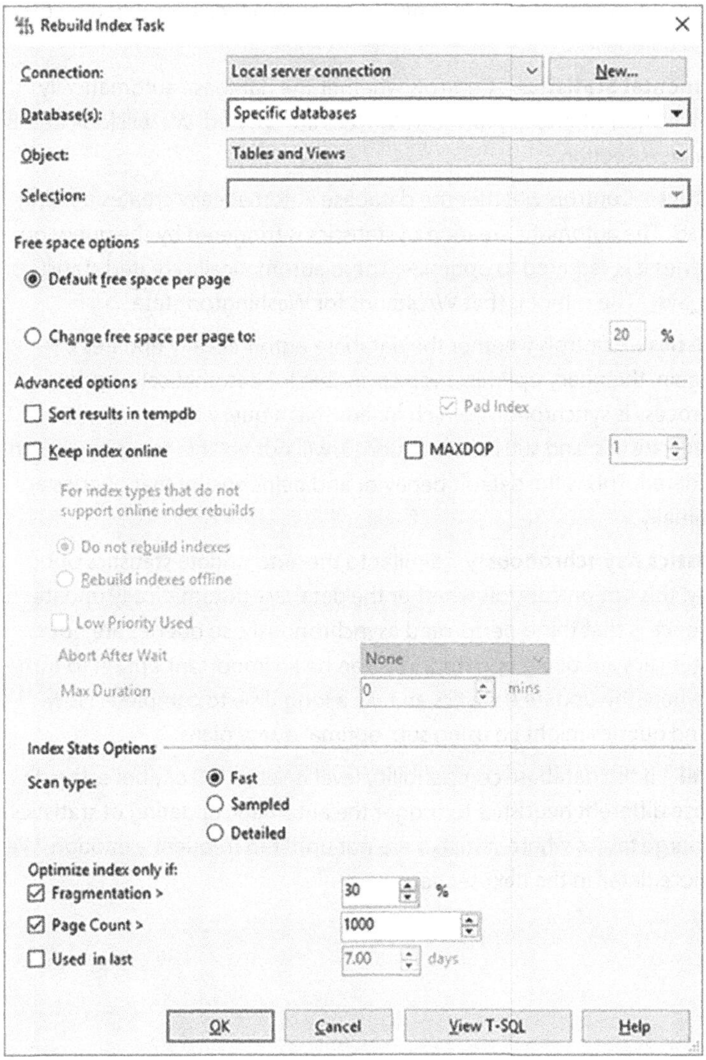

FIGURE 3-26 Rebuild Index Task

Implement Auto Update Statistics

The accuracy of statistics is critical to the correct cardinality estimation and consequently query performance. SQL Server supports a number of options at the database level to implement automatic statistics creation and updating. SQL Server 2016 introduced a change to the algorithm used to determine when automatic updating of statistics kicks in and we will look at that in the next section.

Figure 3-27 shows the options that control how statistics are automatically updated by the database engine for a given database:

- **Auto Create Incremental Statistics** Controls whether the database automatically uses the incremental option when per partition statistics are created. We will look at this in more detail in the next section.

- **Auto Create Statistics** Controls whether the database automatically creates missing optimization statistics. The automatic creation of statistics is triggered by the query optimizer through queries it is required to optimize. These automatically created statistics use a prefix of _WA_Sys_. The rumor is that WA stands for Washington state.

- **Auto Update Statistics** Controls whether the database automatically updates out-of-date statistics. Again, the query optimizer is responsible for automatically updating statistics. This process is synchronous, which means that a query that triggers an automatic update of statistics, and subsequent queries, will not be able to continue until the statistics are updated. This is the default behavior and helps ensure that queries are always running optimally.

- **Auto Update Statistics Asynchronously** Similar to the auto update statistics option discussed previously, this option controls whether the database automatically updates statistics. The difference is that this is performed asynchronously, so queries are not blocked while the statistics are being updated. This can be an important option to turn on for large tables where the update statistics an take a long time to complete. However, the non-blocked queries might be using sub-optimal query plans.

- **Compatibility Level** If the database compatibility level is set to 130 or above, the database engine will use different heuristics to trigger the automatic updating of statistics. This is designed for large tables where statistics are not updated frequently enough. We will look at this in more detail in the next section.

FIGURE 3-27 Database auto update statistics options

For completeness sake don't forget that you can automatically update statistics through scheduled SQL Server Agent jobs or maintenance plans. This is not uncommon in nightly database maintenance plans. Don't forget that you do not have to update statistics on indexes that you have just rebuilt. Also don't forget to update statistics on columns that do not have indexes. These two little tips can drastically reduce the time of your maintenance window and ensure optimal performance.

Implement statistics for large tables

Hardware is getting faster, databases are getting larger, and the database engine is getting older, just like database administrators. These certainties manifest themselves in a series of problems. One of the problems is that statistics for large tables are not updated frequently enough and this results in poor query performance due to poor cardinality estimation by the query optimizer. Another problem is that is takes longer to update statistics, simply due to the size of the tables. Let's examine how you can potentially solve or at least mitigate these problems.

The first problem stems from the fact that the database engine updates statistics automatically based on an algorithm that is represented in Table 3-3. From this table you can see that you only need to modify 20,500 records in a table that contains 100,000 records, 200,500 for 1,000,000 records and 200,000,500 records for 1,000,000,000 records. The problem is that as tables get very large the automatic updating of statistics is not being triggered frequently enough and consequently query performance suffers.

TABLE 3-3 Automatic Statistics Update Thresholds for SQL Server 7.0 to SQL Serer 2014

Table Type	Empty Condition	Threshold When Empty	Threshold When Not Empty
Permanent	< 500 rows	Number of changes >= 500	Number of changes >= 500 + (20% of cardinality)
Temporary	< 6 rows	Number of changes >= 500	Number of changes >= 500 + (20% of cardinality)
Table variables	Change in cardinality does not affect AutoStats generation		

Another closely related problem stems from the fact that queries will be blocked until the statistics are synchronously updated. This can result in very poor query performance as it might take a substantial period of time to update statistics for very large tables. You can address this by enabling asynchronously updating of statistics through the AUTO_UPDATE_STATISTICS_ASYNC database option as discussed in the earlier section.

To solve the problem of statistics not being automatically updated frequently enough for large tables, Microsoft has made the automatic updating of statistics more aggressive for larger tables through a sublinear threshold. In other words, as the table gets larger, less rows need to be modified for statistics to be updated. For a table with 1,000,000 only 3.2% or 32,000 records need to be modified. By 10,000,000 only 1.0% or 100,000 records need to be modified. The configuration option for this is through the database compatibility level as discussed in the earlier section. A database compatibility level of 130 or greater will cause this behavior Of course, you can schedule statistics updates more frequently through the SQL Server Agent, especially for tables that are more important to users.

The other problem we discussed is the length of time that it might take to update the statistics for larger tables. You can address this problem by reducing the sample size, as discussed earlier, but as your table grows larger your returns will diminish.

To help address this problem Microsoft introduced incremental statistics in SQL Server 2014. It only applies to partitioned tables, which are used for very large table scenarios. When INCREMENTAL_STATS is enabled, statistics are generated on a partition level. The major benefit of this is that you can now update statistics at the partition level. Imagine you have a table that is partitioned by month that goes back 10 years in time. If you need to update statistics to optimize performance you do not have to do it across the entie 10 years. Only the data in the current month, or perhaps last 3 months has changed. In this case you can just update the statistics for the 1 or 3 partitions.

Automatic statistics will also trigger earlier as the number of records that need to be modified are now based on the partition size and not the table size.

Unfortunately incremental statistics do not help you get around the 200 step limit that the database engine has for keeping statistics. Although each partition has its own statistics with 200 steps, they are all collectively merged into a single 200 step statitics that is used by the query optimizer.

Don't forget that you can also take advantage of filtered statistics, introduced in SQL Server 2008 to dramatically improve cardinality estimatation. You could for example create statistics just on orders placed this year, or for active orders through a predicate in the statistics creation DDL.

Skill 3.5 Monitor SQL Server instances

This final section is a catchall of features in SQL Server that a database administrator can leverage to monitor their SQL Server instances. A lot of the features that we will be discussing have been in SQL Server for over a decade and are commonly used. Policy Based Management will be the exception, since it might be a new topic for you.

Let's examine how you can configure the SQL: Server Agent to generate alerts and notify you via email when an incident occurs within the database engine. We will then look at Policy Based Management, and finish with a brief discussion on troubleshooting performance in the database engine.

This section covers how to:

- Configure database mail
- Create and manage operators
- Create and manage SQL Agent alerts
- Define custom alert actions
- Define failure actions
- Configure Policy-Based Management
- Identify available space on data volumes
- Identify the cause of performance degradation

Configure database mail

Let's begin with the database mail feature in SQL Server. This is perhaps one of the best administrative capabilities in the database engine. With database mail you can configure the SQL Server Agent to email you whenever a job completes, succeeds, fails, or when an alert fires.

Once configured you can also use the [sp_send_dbmail] system stored procedure to configure the database engine to send you an email with a message, a query result set, or an attachment.

The database mail feature is made up of the following components:

- **Database mail profile**   A database mail profile is a collection of database mail accounts. You send emails in the database engine through database mail profiles. There are two types of profiles:
  - **Private**   Private profiles are defined for security principals in the [msdb] system database and allow only specified database users, roles, and members of the [sysadmin] fixed server role to send emails.
  - **Public**   Public profiles allow all members of the [DatabaseMailUserRole] database role in the [msdb] system database to send emails.
- **Database mail account**   It is a database mail account that stores information required by the database engine to use an SMTP gateway to send email. Each database mail account contains information for one email server.
  - **Anonymous**   Anonymous authentication doesn't try to log into the SMTP gateway.
  - **Basic**   Basic authentication uses a username and password to authenticate against the SMTP gateway.
  - **Windows**   Windows authentication uses the credentials of the database engine to authenticate against the SMTP gateway.

To leverage this poweful capability you need to set up a database mail first. Use the following steps to configure database mail:

1. Connect to your SQL Server instance using SQL Server Management Studio, expand the Management folder, and right-click on Database Mail to start the wizard.
2. Click on Next in the Database Mail Configuration Wizard's welcome screen.
3. Click on Next to set up the initial database mail profile and account, as shown in Figure 3-28.

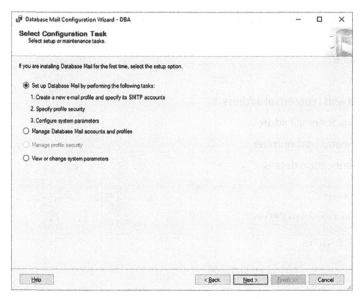

FIGURE 3-28 Database Mail Configuration Wizard: Select Configuration Task

4. Click Yes when prompted to enable the Database Mail features. This enables the Database Mail XPs configuration option.

5. Provide a profile name and description, as shown in Figure 3-29 in the New Profile step and click on Add to add a new SMTP account. Note you can add multiple SMTP accounts and then prioritize them.

FIGURE 3-29 Database Mail Configuration Wizard: New Profile

6. Configure the following details for the database mail account, as shown in Figure 3-30 and click on OK:

   - Account name
   - Description
   - Email adder and reply email address
   - Display name for email address
   - SMTP server and port number
   - SMTP authentication details

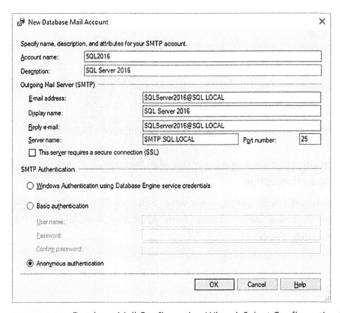

FIGURE 3-30 Database Mail Configuration Wizard: Select Configuration Task

7. Add additional database mail accounts if required and click on Next.
8. Configure the profile security as required and click on Next, as shown in Figure 3-31.

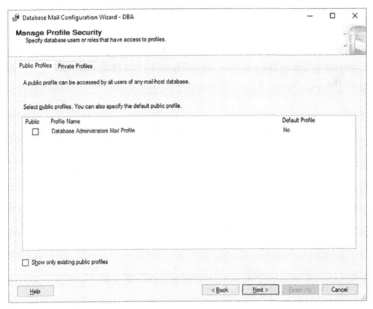

FIGURE 3-31 Database Mail Configuration Wizard: Manage Profile Security

9. Configure the system parameters as shown in Figure 3-32. In this example we have changed the value of the account to retry attempts from 1 to 3. Note, you can also change the maximum file size in bytes for attachments. An important system parameter to remember for troubleshooting is the logging level. Be careful of using verbose because it can generate a lot of logging in the [msdb] system database.

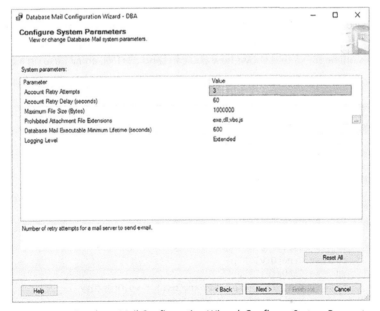

FIGURE 3-32 Database Mail Configuration Wizard: Configure System Parameters

10. Click on Next and then Finish to configure database mail.

Once you have configured database mail you need to configure SQL Server Agent to use the profile you have created. This will light up the ability to use operators, alerts, and configure SQL Server Agent job notification. We will look at this later in this chapter. Figure 3-33 shows you how to configure the SQL Server Agent Properties so that it can use database mail.

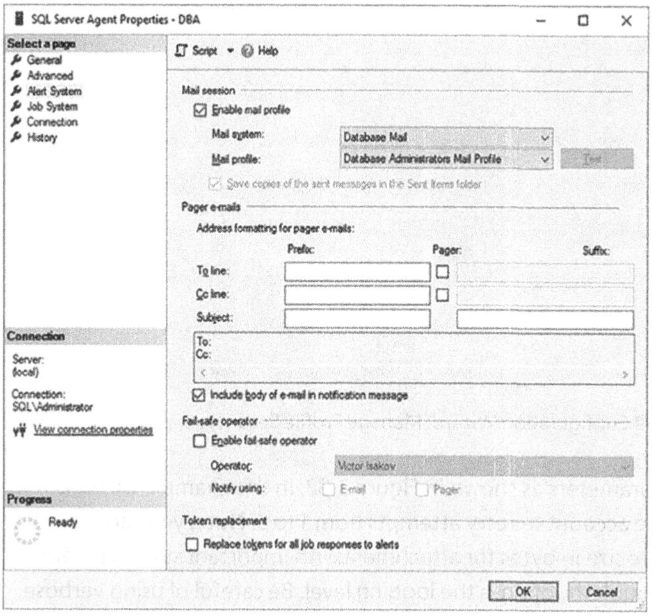

FIGURE 3-33 Configuring SQL Server Agent to use database mail

You can now use database mail on both the database engine using the [sp_send_dbmail] system stored procedure and the SQL Server Agent. Listing 3-23 shows a great example from SQL Server's books online (BOL) that shows how you can send a HTML email base on a query result set.

LISTING 3-23 sp_send_dbmail

```
DECLARE @tableHTML  NVARCHAR(MAX);
SET @tableHTML =
    N'<H1>Work Order Report</H1>' +
    N'<table border="1">' +
    N'<tr><th>Work Order ID</th><th>Product ID</th>' +
    N'<th>Name</th><th>Order Qty</th><th>Due Date</th>' +
    N'<th>Expected Revenue</th></tr>' +
    CAST ( ( SELECT td = wo.WorkOrderID,       '',
                    td = p.ProductID, '',
                    td = p.Name, '',
                    td = wo.OrderQty, '',
                    td = wo.DueDate, '',
                    td = (p.ListPrice - p.StandardCost) * wo.OrderQty
              FROM AdventureWorks.Production.WorkOrder as wo
```

```
            JOIN AdventureWorks.Production.Product AS p
            ON wo.ProductID = p.ProductID
            WHERE DueDate > '2004-04-30'
              AND DATEDIFF(dd, '2004-04-30', DueDate) < 2
            ORDER BY DueDate ASC,
                    (p.ListPrice - p.StandardCost) * wo.OrderQty DESC
            FOR XML PATH('tr'), TYPE
    ) AS NVARCHAR(MAX) ) +
    N'</table>' ;



EXEC msdb.dbo.sp_send_dbmail @recipients='victor.isakov@sql.local',
    @subject = 'Work Order List',
    @body = @tableHTML,
    @body_format = 'HTML' ;
ORDER BY days_past DESC;
```

> **NEED MORE REVIEW?** **[SP_SEND_DBMAIL]**
>
> The [sp_send_dbmail] system stored procedure is very powerful and has a large number of parameters. To learn more about its capabilities visit: *https://docs.microsoft.com/en-us/sql/relational-databases/system-stored-procedures/sp-send-dbmail-transact-sql.*

Database mail has extensive logging capability. It uses the [msdb] system database as its repository so you need to check the disk consumption and potentially clear out the log messages. Figure 3-34 shows an example of the database mail log.

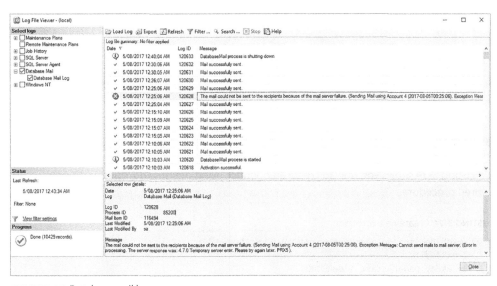

FIGURE 3-34 Database mail log

Create and manage operators

Once you have configured database mail you can add operators, which can can be notified whenever an alert fire or a job finishes. SQL Server Agent only supports operators via email addresses. Use SQL Server Management Studio or the [sp_add_operator] system stored procedure to create an operator.

Figure 3-35 shows how you create an operator via SQL Server Management Studio. You need to provide a name and the email addresses. You can add a second email address by adding it as a pager.

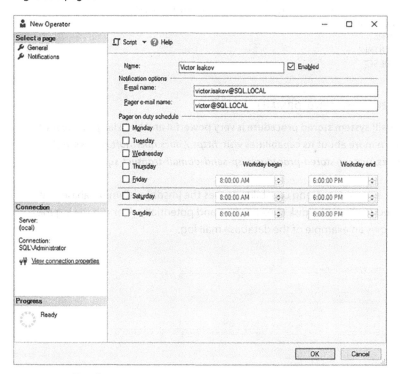

FIGURE 3-35 New Operator

Listing 3-24 shows you how to create an operator using the [sp_add_operator] system stored procedure.

LISTING 3-24 Create new operator

```
EXEC msdb.dbo.sp_add_operator @name=N'Victor Isakov',
    @enabled=1,
    @weekday_pager_start_time=90000,
    @weekday_pager_end_time=180000,
    @saturday_pager_start_time=90000,
    @saturday_pager_end_time=180000,
    @sunday_pager_start_time=90000,
    @sunday_pager_end_time=180000,
    @pager_days=0,
```

```
@email_address=N'victor.isakov@SQL.LOCAL',
@pager_address=N'marcus.isakov@SQL.LOCAL',
@category_name=N'[Microsoft Certified Architect]';
```

Create and manage SQL Agent alerts

SQL Server Agent can create alerts that will fire based on a SQL Server event occurring, and a SQL Server performance object counter meeting a threshold or a WMI event. WMI events are hardly used, but have power capabilities due to the scope of the WMI name space. You can configure an alert to notify an operator or run a SQL Server Agent job. We will have a look at how you can configure an alert action in the next section.

In our first example, shown in Figure 3-36, a SQL Server Agent has been configured to fire when a database's transaction log fills up. This is based on the 9002 error being generated by the database engine whenever a database's transaction log is full. Such event alerts can be based on the database engine's error number, error severity level, or error text. Query the [sys].[messages] system table in the [master] database to examine the different error messages and their severity level. You can scope an alert to a particular database or all databases. It is common to generate alerts for all databases based on any severity of 17 or above as these represent the more serious errors. The Response page allows you to specify which operators will be notifed, as can be seen in Figure 3-36.

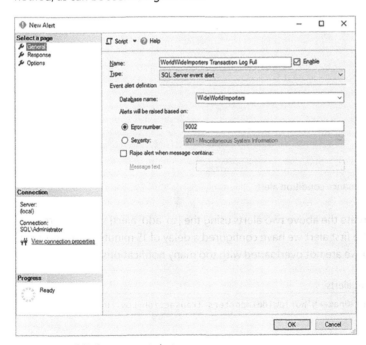

FIGURE 3-36 SQL Server event alert

EXAM TIP

The exam expects you to know common error numbers for errors such as database full (1105), deadlock (1205), log full (9002), and I/O errors (823, 824, 832 and 833).

Our second example in Figure 3-37 shows a SQL Server performance condition alert. Why wait for a database's transaction to be completely full and impact your business when you can alerted when the transction log is over 75%. This enables you to take corrective action. Better still, you can get the SQL Server Agent to automatically take corrective action, and we will look at that in the next section. SQL Server performance condition alerts are based on SQL Server's performance object counters. Unfortunately you cannot leverage the Windows performance object counters.

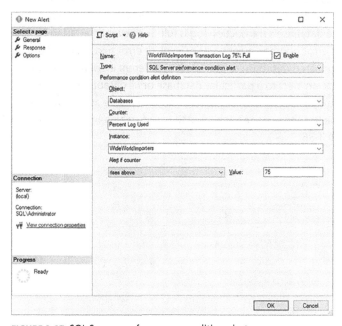

FIGURE 3-37 SQL Server performance condition alert

Listing 3-25 shows to create the above two alerts using the [sp_add_alert] system stored procedure. Note that for the first alert we have configured a delay of 15 minutes (900 seconds) between responses so that we are not overloaded with too many notifications.

LISTING 3-25 Create SQL Agent alerts

```
EXEC msdb.dbo.sp_add_alert @name=N'WorldWideImporters Transaction Log Full',
    @message_id=9002,
    @severity=0,
    @enabled=1,
    @delay_between_responses=900,
    @include_event_description_in=1,
    @database_name=N'WideWorldImporters',
```

```
        @category_name=N'[DBA]',
        @job_id=N'00000000-0000-0000-0000-000000000000';
GO

EXEC msdb.dbo.sp_add_alert @name=N'WorldWideImporters Transaction Log 75% Full',
        @message_id=0,
        @severity=0,
        @enabled=1,
        @delay_between_responses=0,
        @include_event_description_in=0,
        @category_name=N'[DBA]',
        @performance_condition=N'Databases|Percent Log Used|WideWorldImporters|>|75',
        @job_id=N'f857a2e0-f118-4cf4-82d5-277a52941d80';
```

Define custom alert actions

As discussed in the previous section you can configure an alert to execute a custom action via a SQL Server Agent job. Considering the flexibility and capability of SQL Server Agent jobs this represents a powerful capability. SQL Server Agent jobs can execute multiple operating system, PowerShell, Transact-SQL, and SSIS packages steps.

To configure an alert to execute a SQL Server Agent job simply choose the job in the drop-down list on the Response page as shown in Figure 3-38. In this example the transction log will be automatically backed up when it grows above 75%. Listing 3-21 shows what happens behind the scene with the job's GUID is bound to the job.

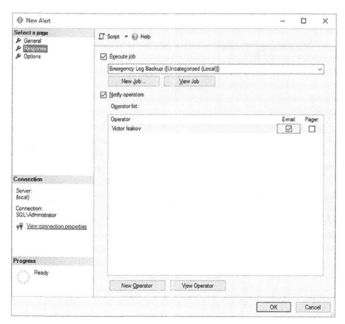

FIGURE 3-38 Response page of SQL Server Agent alert

Define failure actions

There a number of places in the SQL Server Agent where you can define what actions to take when a job fails. Let's have a quick look at them.

Figure 3-39 shows how you can control the failure actions when a job step fails in a SQL Server Agent job. Your valid options are listed below. You can also configure anumber of retry attempts and how long to wait between them whe a job step initially fails.

- Quit the job reporting failure
- Go to the next step
- Quit the job reporting success
- Go to step: [x] xxx

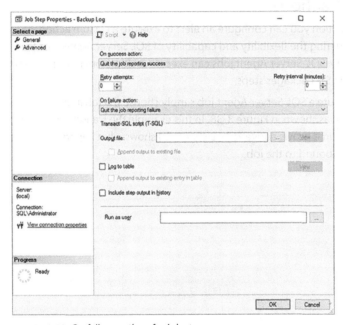

FIGURE 3-39 On failure actions for job steps

In the case of failures it is important to log such incidents. Figure 3-40 shows how you can configure a job to send an email or send a page or write to the Windows Application event log when a job completes, fails or succeeds.

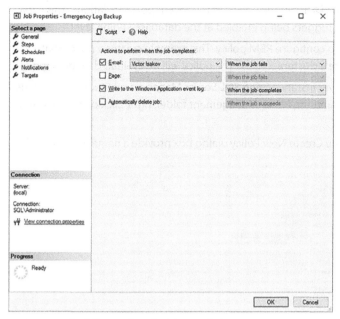

FIGURE 3-40 On failure actions for job completion

Configure policy based management

Policy based management (PBM) provides a framework that allows you to evaluate a single SQL Server instance to see if it confirms to a standard operating environment, or violates any standards or policies that might have a place. Introduced in SQL Server 2008, it is a highly underutilized capability in SQL Server in the industry.

Using PBM you can create a number of different policies that you can then evaluate as required. A policy is made of the following key components:

- **Condition** A condition is a Boolean expression made up of predicate functions or scripts that are used to evaluate whether your policy has been violated:
- **Facet** A facet is a set of logical properties that can be evaluated within the database engine. Examples of facets inside the database engine include availability groups, certificates, databases, endpoints, indexes, tables, and table options.
- **Evaluation mode** Four evaluation modes are supported, although only three of these can be automated:
  - **On demand** The policy is evaluated manually by the database administrator.
  - **On schedule** A SQL Server Agent schedule job periodically evaluates the policy.
  - **On change: log only** Event notifications are used to evaluate a policy when a relevant change is made.

- **On change: prevent** DDL triggers are used to prevent policy violations. This capability relies on nested triggers being enabled at the database engine level.

Use the the following steps to configure PBM policy. This example creates a policy that checks to see that all tables have a clustered index. The policy will be evaluated on demand.

1. Connect to your SQL Server instance using SQL Server Management Studio, expand the Management folder, expand the Policy Management folder, right-click on Policies, and select New Policy.

2. In the General page of the Create New Policy dialog box provide a name for your policy, as shown in Figure 3-41.

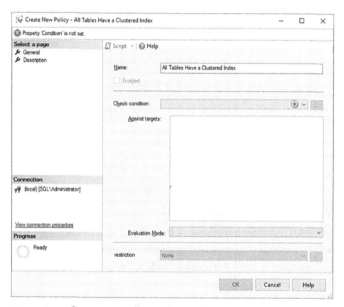

FIGURE 3-41 Create new policy

3. Click on the Check condtion drop down list and select New Condition.

4. In the Create New Condition dialog box configure a new condition with the following properties, as shown in Figure 3-42:

- A name for the condition
- Uses a Table facet
- Uses the "@HasClusteredIndex field = True" expression

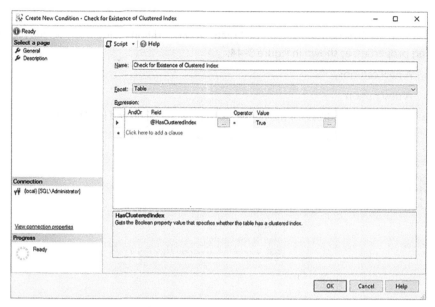

FIGURE 3-42 Create New Condition

5. Back in the Create New Policy dialog box configure the following properties, as shown in Figure 3-43:

   ■ On demand evaluation mode

   ■ Restrict to Enterprise or Standard Edition of SQL Server

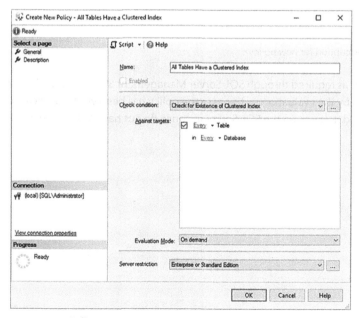

FIGURE 3-43 Policy target

6. Click on the Description page of the Create New Condition dialog box with the following properties, as shown in Figure 3-44:

- A new category

- A description

- The text and address for the hyperlink that will be displayed in SQL Server Management Studio

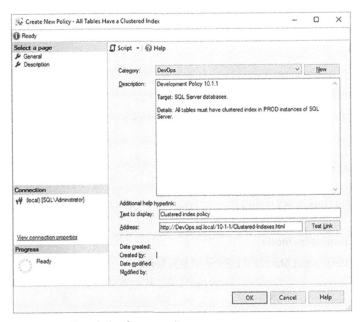

FIGURE 3-44 Description for new policy

Evaluate the policy as required through SQL Server Management Studio. Figure 3-45 shows the output generated by the evaluation. In this case the policy has been violated, because some tables across all databases on the SQL Server instance do not have a clustered index.

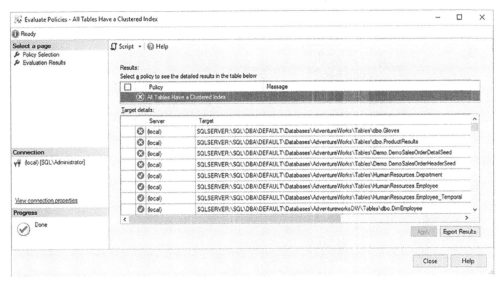

FIGURE 3-45 Policy evaluation

SQL Server ships with a number of pre-defined policies for the database engine, the Analysis Services, and the Reporting Services. Unfortunately, these policies are not automatically installed and need to be imported. The policies for the database engine can be imported from the C:\Program Files (x86)\Microsoft SQL Server*xxx*\Tools\Policies\DatabaseEngine\1033\ folder.

The policy that we created in Figure 3-45 used a predefined property (@HasClusteredIndex). PBM is much more powerful because it allows you to execute any Transact-SQL script through the ExecuteSql() function. This function allows you to run a scalar-valued query against a target SQL Server instance. For obvious reasons only one column can be specified in a SELECT statement (additional columns are ignored) and only one row must be returned. Figure 3-46 show an example of the ExecuteSql() for the predefined Database Page Status policy that can be imported.

FIGURE 3-46 Condition using the ExecuteSql() function

PBM really shines when used in conjunction with a central management server (CMS). A CMS is a SQL Server instance that you configure to store a central repository of all the SQL Server instances you want to manage. Once configured you can execute Transact-SQL scripts and PBM policies, and view log files against a set of your managed instances.

Instead of importing the individual PBM policies into all your managed SQL Server instances, you can import them into your CMS. You can then evaluate polcies against all your SQL Server instances, or a subset through folders, as required. Figure 3-47 shows the Database Page Suspect policy being evaluated against all of the SQL Server instances that have been registered in the CMS.

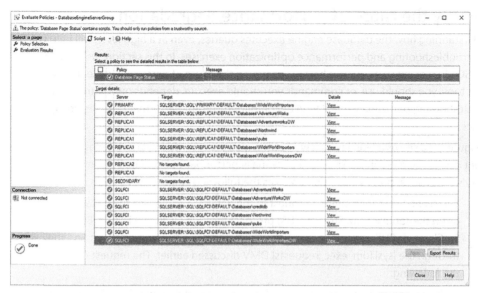

FIGURE 3-47 Policy evaluation across SQL Server instances registered in a CMS

Identify available space on data volumes

The database engine has limited capability to query the operating system due to security reasons. Furthermore, a database administrator might not have the security privileges to administer the operating system. Consequently, it was important for Microsoft to give database administrators the ability to identify the available space on the database engine's data volumes in particular.

In the past, database administrators used the [xp_fixeddrives] extended store procedure or shelled out using the [xp_cmdshell] extended stored procedures. Both of these techniques have superceded with the [sys].[dm_os_volume_stats] DMV.

Listing 3-26 shows an example of a query that returns all the database names and space consumption on the volumes used by the database engine. Note, the [percent_free] is a calculated field.

LISTING 3-26 Identifying available space on CSVs

```
SELECT DISTINCT DB_NAME(s.database_id) AS database_name,
    s.database_id, s.volume_mount_point, s.volume_id,
    s.logical_volume_name, s.file_system_type, s.total_bytes, s.available_bytes,
    ((s.available_bytes*1.0)/s.total_bytes) as percent_free
FROM sys.master_files AS f
CROSS APPLY sys.dm_os_volume_stats(f.database_id, f.file_id) AS s;
```

There's not much more to add, but the [xp_fixeddrives] extended stored procedure returns the free space for all disk drives, and not just for the volumes used by the database engine.

Identify the cause of performance degradation

Understanding how the database engine executes queries, even at a high level, will help you with troubleshooting and performance optimization exercises. In this section, we will cover how SQL Server executes queries before examining the cause of performance degradation. What tools you should use, or commands you should execute, depends on whether you are troubleshooting performance real time or comparing current performance to historical performance.

Figure 3-48 shows a high level view of how a query is executed by the database and the different components involved. There are potentially performance bottlenecks at every stage in a query's life cycle. A query's execution involves the following steps:

1. The client application sends a request to the database engine via the network stack using the Tabular Data Stream (TDS) protocol through ODBC, OLEDB, JDBC, managed SqlClient, or PHP driver for SQL Server. You can query what requests exist and their state through the [sys].[dm_exec_requests] DMV discussed earlier. The request can be one of the following:

   - **Batch request**   Request used by Transact-SQL batches, which are made up of statements.

   - **Bulk load request**   Special type of requests used by bulk insert operations.

   - **RPC request**   Used by remote procedure calls to call one of a number of identifying special stored procedures such as [Sp_ExecuteSql], [Sp_Prepare], and [Sp_Execute].

2. A task is created by the database engine with a unique handle. Its state will be PENDING. Query the [sys].[dm_os_tasks] DMV to see the list of tasks in the database engine.

3. An idle worker from the database engine's worker thread pool takes the pending task and starts to execute it. You can control the worker threads in SQL Server through the max worker threads configuration option. Query the [sys].[dm_os_workers] for more information about their state.

4. The database engine parses, compiles, and optimizes the entire batch. If the batch contains an error the request is terminated and an error message is returned. The database engine also sees if an existing query plan that is cached in the procedure cache can be reused. Otherwise the optimization phase will generate a query plan.

   - There are a number of phases in the optimization phase that will generate either a trivial, serial, or parallel execution plan.

   - SQL Server uses a cost-based optimizer. This is why it is critical to have your statistics up to date. Statistics drives cardinality estimation which affects query plan generation and memory grant requests.

   - The optimization phase looks for search arguments and join predicates because they are the primary drivers for what join types to use, what indexes to seek or scan, and the order in which to do these operations.

- The database engine supports nested loop, merge, and hash joins. Hash joins can be very expensive operations.
- You can view the estimated or actual execution plan via SQL Server Management Studio and DMVs.

5. The query plan is executed by the database engine.

- The execution plan is made up of a number of operations that need to be executed in a particular order. Some operators might need a significant amount of memory. The total amount of memory required by an execution plan is referred to as a memory grant. The exam might ask you to analyze an execution plan, so be familiar with that analysis.
- The database engine uses the access methods to access the data required from a table or index in the form of a bookmark lookup, a scan, or a seek operator. Watch out for excessive bookmark lookup and needless scans on unindexed tables.
- If all the data is in the buffer pool you will only see logical reads. If the database engine needs to read data from the disk subsystem, you will see physical reads.
- The database engine might not have sufficient memory to executing pending queries. The resource semaphore is responsible for satisfying memory grant requests while keeping overall memory grant usages within the database engine's limit. Query the [sys].[dm_exec_query_memory_grants] DMV to see the current status of memory grants. Waiting queries will have a NULL returned for the [grant_time] column.
- Queries that use parallelism will use Exchange operators. You will see CXPACKET waits for parallel queries in DMVs like [sys].[dm_os_wait_stats].
- Skill 3.2 discussed the various DMVs, like [sys].[dm_exec_cached_plans], and tools, like Live Query Stats, that you can use to determine what query plans are in memory, their plan shape, their properties and whether they need to be optimized.
- Watch out for operators that spill to disk due to insufficient memory grants. Spilling to disk can be either an Exchange Spill (*https://docs.microsoft.com/en-us/sql/relational-databases/event-classes/exchange-spill-event-class*), Sort Warning (*https://docs.microsoft.com/en-us/sql/relational-databases/event-classes/sort-warnings-event-class*) or Hash Warning (*https://docs.microsoft.com/en-us/sql/relational-databases/event-classes/hash-warning-event-class*).
- The database engine uses latches to physically protect pages from concurrent I/O requests, to prevent data corruption/inconsistency. Data modification requests will require an EX page latch. Read operation requests can get away will a SH page latch. These two types of requests show up as PAGELATCH_SH and PAGELATCH_EX wait types. The database engine also maintains a [sys].[dm_os_latch_stats] for troubleshooting latches. High PAGEIOLATCH_SH waits per database might indicate a lack of indexes.
- The database engine uses locks to logically protect data and schema from concurrent queries. We discussed locking and blocking in Skill 3.1. The [sys].[dm_tran_locks]

keeps track of the locks being maintained by the lock manager. Otherwise you can analyze the [sys].[dm_os_wait_stats] DMV for high counts and durations of the LCK_M_X and other lock wait types. For real-time troubleshooting query the [sys].[dm_os_waiting_tasks] discussed above to determine the resource being waited on.

6. The result set is streamed to the client as it is being generated by the worker for the task.

   ■ The database engine predominantly uses a cooperative multitasking model through the SQLOS and limits the quantum of time that a task's thread can spend executing on a scheduler. The quantum in SQL Server is 4 milliseconds. Threads that exhaust their quantum register a SOS_SCHEDULER_YIELD wait type.

   ■ Otherwise, threads are executed asynchronously on the schedulers, which frees up the scheduler to service another thread if the task needs to wait for a resource. The database engine keeps track of these waits via the [sys].[dm_os_waits] DMV.

   ■ A task can be waiting for a worker thread (PENDING); runnable, but waiting to receive a quantum (RUNNABLE); currently running on the scheduler (RUNNING); has a worker but is waiting for an event (SUSPENDED): stuck in a spinlock (SPINLOCK): or completed (DONE).

7. When the worker completes executing on a scheduler it is returned to the worker pool.

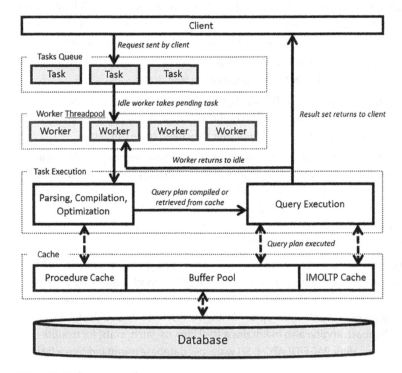

FIGURE 3-48 Query execution

Identifying the cause of performance degradation pre-supposed that you knew what your performance was like in the past, compared to the present. This emphasizes the need for you to capture some form of baseline using either Windows Performance Monitor or any of the other tools we have examined earlier in this chapter such as Query Store or Management Data Warehouse. Without a baseline, it is very difficult to perform a root cause analysis on the cause of the performance degradation because you will not be able to compare metrics between how a query is performing now compared to the past.

Obviously, Microsoft's strategic direction is Query Store. In SQL Server 2016 there are a number of reports that you can leverage to help you identify the cause of performance degradation:

- **Regressed Queries**   Identifies queries for which the execution metrics have recently regressed. Use this report to correlate your observed application performance problems with the actual queries whose performance needs to be improved.

- **Top Resource Consuming Queries**   Analyzes the total resource consumption for the database by any of the following metrics: execution count, duration, CPU time, logical reads, logical writes, physical reads, CLR time, degree of parallelism, memory consumption, or row count. Use this report to identify resource patterns over time and optimize overall consumption for your database. There is an option in this report to track a specific query.

- **Top Resource Consuming Queries**   Identifies the queries that consume the most resources based any of the following dimensions: execution count, duration, CPU time, logical reads, logical writes, physical reads, CLR time, degree of parallelism, memory consumption, or row count. Use this report to focus your attention on the queries that have the biggest impact on resource consumption. There is an option in this report to track a specific query.

- **Queries With High Variance**   Identifies queries with high execution variation by the dimensions for a specified time interval. Variation and standard deviation are supported in the analysis. Use this report to identify queries with widely variant performance that can be degrading performance.

- **Tracked Queries**   Tracks the execution of a specified query in real-time. Use this report to see the performance degradation.

In SQL Server 2017 Query Store was enhanced further with its ability to capture wait stats summary information. Being able to track wait stats categories per query in Query Store tremendously improves the database administrator's ability to performance troubleshoot query performance and bottlenecks. SQL Server 2017 can automatically tune your queries by identifying and fixing query regression, interleaved execution of multi-statement table values functions, batch mode memory grant feedback and batch mode adaptive joins.

In this chapter, there are a couple of tools that will help with performance troubleshooting that we have not covered yet. So, let's cover them now because there is a high probablity of them being in the exam.

The first tool is Performance Monitor, a Windows tool that enables you to monitor both operating system and database engine performance object counters. The great thing about Performance Monitor is that is can collect a phenomenal amount of metrics with very little overhead to files that can automatically restart after they reach a certain size and date. You can also correlate SQL Server Profiler traces with the Performance Monitor logs. For the exam make sure you understand the following object counters:

- **Database engine**   The following counters represent a good start for monitoring the database engine: Batch Requests/sec, Errors/sec, Page lookups/sec, Processes Blocked, Log growths, and Transactions.

- **Processor subsystem**   The following counters represent a good start for monitoring the CPUs: % Processor Time and % Privileged Time.

- **Memory**   The following counters represent a good start for monitoring the memory subsystem: Memory Grants Pending, Memory grant queue waits, and Memory Page Life Expectancy.

- **Disk subsystem**   The following counters represent a good start for monitoring the I/O subsystem: Backup/Restore throughput/sec, Checkpoints/sec, Log flushes/sec, Log writes/sec, Logical Disk, Page IO latches/sec, Page reads/sec, Page writes/sec, and Pages/sec.

- **Contention**   The following counters represent a good start for monitoring contention issues: Num Deadlocks/sec, SQL Server:Latches, SQL Server:Locks, SQL Server:Wait Statistics.

You can query performance monitor counters through the [sys].[dm_os_performance_counters] DMV. Unfortunately, you are constrained to the SQL Server performance object counters only.

You should also be very familiar with analyzing the output of the [sys].[dm_os_wait_stats] DMV. The database engine tracks what resources the tasks have been waiting on during query execution. For the exam be aware of the following common waits:

- **ASYNC_IO_COMPLETION**   Generally seen due to backup, restore, and database file operations.

- **ASYNC_NETWORK_IO**   A lot of database administrators jump the gun here and assume it's a network issue, but it is more commonly due to poor application design.

- **BACKUPIO**   Self-evident.

- **CXPACKET**   Occurs with parallel query plans when trying to synchronize the query processor exchange iterator.

- **IO_COMPLETION**   Tasks are waiting for some other I/O to complete, such as those related to DLLs, [tempdb] sort files and certain DBCC operations.

- **LCK_*** Tasks are waiting on a specific lock.

- **LATCH_*** Tasks are waiting on some internal database engine resource, as opposed to data in the buffer pool.

- **OLEDB** Occurs when SQL Server calls the SQL Server Native Client OLE DB Provider, so most database administrators assume its related to linked servers. However, OLEDB is also used by all DMVs and by the DBCC CHECKDB operations.

- **PAGEIOLATCH_*** Tasks blocked by these wait types are waiting for data to be transferred between the disk and the buffer pool.

- **PAGELATCH_*** Tasks are waiting on a latch for a buffer that is not in an I/O request.

- **RESOURCE_SEMAPHORE** Queries are waiting for memory grants.

- **RESOURCE_SEMAPHORE_QUERY_COMPILE** Tasks are waiting to compile their request.

- **SOS_SCHEDULER_YIELD** Tasks have voluntarily yielded on the scheduler for other tasks to execute and are waiting for its quantum to be renewed. This could indicate spinlock contention.

- **THREADPOOL** Tasks are waiting to be assigned to a worker thread.

- **WRITELOG** Tasks are waiting to write transaction commit log records to the disk.

> **NEED MORE REVIEW?** **SQL SERVER WAITS**
>
> For a complete list of the different waits and their description visit: *https://docs.microsoft. com/en-us/sql/relational-databases/system-dynamic-management-views/sys-dm-os-wait- stats-transact-sql.*

Finally, the [sys] [dm_io_virtual_file_stats] DMV is extremely useful for analyzing I/O metrics and potential bottlenecks of the database data and log files. The [io_stall_read_ms] and [io_stall_write_ms] columns are particularly useful for determining how often user queries are stalled waiting for I/O requests to be completed against the database files. Query this DMV to calculate the average I/O latency and compare them against Microsoft's recommendations:

- < 8ms: excellent

- < 12ms: good

- < 20ms: fair

- > 20ms: poor

EXAM TIP

For the exam it would be worth your while to to visit: *https://docs.microsoft.com/en-us/sql/ relational-databases/performance/performance-monitoring-and-tuning-tools.* This ensures you are familiar with all the performance monitoring and tuning tools that are available in SQL Server and what their use cases are.

Thought experiment

In this thought experiment, demonstrate your skills and knowledge of the topics covered in this chapter. You can find answers to this thought experiment in the next section.

You work as a database administrator for World Wide Importers, which has an online transactional database that used for human resources, sales and customer relationship management.

1. Users are complaining about poor query performance for queries that query the [Sales_History] table. The table is 400GB in size. It is not partitioned. After performing a root cuase analysis you have determined that the poor query performanc is due to outdated statistics. You need to update the statistics in the least possible time for the table What statistic update option should you use?

   A. FULLSCAN

   B. SAMPLE

   C. INCREMENTAL

   D. NORECOMPUTE

2. You need to analyze which queries are consuming the most memory by their query plans. What DMV should you query?

   A. [sys].[dm_db_task_space_usage]

   B. [sys].[dm_db_session_space_usage]

   C. [sys].[dm_exec_cached_plans]

   D. [sys].[dm_exec_query_stats]

3. Management wants you to configure a monitoring solution that will trakc query execution plans and server-level wait stats so that your junior database administrators can troubleshoot performance and identify query execution times historically for a year. What technology should you use?

   A. The default system_health extended event session

   B. Policy Based Managment.

   C. Query Store.

   D. Data Collector and Management Data Warehouse.

Thought experiment answers

This section contains the solution to the thought experiment. Each answer explains why the answer choice is correct.

1. **Correct answer:** B

   A. **Incorrect:** The FULLSCAN option will take too long on a 400GB table.

   B. **Correct:** The SAMPLE option will allows you scan a smaller percentage of the table. With SQL Server 2016 this is parallelized.

   C. **Incorrect:** The INCREMENTAL option does not apply to non-partitioned tables.

   D. **Incorrect:** The NORECOMPUTE option disables automatic statistics update.

2. **Correct answer:** C

   A. **Incorrect:** The [sys].[dm_db_task_space_usage] DMV does not track query plans.

   B. **Incorrect:** The [sys].[dm_db_session_space_usage DMV does not track query plans.

   C. **Correct:** The [sys].[dm_exec_cached_plans] DMV tracks query plan's memory usage.

   D. **Incorrect:** The [sys].[dm_exec_query_stats] DMV does not track the query plan's memory usage.

3. **Correct answer:** D

   A. **Incorrect:** The system_health extended event session will not collect the required information. Nor does it have the required repository.

   B. **Incorrect:** Policy Based Management only evaluates custom polcies for compliance.

   C. **Incorrect:** Query Store will not collect wait stats.

   D. **Correct:** The Data Collectors will capture both query execution metrics and wait stats.

Chapter summary

- Query the [sys].[dm_exec_requests] DMV to troubleshoot what requests are currently executing with the database engine.

- Query the [sys].[dm_os_waiting_tasks] DMV to troubleshoot what requests are being blocked or are blocking You can also leverage the Activity Monitor or blocke process report capability in SQL Server.

- Query the [sys].[dm_db_file_space_usage], [sys].[dm_db_session_space_usage], [sys].[dm_db_task_space_usage], [sys].[dm_tran_active_snapshot_database_transactions] and [sys].[dm_tran_version_store] DMVs to identify sessions that are consuming resources in thte [tempdb] system database.

- Configure the data collector to collect telemetry information about server resource usage, query execution and disk utilization into a repository. This includes wait stats. The data in the repository can be used primarily for historical troubleshooting, query tuning and server performance analysis.

- Use the Query Store for capturing detailed query metrics at the database level. The Query Store can be used for detecting query regression and identifying problematic queries.

- Use extended events to troubleshoot the database engine in realtime. Be careful using extended events because it can potentially impact performance.

- The best way to detect deadlocks and capture information about them for trouble-shooting purposes is through extended events.

- Query the [sys].[dm_exec_cached_plans], [sys].[dm_exec_query_plan] and [sys].[dm_exec_query_stats] to analyse the procedure cache and identify problematic execution plans.

- The database engine has a default extended event session, called the system_health, running that automatically tracks the most important errors and incidents, including deadlocks. Querying the system_health session periodically is a great, easy way to detect deadlocks.

- Query the [sys].[dm_db_index_physical_stats] DMV to detect the level of fragmentation within a table or index.

- Microsoft recommends reorganizing indexes that are fragmented between 5% and 30%. Indexes fragemented over 30% need to be rebuilt. These thresholds are somewhat arbitrary, and not applicable in the real-world, but you should use them in the exam.

- Query the [sys].[dm_db_missing_index_details], [sys].[dm_db_missing_index_columns] and [sys].[dm_db_missing_index_groups] to see what missing indexes the database engine recommends.

- Query the [sys].[dm_db_index_usage_stats] DMV to how indexes are being used and identify if they are underutilized.

- From SQL Server 2016 you should use ALTER INDEX REORGANIZE for fragemented columnstore indexes as it is performed online and is effectively an index rebuild.

- Query the [sys].[stats] DMV and [sys].[dm_db_stats_properties] DMF to help you determine if statistics need updating. Alternatively you can use the DBCC SHOW_STATISTICS command.

- Automatic asynchronous statistics update (AUTO_UPDATE_STATISTICS_ASYNC) will not block queries that have trigger automatic updating of statistics.

- You do not need to update statistics for indexes that you have rebuilt.

- With a database compatibility level set to 130 the database engine updates statistics more aggressively for larger tables.

- For large tables that are partitioned you can enable incremental statistics update. The database engine will then be able to update statistics at the partition level.

- Policy Based Management allows you evaluate whether your SQL Server instances conform to a configurable policy that you have set.

CHAPTER 4

Manage high availability and disaster recovery

I t is important to understand the difference between high availability and disaster recovery. It is not uncommon for management in organizations to misunderstand these concepts and use the wrong technology for their SQL Server infrastructure. In this last chapter, we examine the high availability technologies available in SQL Server, as promised in Chapter 2, "Manage backup and restore of databases."

With high availability, you are using technology in SQL Server to minimize the downtime of a given database solution to maximize its availability. With disaster recovery, however, you are using technology to recover from a disaster incident, potentially minimizing the amount of data lost. In some cases, data loss is acceptable, because the imperative is to get your database solution online as soon as possible. That is why it is critical to engage with all stakeholders to determine the business requirements. With both high availability and disaster recovery people and processes play a key part, so make sure you don't focus solely on the technology.

The exam will test your ability to design the appropriate high availability solution for a given scenario, which is why Skill 4.1 starts with a discussion about high availability and the primary considerations for designing a particular solution. Skill 4.2 then covers the designing of a disaster recovery solution, which commonly goes hand-in-hand with a high availability solution. Given how we covered disaster recovery in Chapter 2, a detailed discussion will not be required here. Skill 4.3 examines the log shipping technology in SQL Server and how it is primarily used to provide disaster recovery. Skill 4.4 then details Availability Groups and examines how they can be used to provide both high availability and scale-out capability to your databases. Finally, in Skill 4.5 we implement failover clustering solutions. Although this high availability technology has been available since SQL Server 2000, it's commonly used in the industry and should not be discounted as an old, unused technology. Microsoft keeps investing in failover clustering, and we will learn about how SQL Server can take advantage of cluster shared volumes.

High availability technologies are complex and involve a lot of set up and configuration, so this chapter has many figures that show you their installation, configuration, and administration processes. Make sure you examine the various options in the figures and listings in this chapter to best prepared for the exam.

Skills covered in this chapter:

- Design a high availability solution
- Design a disaster recovery solution
- Implement log shipping
- Implement Availability Groups
- Implement failover clustering

Skill 4.1: Design a high availability solution

High availability, as the name suggests, is concerned with making sure that your database is highly available. The cost of an unavailable database solution, in today's modern, globalized 24x7, Internet connected world can be catastrophic to your organization.

One of the first questions you should be asking of your organization is what availability is required for your database solution. This will form part of your Service Level Agreement (SLA) for your database solution. Availability is usually expressed as a percentage of uptime in a given year, and can be expressed as follows:

$$\text{Availability} = \frac{\text{Actual uptime}}{\text{Expected uptime}} \times 100\%$$

This is commonly referred to as the number of nines required. Table 4-1 shows the availability, the number of nines, and how much down time that corresponds to annually.

TABLE 4-1: Number of nines for high availability.

Availability	Nines	Annual downtime	Monthly downtime	Weekly downtime	Daily downtime
90%	1	36.5 days	72 hours	16.8 hours	2.4 hours
95%	1.5	18.25 days	36 hours	8.4 hours	1.2 hours
99%	2	3.65 days	7.20 hours	1.68 hours	14.4 minutes
99.5%	2.5	1.83 days	3.60 hours	50.4 minutes	7.2 minutes
99.9%	3	8.76 hours	43.8 minutes	10.1 minutes	1.44 minutes
99.95%	3.5	4.38 hours	21.56 minutes	5.04 minutes	43.2 seconds
99.99%	4	52.56 minutes	4.38 minutes	1.01 minutes	8.66 seconds
99.995%	4.5	26.28 minutes	2.16 minutes	30.24 seconds	4.32 seconds
99.999%	5	5.26 minutes	25.9 seconds	6.05 seconds	864.3 milliseconds
99.9999%	6	31.5 seconds	2.59 seconds	604.8 milliseconds	86.4 milliseconds
99.99999%	7	3.15 seconds	262.97 milliseconds	60.48 milliseconds	8.64 milliseconds
99.99999999%	8	315.569 milliseconds	26.297 milliseconds	6.048 milliseconds	0.864 milliseconds
99.999999999%	9	31.5569 milliseconds	2.6297 milliseconds	0.6048 milliseconds	0.0864 milliseconds

As you can see, achieving even four nines might be difficult. Four nines represents only 4.38 minutes of downtime per month. Now consider how long it takes for your servers to be rebooted. On modern servers, that have a large amount of memory, it might take you 15-30 minutes for them to boot up, as they run through their BIOS memory checks. In most cases these BIOS memory checks cannot be turned off. Consider further how often you patch your Windows environment, which typically requires a reboot, and how long that takes. Do not underestimate the potential complexity of achieving anything beyond three nines.

When determining your SLA you should also define what constitutes downtime in the context of your SLA. There are two types of downtime:

- **Planned downtime** Planned downtime refers to the downtime incurred by your maintenance tasks. These maintenance tasks might include patching hardware or software, hardware maintenance, patching the Windows operating system, or patching SQL Server. Planned downtime is typically scheduled and controlled through business processes. Consequently, there is typically no data loss.

- **Unplanned downtime** Unplanned downtime refers to downtime that is incurred due to an unexpected incident that causes outage. Examples include:

  - Hardware failures, such as with a disk drive or power supply unit failing or bad firmware in a hardware vendor's HBA.

  - Data center failure, such as with a power failing, or flooding occurring.

- Software failure, such as with Windows crashing, SQL Server hanging, or a corrupt database.

- User error, such as dropping a database, or accidentally deleting data.

In some SLAs there are only penalties enforced for unplanned downtime.

Once you have determined your organizations availability requirements you can assess which SQL: Server high availability technology fits your business requirements. You might need to take in multiple factors, including:

- **Whether automatic failover is required**   Certain high availability technologies and configurations do not offer automatic failover. In certain use cases an organization might not require high availability.

- **Failover speed**   Different high availability technologies offer different failover speeds, so understanding how quickly a failover needs to take will help you choose the appropriate solution.

- **Scalability**   Whether or not you need to scale out your database solution impacts your high availability technology selection. Scaling out your database can provide both performance and uptime benefits. Availability Groups offer the best scale-out capability.

- **Infrastructure between data centers**   The latency and throughput between sites/data centers will directly impact what high availability technologies can be implemented. Latency is more important than distance. You do not want automatic fail overs to be performed due to slow response times between data centers. In this case automatic failover might not be required.

- **Connecting applications**   What applications are accessing the database and what network libraries they use to connect to the databases will also play an important factor in any design. Certain high availability technologies might not work as well with older applications.

- **Recovery model**   This is a very important consideration. What recovery model is being used by a database and the volume of transactions experienced by the database will dictate what high availability technology can be used. Remember that Availability Groups require the databases to be using the full recovery model. We covered recovery models in Chapter 2.

- **Number of databases**   Whether the database solution involves multiple databases that need to fail over as a single unit is another important factor and design consideration.

- **Database size**   This covers the size of the databases and how much it will cost to potentially replicate those databases on multiple instances of SQL Server. Very Large Databases (VLDBs) might be too expensive to host on multiple SQL Server instances. They might also be larger than what is possible to fit locally on a server, for example.

- **Database administrator skill set**   Determine whether your organization has a team of database administrators and how experienced they are. Certain high availability technologies are more complex to administer.
- **SQL Server Edition**   The SQL Server licensing implications and associated costs with a different edition is a very important factor in organizations. Certain high availability technologies are only available in the Enterprise Edition.

> **IMPORTANT   DESIGNING A HIGH AVAILABILITY SOLUTION**
>
> When designing a high availability solution, you need to take into account all the things that can possibly fail. You also need to provide redundancy at every level that is cost effective for your organization. There a plenty of tales/urban myths about multi-million dollar highly available solutions failing due to a non-redundant component that cost an insignificant amount. Some of those tales are true!

SQL Server supports the following high availability technologies:

- **Failover clustering**   With failover clustering you rely on the features of the Windows operating system to build a cluster of separate nodes that together provide redundancy at the hardware and software levels.
- **Transactional replication**   With transactional replication various replication agents are reading a database's transaction log, storing those captured transactions in a separate database, and then replicating those transactions to other databases located on different servers.
- **Database mirroring**   With database mirroring the database engine automatically transmits the transaction log to one other server when the same database exists.
- **Availability groups**   Availability groups are an evolution of Database Mirroring where the transaction log can be transmitted in real time to multiple servers that maintain a copy of the database.
- **Log shipping**   With log shipping multiple copies of the database are kept on multiple servers through scheduled log backups and restores.

Each high availability technology will have its own set of associated costs, and pros, and cons. As a database administrator, it is up to you to assess your business requirements and architect the appropriate high availability solution. In this book, we will focus on Log Shipping, Availability Groups and Failover Clustering.

Don't forget that you can combine high availability technologies. For example, you can take advantage of failover clustering locally in one data center to provide high availability and use log shipping to another data center for disaster recovery purposes.

> **IMPORTANT** **IMPLEMENTING A PROOF-OF-CONCEPT FOR YOUR HIGH AVAILABILITY SOLUTION**
>
> There is no substitute for implementing a Proof-of-Concept (POC) for your high availability solution to ensure that it will work exactly as you expect it to. It will also allow you to test your processes and determine whether the high availability technology will impact your databases solution. Implementing a POC is so easy these days with virtualization and the cloud. Just do it!

Skill 4.2: Design a disaster recovery solution

Whereas high availability is concerned about mitigating against different types of failures, disaster recovery is concerned about what to do in the case of a failure occurring. A disaster recovery solution involves technology and processes that will enable you to restore your availability with an appropriate data loss in an appropriate timeframe.

To design an appropriate disaster recovery plan, you need to engage the appropriate stakeholders in your organization to articulate the following requirements:

- Recovery Time Objective (RTO)
- Recovery Point Objective (RPO)
- Recovery Level Objective (RLO)

When designing your disaster recovery plan you need to take in multiple additional factors, including:

- The size of the databases
- How long it will take to restore hardware
- Whether you can take advantage of the cloud
- How long it will take to restore the Windows operating system
- How long it will take to restore the SQL Server environment
- The order in which you will need to perform the various tasks in your disaster recovery plan

These considerations and others were covered in depth in Chapter 2. Make sure you understand the concepts and considerations covered there, because they will impact your high availability design. The exam might ask you to design a high availability and disaster recovery solution for the same given scenario.

In a lot of organization's cases their database solutions are "too big to fail." In such cases you need to rely more on high availability, redundancy, and processes to ensure that you never have to recovery from a disaster. Good luck!

```
EXEC msdb.dbo.sp_attach_schedule
        @job_id = @LS_BackupJobId
        ,@schedule_id = @LS_BackUpScheduleID

EXEC msdb.dbo.sp_update_job
        @job_id = @LS_BackupJobId
        ,@enabled = 1

END

EXEC master.dbo.sp_add_log_shipping_alert_job

EXEC master.dbo.sp_add_log_shipping_primary_secondary
        @primary_database = N'WideWorldImporters'
        ,@secondary_server = N'SECONDARY'
        ,@secondary_database = N'WideWorldImporters'
        ,@overwrite = 1

-- ****** End: Script to be run at Primary: [PRIMARY]  ******

-- Execute the following statements at the Secondary to configure Log Shipping
-- for the database [SECONDARY].[WideWorldImporters],
-- the script needs to be run at the Secondary in the context of the [msdb] database.
--------------------------------------------------------------------------------------
-- Adding the Log Shipping configuration

-- ****** Begin: Script to be run at Secondary: [SECONDARY] ******

DECLARE @LS_Secondary__CopyJobId   AS uniqueidentifier
DECLARE @LS_Secondary__RestoreJobId     AS uniqueidentifier
DECLARE @LS_Secondary__SecondaryId      AS uniqueidentifier
DECLARE @LS_Add_RetCode      As int

EXEC @LS_Add_RetCode = master.dbo.sp_add_log_shipping_secondary_primary
        @primary_server = N'PRIMARY'
        ,@primary_database = N'WideWorldImporters'
        ,@backup_source_directory = N'\\STORAGE\Log_Shipping'
        ,@backup_destination_directory = N'B:\PRIMARY_LOG_SHIPPING'
        ,@copy_job_name = N'[LOGSHIP] Copy PRIMARY WideWorldImporters'
        ,@restore_job_name = N'[LOGSHIP] Restore PRIMARY WideWorldImporters'
        ,@file_retention_period = 4320
        ,@overwrite = 1
        ,@copy_job_id = @LS_Secondary__CopyJobId OUTPUT
        ,@restore_job_id = @LS_Secondary__RestoreJobId OUTPUT
        ,@secondary_id = @LS_Secondary__SecondaryId OUTPUT

IF (@@ERROR = 0 AND @LS_Add_RetCode = 0)
BEGIN

DECLARE @LS_SecondaryCopyJobScheduleUID     As uniqueidentifier
DECLARE @LS_SecondaryCopyJobScheduleID      AS int

EXEC msdb.dbo.sp_add_schedule
        @schedule_name =N'Every 15 minutes'
        ,@enabled = 1
        ,@freq_type = 4
```

```
            ,@freq_interval = 1
            ,@freq_subday_type = 4
            ,@freq_subday_interval = 15
            ,@freq_recurrence_factor = 0
            ,@active_start_date = 20170302      -- Change as appropriate
            ,@active_end_date = 99991231
            ,@active_start_time = 0
            ,@active_end_time = 235900
            ,@schedule_uid = @LS_SecondaryCopyJobScheduleUID OUTPUT
            ,@schedule_id = @LS_SecondaryCopyJobScheduleID OUTPUT

    EXEC msdb.dbo.sp_attach_schedule
            @job_id = @LS_Secondary__CopyJobId
            ,@schedule_id = @LS_SecondaryCopyJobScheduleID

    DECLARE @LS_SecondaryRestoreJobScheduleUID     As uniqueidentifier
    DECLARE @LS_SecondaryRestoreJobScheduleID      AS int

    EXEC msdb.dbo.sp_add_schedule
            @schedule_name =N'Every 15 minutes'
            ,@enabled = 1
            ,@freq_type = 4
            ,@freq_interval = 1
            ,@freq_subday_type = 4
            ,@freq_subday_interval = 15
            ,@freq_recurrence_factor = 0
            ,@active_start_date = 20170302      -- Change as appropriate
            ,@active_end_date = 99991231
            ,@active_start_time = 0
            ,@active_end_time = 235900
            ,@schedule_uid = @LS_SecondaryRestoreJobScheduleUID OUTPUT
            ,@schedule_id = @LS_SecondaryRestoreJobScheduleID OUTPUT

    EXEC msdb.dbo.sp_attach_schedule
            @job_id = @LS_Secondary__RestoreJobId
            ,@schedule_id = @LS_SecondaryRestoreJobScheduleID

END

DECLARE @LS_Add_RetCode2  As int

IF (@@ERROR = 0 AND @LS_Add_RetCode = 0)
BEGIN

EXEC @LS_Add_RetCode2 = master.dbo.sp_add_log_shipping_secondary_database
        @secondary_database = N'WideWorldImporters'
        ,@primary_server = N'PRIMARY'
        ,@primary_database = N'WideWorldImporters'
        ,@restore_delay = 0
        ,@restore_mode = 0
        ,@disconnect_users  = 0
        ,@restore_threshold = 45
        ,@threshold_alert_enabled = 1
        ,@history_retention_period   = 5760
        ,@overwrite = 1
```

```
END

IF (@@error = 0 AND @LS_Add_RetCode = 0)
BEGIN

EXEC msdb.dbo.sp_update_job
        @job_id = @LS_Secondary__CopyJobId
        ,@enabled = 1

EXEC msdb.dbo.sp_update_job
        @job_id = @LS_Secondary__RestoreJobId
        ,@enabled = 1

END
-- ****** End: Script to be run at Secondary: [SECONDARY] ******
GO
```

EXAM TIP

Make sure you familiarize yourself with the key statements and parameters in the log shipping creation script for the exam.

Figure 4-7 shows the log shipping backup job and step created on the primary server. Note how the log shipping back up job does not run any Transact-SQL commands. Instead it invokes the **sqllogship.exe** agent with a number of parameters. The copy and the backup jobs are also run on the secondary server. If you connect to the secondary server in SQL Server Management Studio, the secondary database is permanently in a restoring state.

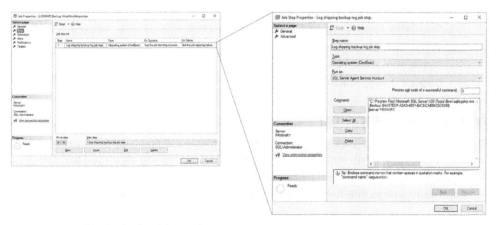

FIGURE 4-7 Log shipping backup job on primary server

> **NOTE   CUSTOMIZING LOG SHIPPING JOBS**
>
> There is nothing preventing you from customizing the log shipping jobs created by SQL
> Server Management Server. For example, you could robocopy the log backups immediately
> after the log copy job step completes to your disaster recovery server.

Because log shipping uses an agent, it is difficult to customize log shipping. That is why it is
not uncommon for database administrators to develop and implement their own custom log
shipping through Transact-SQL scripts.

The sqllogship.exe agent supports the following parameters:

```
sqllogship
    -server instance_name
{
    -backup primary_id |
    -copy secondary_id |
    -restore secondary_id
}
[ -verboselevel level ]
[ -logintimeout timeout_value ]
[ -querytimeout timeout_value ]
```

To help troubleshoot log shipping you can change the -verboselevel parameter as required.
Table 4-2 shows the different levels supported. The default value used is 3.

TABLE 4-2 SQLLOGSHIP.EXE -VERBOSELEVEL PARAMETER OPTIONS

Level	Description
0	Output no tracing and debugging messages
1	Output error-handling messages
2	Output warnings and error-handling messages
3	Output informational messages, warnings, and error-handling messages
4	Output all debugging and tracing messages

Monitor log shipping

It is important to monitor your log shipping to ensure that log shipping is working as expected,
because it could potentially impact your RPO/RTO SLAs. Log shipping allows you to create
a separate monitor server that will monitor log shipping jobs on the primary and secondary
servers. If a customized threshold expires, an alert will be generated to indicate that a job has
failed.

The following steps show how to configure a monitor server for your log shipping solution.

1. Open SQL Server Management Studio and connect to the primary SQL Server instance.

2. Expand the Databases folder.

3. Right-click on the primary database and click on the Transaction Log Shipping page.

4. Check the Use A Monitor Server Instance check box.

5. Click on the Settings button to configure the monitor server.

6. Click on the Connect button to authenticate against the monitoring server.

7. Provider the server name and authentication details for the monitor server in the Connect to Server dialog box and click the Connect button.

8. Configure the following details, as shown in Figure 4-8, to configure the monitor server:

- Credentials to be used by the monitor server. The best and easiest set up is to impersonate the proxy account of the log shipping jobs.

- The history retention after which history will be deleted.

    - In a production environment, it is not uncommon to configure such information for a number of years.

- The name of the alert job.

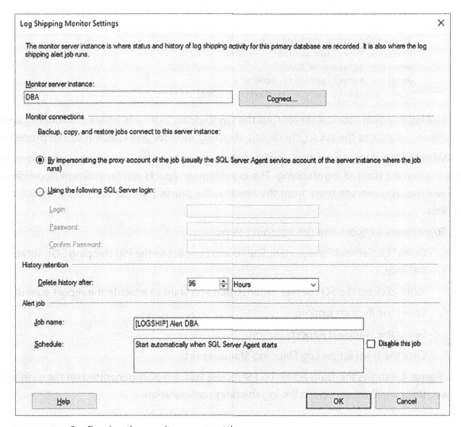

FIGURE 4-8 Configuring the monitor server settings

9. Click on the OK button to close the Log Shipping Monitor Settings dialog box.

10. Click on the OK button for SQL Server Management Studio to configure the log shipping monitor.

Listing 4-2 shows the Transact-SQL script that was generated to configure the log shipping monitor server.

LISTING 4-2 Log shipping configuration.

```
-- ****** Begin: Script to be run at Monitor: [DBA] ******

EXEC msdb.dbo.sp_processlogshippingmonitorsecondary
        @mode = 1
        ,@secondary_server = N'SECONDARY'
        ,@secondary_database = N'WideWorldImporters'
        ,@secondary_id = N''
        ,@primary_server = N'PRIMARY'
        ,@primary_database = N'WideWorldImporters'
        ,@restore_threshold = 45
        ,@threshold_alert = 14420
        ,@threshold_alert_enabled = 1
        ,@history_retention_period    = 5760
        ,@monitor_server = N'DBA'
        ,@monitor_server_security_mode = 1
-- ****** End: Script to be run at Monitor: [DBA] ******
```

The log shipping monitor server runs the log shipping alert job. Instead of running an executable, it executes the sys.sp_check_log_shipping_monitor_alert system stored procedure.

With the log shipping monitor configured you can now execute a number of reports to see the current state of log shipping. The log shipping reports will be different depending on whether you execute them from the monitor, the primary, or the secondary log shipping server.

To generate a report, use the following steps:

1. Open SQL Server Management Studio and connect to the log shipping SQL Server instance.

2. Right-click on the SQL Server instance that you want to execute the report against.

3. Select the Reports option.

4. Select the Standard Reports option.

5. Click the Transaction Log Shipping Status report.

Figure 4-9 shows the Transaction Log Shipping Status report generated on the monitoring server. It shows all the servers in the log shipping configuration.

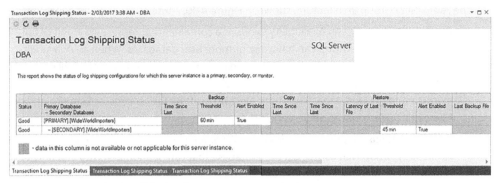

FIGURE 4-9 Transaction Log Shipping Status report on monitoring server

Skill 4.4: Implement Availability Groups

Introduced in SQL Server 2012, Availability Groups revolutionized high availability by drop-ping the reliance on specific hardware and giving you the option of scaling out your database solution. With Availability Groups, high availability is achieved by combining the capabilities of Windows with the Database Engine. Consequently, Availability Groups are hardware, shared storage, and cloud provider agnostic. Don't automatically use Availability Groups because they are "better than clustering", or because "clustering is going away." Both of those assertions are false.

This objective covers how to:

- Architect Availability Groups
- Configure Windows clustering
- Create an Availability Group
- Configure read-only routing
- Manage failover
- Create distributed Availability Group

Architect Availability Groups

Availability Groups have the most complex architecture out of all the high availability technolo-gies, so make sure you understand how they work, their limitations and how best to implement them. Do not be seduced by automatically using Availability Groups because they represent new technology. It is perfectly valid to continue using Failover Clustering as a high availability solution, because it is not going away and Microsoft continues to improve it in every release of Windows Server. An organization should have some operational maturity to successfully manage Availability Groups. Furthermore, certain edge cases may degrade performance. Ide-ally you should perform a Proof-of-Concept (POC) before deploying Availability Groups into production.

The Availability Group architecture, shown in Figure 4-10, contains the following elements:

- **Availability group** An Availability Group is a container that represents a unit of fail over. An Availability Group can have one or more user databases. When an Availability Group fails over from one replica (a SQL Server instance) to another replica, all of the databases that are part of the Availability Group fail over. This might be particularly important for multi database solutions like Microsoft Biztalk, Microsoft SharePoint, and Microsoft Team Foundation Server (TFS).

- **Primary replica** A primary replica is a SQL Server instance that is currently hosting the Availability Group that contains a user database that can be modified. You can only have one primary instance at any given point in time.

- **Secondary replica** A secondary replica is a SQL Server instance that is hosting a copy of the Availability Group. The user databases within the Availability Group hosted on a secondary replica can't be modified. Different versions of SQL Server support a different maximum number of secondary replicas:

  - SQL Server 2012 supports four secondary replicas
  - SQL Server 2014-2016 supports eight secondary replicas

- **Failover partner** A failover partner is a secondary replica that has been configured as an automatic failover destination. If something goes wrong with a primary replica the Availability Group will be automatically failed over to the secondary replica acting as a failover partner. Different versions of SQL Server support a different maximum number of failover partners:

  - SQL Server 2012-2016 supports one failover partner
  - SQL Server 2016 supports two failover partners

- **Readable secondary replica** A readable secondary replica is a secondary replica that has been configured to allow select queries to run against it. When a SQL Server instance acts as a readable secondary the database engine will automatically generate temporary statistics in the [tempdb] system database to help ensure optimal query performance. Furthermore, row-versioning, which also uses the [tempdb] system database, is used by the database engine to remove blocking contention.

- **Availability group listener** An Availability Group listener is a combination of a virtual network name (VNN) and virtual IP (VIP) address that can be used by client applications to connect to the databases hosted within the Availability Group. The VNN and its VIP is stored as a DNS entry in Active Directory (AD). An Availability Group can have multiple Availability Group listeners. The primary use of an Availability Group listener is to provide a level of abstraction from the primary replica. Applications connect to the Availability Group listener and not the current primary replica's physical server name.

- **Primary database** A primary database is a user database hosted on the primary replica of an Availability Group replica.

- **Secondary database** A secondary database is a user database hosted on any of the secondary replicas of an Availability Group.

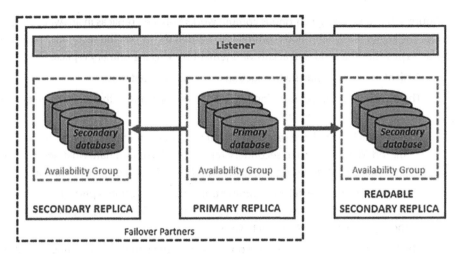

FIGURE 4-10 Availability group architecture

The primary replica can have multiple roles. Any given SQL Server instance could be both a readable secondary and a failover partner.

Availability Groups work by automatically transmitting up to 60KB transaction log buffers (in memory structures, also referred to as log blocks, that are written to first, before they are flushed to disk using the Write-Ahead-Logging (WAL) protocol) as they fill up or when a commit transaction event occurs. Consequently, the primary database and secondary database can be synchronized in real-time.

Availability groups support two different synchronization modes:

- **Synchronous commit** With synchronous commit mode the secondary replica is kept synchronized synchronously, in real-time. The secondary database is an exact binary match of the primary database. Because the databases are kept in sync, this implies a performance overhead on primary, which can effect performance; both databases wait to be in sync before the commit. Synchronous mode facilitates the failover capability of Availability Groups. Ideally, with synchronous mode you have very low network latency between the primary replica and secondary replica. If there is a network issue between the primary replica and the secondary replica the Availability Group will automatically switch over to asynchronous mode. This allows transactions to still be completed on the synchronous replica if the secondary replica is offline or there is a network issue.

- **Asynchronous commit** With asynchronous mode the secondary replica is kept synchronized asynchronously with no guarantee that the primary database and secondary database are an exact match at any given point in time and space. The primary replica transmits the log buffers as quickly as it can. There should be minimal or no impact to the transactions running in the primary database. Asynchronous mode tolerates a higher network latency, and is typically used between data centers.

Figure 4-11 shows how synchronous commit works between replicas in an Availability Group. The key to the synchronous commit is to harden the log on the secondary replica as quickly as possible and send that acknowledgement back to the primary replica.

1. A client application starts a transaction in the primary database.

2. The transaction starts consuming log blocks with operations that need to be performed to complete the transaction.
   - In the background, the secondary replica is requesting the Log Blocks to be transmitted. The primary and secondary replica need to coordinate what needs to be transmitted using the Log Sequence Number (LSN) and other information.

3. The log block becomes full or a commit transaction operation is performed. The database engine's Log Manager persists (flushes) the Log Block to the log file on the disk and to the *Log Pool* used by Availability Groups.

4. The *Log Capture* thread reads the Log Block from the Log Pool and sends it to all secondary replicas.
   - There is a separate log capture thread for each secondary replica. This allows for parallel updating of secondary replicas.
   - The log content is compressed and encrypted before being sent out on the network.
   - The log content is compressed and encrypted before it gets sent to the secondary replica.

5. The *Log Receive* thread on the secondary replica receives the Log Block.

6. The Log Receive thread writes the Log Block to the Log Cache on the secondary replica.

7. The Redo thread applies the changes from the Log Block to the database as the Log Cache is being written to:
   - There is a separate redo thread per secondary database.
   - When the Log Block fills, or a commit log operation is received, the Log Cache is hardened onto the disk where the transaction log of the secondary database is located.

8. An acknowledgement is sent by the synchronous secondary replica to the primary replica to acknowledge that the log has been hardened. This is the key step because it guarantees that no data loss is possible.

IMPORTANT **HARDENING THE LOG ON THE SECONDARY REPLICAS**
Hardening the log buffers on the secondary represents the key operation in Availability Groups as it means no data loss is possible, even if the secondary replica crashes.

---

9. If the Redo thread falls behind the rate at which the Log Blocks are being written to and flushed out of the log cache, it starts reading the log blocks from the transaction log on disk and apply them to the secondary database.

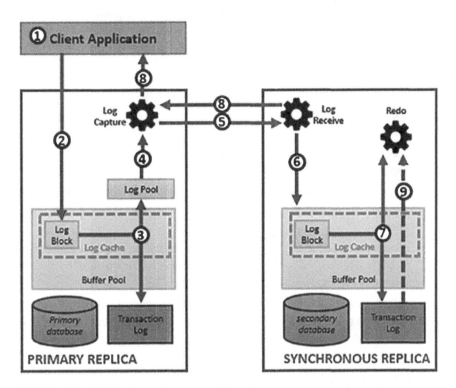

FIGURE 4-11 Availability Group Synchronous Commit

Figure 4-12 shows how asynchronous commit works between replicas in an Availability Group. The process is similar to the synchronous commit process, except that the acknowledgement message of a successful commit is sent after the log blocks are persisted locally on the Primary Replica. The key to the asynchronous commit is to minimize the impact on the Primary Replica.

1. A client application starts a transaction in the primary database.

2. The transaction starts consuming Log Blocks with operations that need to be performed to complete the transaction.

   ■ In the background, the secondary replica requests the Log Blocks to be transmitted. The primary and secondary replica needs to coordinate what needs to be transmitted using the Log Sequence Number (LSN) and other information.

3. The Log Block becomes full or a commit transaction operation is performed. The database engine's Log Manager persists (flushes) the Log Blocks to the log file on the disk and to the *Log Pool* used by Availability Groups.

4. If all of the secondary replicas are using asynchronous commit mode, the acknowledgement of a successful commit is effectively sent to the client application.

- Concurrently, the Log Capture thread reads the Log Blocks from the log pool and transmits them to the secondary replica.
- There is one Log Capture thread per replica, so all replicas are synchronized in parallel.
- The log content is compressed and encrypted before being sent on the network.

5. On the secondary replica, the Log Receive thread receives the Log Blocks from the network.

6. The Log Receive thread writes the received Log Blocks to the Log Cache on the secondary replica.

7. As the Log Blocks are written to the Log Cache, the Redo thread reads the changes and applies them to the pages of the database so that it will be in sync with the primary database.
- When the Log Cache on the secondary becomes full, or a commit transaction log record is received, the contents of the log cache is hardened onto the disk of the secondary replica.

8. If the Redo thread falls behind the rate at which the Log Blocks are being written to and flushed out of the Log Cache, it starts reading the Log Blocks from the transaction log on disk, applying them to the secondary database.

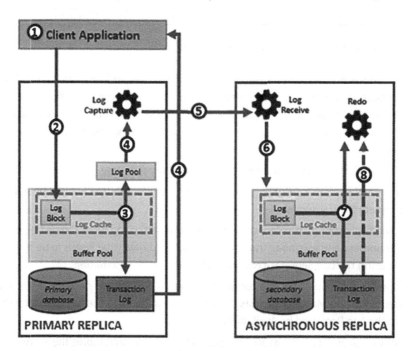

FIGURE 4-12 Availability Group Asynchronous commit

Log stream compression was introduced in SQL Server 2014 as a means of improving the performance of Availability Groups. However, the default behavior of log stream compression has changed in SQL Server 2016:

- Log stream compression is disabled by default for synchronous replicas. This helps ensures OLTP performance is not slowed down on the primary replica. Log stream compression consumes more processor resources and adds a latency.
  - You can change this default behavior by enabling trace flag 9592.
- Log stream compression is enabled by default for asynchronous replicas.
  - You can change this default behavior by enabling trace flag 1462.
- Log stream compression is disabled by default for Automatic Seeding to reduce processor usage on the primary replica.
- You can change this default behavior by enabling trace flag 9567.

The release of SQL Server 2016 brought support for Basic Availability Groups, which are designed to replace Database Mirroring in Standard Edition. You should no longer be implementing Database Mirroring on SQL Server 2016, because it has been deprecated and is scheduled to be dropped from the product in a future release. Basic Availability Groups are considered a replacement for Database Mirroring, so their limitations "mimic" the limitations of Database Mirroring.

Basic Availability Groups have a number of limitations, including:

- Limited to two replicas (primary and secondary).
- Only support one database per Availability Group.
- Can't add a replica to an existing Availability Group.
- Can't remove a replica to an existing Availability Group.
- Can't upgrade a basic Availability Group to an advanced Availability Group.
- Only supported in Standard Edition.
- No read access on secondary replica (no support for readable secondaries).
- Backups cannot be performed on the secondary replica.

The pros of using Availability Groups include:

- Support for any edition of SQL Server
  - SQL Server 2016 Standard Edition only supports Basic Availability Groups
- Provides automatic failover

> **IMPORTANT AUTOMATIC FAILOVER IN AVAILABILITY GROUPS**
>
> Availability groups will not failover with certain issues at the database level, such as a database becoming suspect due to the loss of a data file, deletion of a database, or corruption of a transaction log.

- Typically, provides faster failover when compared to failover clustering. This is because when there is a failover event in a failover cluster the SQL Server instance has to be started on the node to which you are failing over to. This can potentially take longer as the binaries have to load into memory, memory has to be allocated to the Database Engine and the databases have to be automatically recovered. Typically though, this is not an important factor in reality, as there are other considerations that are more important.

- Automatic page repair. Each replica tries to automatically recover from a page corruption incident on its local database. This is limited to certain types of errors that prevent reading a database page.

    - If the primary replica cannot read a page it broadcasts a request for a correct copy to all the secondary replicas and replaces the corrupt page from the first secondary replica that provides the correct page.

    - If a secondary replica can't read a page, it requests a correct copy of the page from the primary replica.

- Supports 2 failover partners (with the release of SQL Server 2016).

- No data loss is possible between two synchronous replicas, since data is modified on both in real-time.

- Does not rely on shared storage, which represents a single point in failure.

    - Each replica has its own separate copy of the database.

- Does not require a SAN, which can be expensive, slow, or not available in various cloud providers.

- Typically, can provide much faster performance due to the ability to use local flash storage attached to very fast buses such as PCIe. SANs cannot provide this level of storage performance.

- Scope of protection is at the database or database group level.

    - A group of databases can be protected together, which can be important for software solutions such as Microsoft SharePoint, Microsoft BizTalk, and Microsoft Team Foundation Services (TFS).

- Support for up to secondary eight replicas.

- Support for both synchronous and asynchronous modes. This flexibility is important for implementing Availability Groups within and between data centers, depending on business requirements and technical constraints.

- Read operations can be offloaded from the primary replica to readable secondaries. This allows you to scale out your database solution in certain use cases. This represents one of the major benefits of Availability Groups over other high availability solutions.

- Backup and database consistency check operations can be offloaded from the primary replica to the secondary replica.

    - Secondary replicas support performing log backups and copy-only backups of a full database, file, or filegroup.

The cons of using Availability Groups include:

- Replica databases have to use the full recovery model.
  - Some production database solutions should not use the full recovery model due to the amount of transaction log activity that they incur. An example of this includes the search and logging databases in Microsoft SharePoint.
- They are much more difficult to manage.
  - Logins are not automatically synchronized between replicas. You can take advantage of contained databases to help mitigate this.
  - SQL Server Agent jobs, alerts, and operators are not automatically synchronized between replicas.
  - Patching SQL Server instances are more complicated than failover clustering, especially where there is a lot of database modification during any potential outage window. You don't want the Availability Groups to send a queue to grow to a size such that it can never synchronize, and you will be forced to re-initialize the replica database.
- No support for providing a delay between when changes are made on the primary database and the secondary database.
- Impacting database performance in certain highly transactional workloads in OLTP database scenarios.
- Might not support synchronous mode where your network is unreliable or has a high latency, as in the case between data centers.
- Might not be supported by certain applications. Engage your application developers or vendor to determine whether there are potentially any issues.
- You are limited with what operations can be performed on a database replica. In such cases, you have to remove the database from the Availability Group first. For example, the following operations can't be performed on a database that is part of an Availability Group:
  - Detaching the database
  - Taking a database offline
- Does not fully support Microsoft Distributed Transaction Coordinator (DTC or MSDTC). This depends on the version of SQL Server that you are using and how your applications used the DTC.
  - SQL Server 2016 has *limited support for DTC*.

Use Availability Groups for the following use cases:

- Providing a high availability solution where there is no shared storage.
- Providing a high availability solution where the business does not want to use shared storage. Different reasons include:
    - Poor performance of your shared storage.
    - Expense of your shared storage.
    - Shared storage represents a single point of failure.
- Providing high availability or disaster recovery between data centers without having to rely upon geo-clustering/stretch clusters that rely on more complicated and expensive storage synchronization technology.
- Offloading reporting from the primary OLTP database. This is where Availability Groups really shine, as they represent the only scale-out technology within SQL Server. This can also be implemented between different sites if users don't require the data to be 100% up to date, as in the case of a data warehouse where they are reporting on historical data.
- Providing high availability between more than three data centers. With SQL Server 2016's ability to have two failover partners, you can effectively build a triple redundant solution.

SQL Server 2014 introduced the following enhancements to Availability Groups:

- Number of secondary replicas was increased to eight.
- Increased availability of readable secondaries, such as if the primary replica became unavailable.
- Enhanced diagnostics through new functions like is_primary_replica.
- New DMVs, such as sys.dm_io_cluster_valid_path_names.

SQL Server 2016 added the following:

- Basic Availability Groups with Standard Edition
- Distributed Availability Groups
- Domain-independent Availability Groups (Active Directory is no longer required)
- Improvements in the log transport's performance
- Load balancing between readable secondary replicas
- Support for Group Managed Service Accounts (GMSA)
- Support for two automatic failover targets

- Automatic seeding of databases through the log transport

- Limited Microsoft Distributed Transaction Coordinator (MSDTC) support

- Support for updatable columnstore indexes on secondary replicas

- Support for encrypted databases

- Support for SSIS Catalog

- Improvements in database level failover triggers

EXAM TIP

Make sure you familiarize yourself, at least at a high level, with the new Availability Groups features in SQL Server 2016. Undoubtedly, the exam writers will be seduced by writing exam questions that will test on the new SQL Server 2016 features.

Architect readable secondaries

One of the major benefits of Availability Groups is to offload your reports and read-only operations from the primary replica. By offloading read operations to these secondary replicas you remove the contention created readers blocking writers and vice versa. Your read operations are also not competing for the same processor, memory and storage resources as your OLTP operations.

Readable secondaries create temporary statistics inside the [tempdb] system database to help optimize query performance on that particular readable secondary. If you have multiple readable secondaries servicing different reports it is quite possible for each readable secondary to have a different set of temporary statistics.

Readable secondaries do not block the primary replica from continually updating the secondary database. The readable secondary replicas achieve this by taking advantage of snapshot isolation, which in turn relies on row-versioning. Row-versioning heavily relies on the [tempdb] system database, so make sure it is optimally configured on fast storage.

> ***IMPORTANT*** **READABLE SECONDARY OVERHEAD**
>
> Because readable secondaries take advantage of row-versioning inside the database engine, they introduce a 14 byte overhead on the primary database. Remember, the primary and secondary databases have to be a binary identical copy of each other. So, the secondary database can never be modified directly. Consequently, when you configure a readable secondary the primary replica starts to automatically add the 14 byte overhead to all data and index pages as they get modified. This can potentially degrade performance, and cause more page splits and fragmentation in your primary database.

Availability groups allow you to fine tune how applications will be able to connect to these read-only replicas. When you configure a replica to be a readable replica you have the following options:

- **Read only** With a read only secondary database any application will be able to connect to the secondary database.

- **Read only intent** With a read only intent secondary database only "modern" applications that support the ApplicationIntent=ReadOnly or Application Intent=ReadOnly connection string parameter will be able to connect to the secondary database.

If you have a number of readable replicas in your Availability Group you can set up routing rules for how applications will be automatically redirected to a readable secondary when they connect to the Availability Group via the listener.

SQL Server 2016 introduced the ability to configure load-balancing across a set of your readable secondary replicas.

Configure Windows clustering

Availability groups rely on the Windows Server Failover Clustering (WSFC) feature to help facilitate high availability and automatic failover. You need to install WSFC on all of the nodes of your failover cluster, and create a cluster before you can configure an Availability Group in SQL Server.

To practice setting up Availability Groups, set up the following VMs in Hyper-V:

1. A domain controller (ADDS) for the SQL.LOCAL domain

2. A SQL Server instance (REPLICA1) joined to SQL.LOCAL

3. A SQL Server instance (REPLICA2) joined to SQL.LOCAL

4. A SQL Server instance (REPLICA3) joined to SQL.LOCAL

5. A Windows file server (STORAGE) joined to the domain:

6. This server is optional

7. It is used for the backup files

8. You could use a share created on the domain controller instead, or either of the SQL Server instances

The following steps show how to install the Windows failover clustering feature

1. Log into the first node that you plan to set up as an Availability Group as a domain administrator.

2. Open up Server Manager.

3. Choose Add Roles And Features from the Manage drop-down list.

4. In the Add Roles And Features Wizard select the Next button.

5. Choose the Role-Based Or Feature-Based Installation type and click on Next.

6. Ensure that the local server is selected in the Server Pool and click on the Next button.

7. Do not install any roles. Click on the Next button in the Select Server Roles page.

8. Select the Failover Clustering check box to install the Failover Clustering feature.

9. The Add Roles And Features Wizard will, by default, want to install the Failover Clustering tools and Powershell modules. Confirm this action by clicking on the Add Features button.

10. Confirm that you are installing Failover Clustering and the related tools before clicking on the Install button to begin the installation.

11. Confirm that the installation was successful and click on the Close button to finish the installation. (A reboot might be required, in which case the wizard will prompt you to do that.)

12. Repeat the above steps on the remaining nodes that will make up the Availability Group replicas. In this chapter, we will be configuring an Availability Group across 3 replicas.

After installing the failover clustering feature on all the planned Availability Group replicas, you need to create a failover cluster.

The following steps show how to install the Windows failover clustering feature:

1. Open Failover Cluster Manager, which has now been installed on your server.

2. Click on the Create Cluster action in the right-most pane. This will start the Create Cluster Wizard.

3. Click on the Next button in the Before You Begin page of the Create Cluster Wizard.

4. Enter the name of the server that you want to add to the failover cluster and click on the Add button. The Create Cluster Wizard will validate the server's existence and add it to the bottom text box using its fully qualified domain name (FQDN).

5. Repeat Step 4 for all of the servers that you wish to add.

6. Click on the Next button as shown in Figure 4-13.

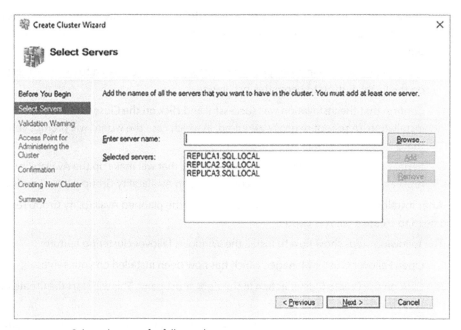

FIGURE 4-13 Selected servers for failover cluster

7. You need to validate that your Windows servers are capable of running a failover cluster that will be supported by Microsoft. Click on the Next button to run the configuration validation tests.

8. Click on the Next button in the Before You Begin page of the Validate A Configuration Wizard.

9. It is a best practice to run all of the cluster validation tests. In your case, as there is no shared stored used in Availability Groups, the validation test might generate some warnings. Click on the Next button to start the validation tests.

10. Review the servers to test and the tests that will be run. Click on the Next button to start the failover cluster validation tests. Figure 4-14 shows the cluster validation tests executing.

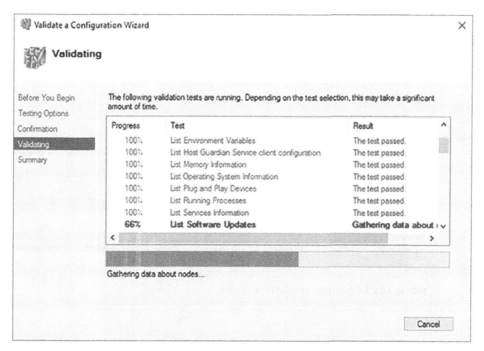

FIGURE 4-14 Cluster validation tests executing

11. As expected, the shared disk validation test has failed, because there are none. Click on the View Report button to see if there are any other problems.

12. Review the Failover Cluster Validation Report, shown in Figure 4-15. In this case the failed storage tests, shown in Figure 4-16, are fine because you will not be using shared disks. The network communication warnings, shown in Figure 4-17, are highlighting the lack of redundancy at the network level between the failover cluster's node. This should be fine. You could, for example, provide redundancy by having multiple NICs in a Windows Server NIC team.

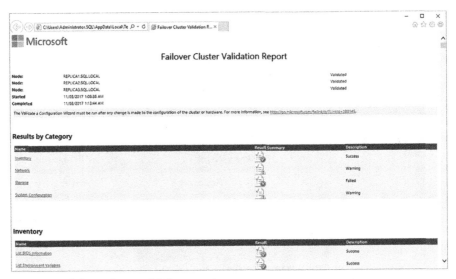

FIGURE 4-15 Failover cluster validation report

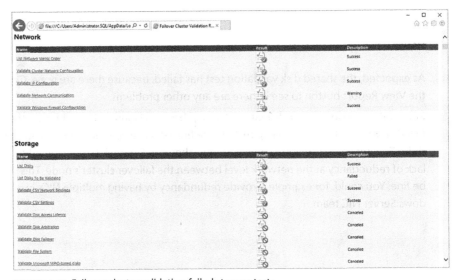

FIGURE 4-16 Failover cluster validation failed storage tests

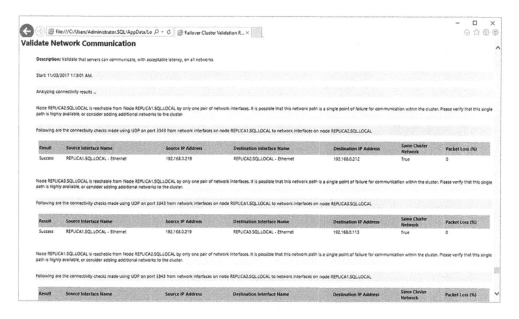

FIGURE 4-17 Failover cluster validation network communication test warnings

13. Address any errors in the Failover Cluster Validation Report, if any.

14. Re-run the Failover Cluster Validation Report, as necessary.

15. Save the Failover Cluster Validation Report. It can be re-run at any time.

16. Close the Failover Cluster Validation Report.

17. Close the Validate a Configuration Wizard by clicking on the Finish button.

18. Provide a NetBIOS name and IP address for the failover cluster, as shown in Figure 4-18.

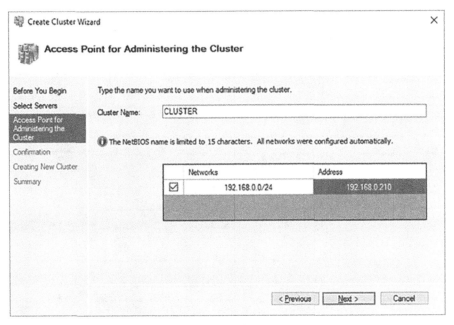

FIGURE 4-18 Availability Group Synchronous Commit

19. Uncheck the Add All Eligible Storage To The Cluster option, review and then confirm the creation of the failover cluster by clicking on the Next button.

20. Wait for the failover cluster to be created.

21. Review the failover cluster creation Summary page. Click on the View Report button to view the detailed failover cluster creation report.

22. Review and save the Create Cluster report looking out for any errors and warnings.

23. Close the Create Cluster report.

24. Click on the Finish button to close the Create Cluster Wizard

You can now leverage your failover cluster to create an Availability Group.

Create an Availability Group

To create an Availability the following prerequisites, need to have been met:

- A SQL Server instance must have been installed on all the servers that you plan to be part of an Availability Group.
- A failover cluster must have been created.
- Availability Groups must be enable for each SQL Server instance.

The following steps show how to enable Availability Groups for a SQL Server instance

1. Open up SQL Server Configuration Manager.

2. Right-click on the SQL Server instance and select Properties.

3. Select the Enable AlwaysOn Availability Group check box, as shown in Figure 4-19. Note the name of the failover cluster that you created earlier.

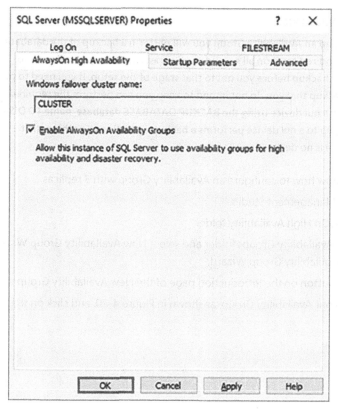

FIGURE 4-19 Enabling Availability Group at the SQL Server instance level

4. Click on the OK button to close the properties dialog box

5. Click on the OK button to close the warning. Note that SQL Server Configuration Manager does not automatically restart SQL Server whenever it is required for a change to take effect.

6. Right-click on the SQL Server instance and restart SQL Server.

You can now install an Availability Group within your SQL Server instances. To be able to add a database to an Availability Group the following pre-requisites must be met:

■ The database must be using full recovery model

■ A full database backup must have been performed, so that it's transaction log is not in auto-truncate mode.

■ The database cannot be in read-only mode

■ The database cannot be in single-user mode

■ The database cannot be in auto-close mode

■ The database cannot be part of an existing Availability Group. Databases can only belong to a single Availability Group at any point in time and space.

TIP **BACKING UP TO NUL DEVICE**

Typically, when setting up an Availability Group you will perform a backup of the database on the primary server and restore it on all secondary replicas. However, you still need to perform a full database backup before you get to that stage of the setup. If you need to perform a full database backup that you do not intend to keep you can perform the required full database backup to a nul device using the BACKUP DATABASE database_name TO DISK = 'nul' syntax. Backing up to a nul device performs a backup operation to nothing, so it is incredibly quick as there is no destination I/O.

The following steps show how to configure an Availability Group with 3 replicas.

1. Open SQL Server Management Studio.
2. Expand the AlwaysOn High Availability folder
3. Right-click on the Availability Groups folder and select New Availability Group Wizard to start the New Availability Group Wizard.
4. Click on the Next button on the Introduction page of the New Availability Group wizard.
5. Enter a name for your Availability Group, as shown in Figure 4-20, and click on the Next button.

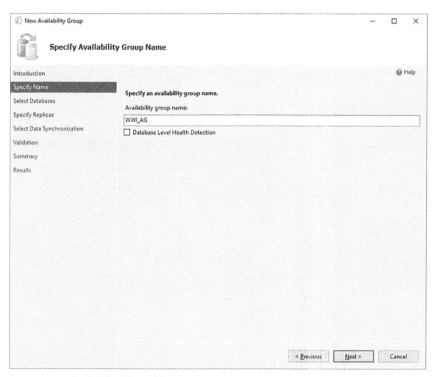

FIGURE 4-20 Availability Group Name

6. Select the Database Level Health Detection if you want the Availability Group to auto-matically failover if the Database Engine notices that any database within the Availability Group is no longer online. Although not fool-proof this new feature in SQL Server 2016 is worth enabling for Availability Groups that have multiple databases that represent a multi-database solution.

7. The Select Databases page allows you to select which databases will be part of the Avail-ability Group. Only databases that meet the pre-requisites will be selectable. Select your database, as shown in Figure 4-21 and click on the Next button.

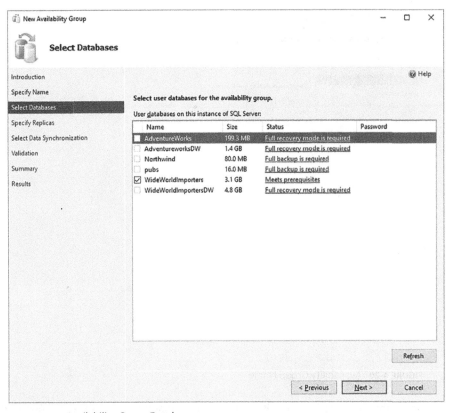

FIGURE 4-21 Availability Group Databases

8. The Specify Replicas page allows you to select up to 8 replicas for your Availability Group. You can select up to 3 replicas that will provide automatic failover, if required. You are further limited to only 3 synchronous replicas. Click on the Add Replica... button to add a secondary replica.

9. Connect to the replica by providing the server name and authentication details.

10. Repeat the above step for any other replicas that you wish to add to the Availability Group.

11. Check the Automatic Failover (Up to 3) check box for all your failover partner replicas, as shown in Figure 4-68. Notice how the replicas are automatically configured to use synchronous mode.

12. Select your readable secondaries, as shown in Figure 4-22. Readable secondaries have the following options:

- **Yes** When in a secondary role, allow all connections from all applications to access this secondary in a readable fashion.

- **Read-only intent**   When in a secondary role, only allow connections from "modern" applications that support the ApplicationIntent=ReadOnly or Application Intent=ReadOnly connection string parameter.

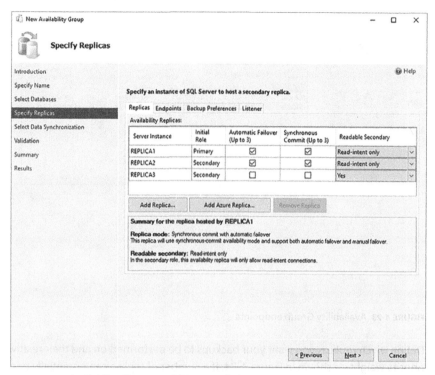

FIGURE 4-22 Availability Group readable secondaries

13. Click on the Next button.
14. Review the endpoint configuration for your replicas, as shown in Figure 4-23. Note that by default the endpoints will be encrypted. The default endpoints are fine in most cases. You will need to change the endpoints if your replicas are hosted on the same Window Operating System Environment (OSE). Click on the Next button when you are done.

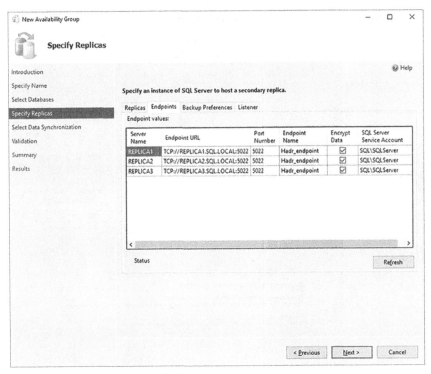

FIGURE 4-23 Availability Group endpoints

15. Define which replicas you want your backups to be performed on and their relative priority weight, as shown in Figure 4-24. If a number of replica can potentially perform the automated backup based on your preferences, the one with the highest priority will perform the backup. With Availability Groups backups can be performed on different replicas depending on where you want them performed. You backup preference choices are:

- **Prefer Secondary** Automated backups will occur on a secondary replica. If no secondary replica is available, backups will be performed on the primary replica.

- **Secondary Only** Automated backups for this Availability Group must occur on a secondary replica.

- **Primary Only** Automated backups for this Availability Group must occur on a primary replica. Don't forget that non copy-only full database backups can only be performed on the primary replica.

- **Any Replica** Automated backups for this Availability Group can occur on any replica.

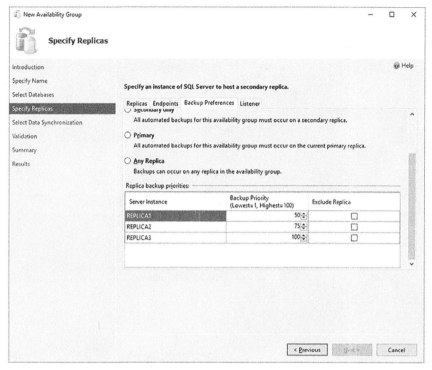

FIGURE 4-24 Availability Group backup preferences

16. Click on the Listener tab.

17. Configure the listener by providing the following information, as shown in Figure 4-25, and then click on the Next button:

- DNS name
- IP address
- Port number

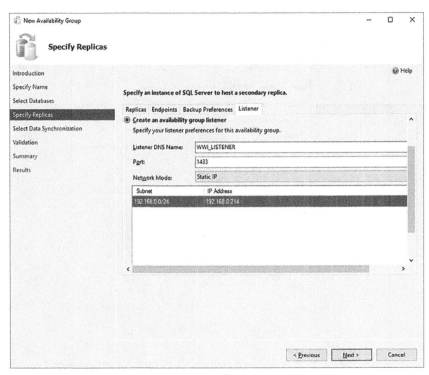

FIGURE 4-25 Availability Group listener configuration

18. The Create New Availability Group Wizard by default will synchronize the database from the primary replica to all of the secondary replicas through backup and restore operations. Provide the shared network location that will be used to store the database backups, as shown in Figure 4-26. Make sure that all replicas have access to this location.

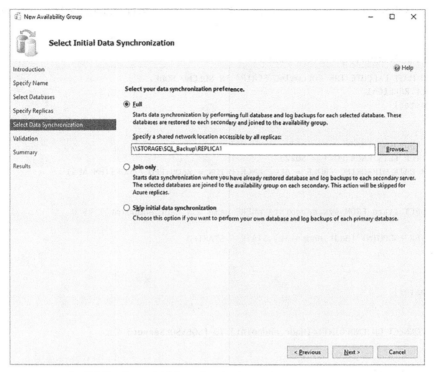

FIGURE 4-26 Availability Group initial synchronization options

---

NOTE **DIRECT SEEDING**

With the release of SQL Server 2016 you have the option of creating the replica of the primary database on the secondary replicas through the endpoints created by the Availability Group, instead of through backup and restore operations. This is done through the `SEEDING_MODE = AUTOMATIC` option of the **CREATE AVAILABILITY GROUP** statement. Direct seeding will not be as efficient as the backup and restore operations, and is designed for specific use cases where the backup/restore process will not work.

---

19. Click on the Next button when the Create New Availability Group Wizard finishes validating the Availability Group creation.

20. Review the Availability Group creation summary to make sure that all of the configuration details are correct.

21. Click on the Script drop down list and save the Availability Group creation script for review and change management reasons.

22. Click on the Finish button to start the Availability Group creation.

23. This will take some time.

24. Confirm that the Availability Group was successfully created.

Listing 4-3 shows the Transact-SQL script that was generated to configure the Log Shipping solution.

LISTING 4-3 Availability group configuration

```
--- YOU MUST EXECUTE THE FOLLOWING SCRIPT IN SQLCMD MODE.
:Connect REPLICA1
USE [master]
GO

CREATE ENDPOINT [Hadr_endpoint]
    AS TCP (LISTENER_PORT = 5022)
    FOR DATA_MIRRORING (ROLE = ALL, ENCRYPTION = REQUIRED ALGORITHM AES)
GO

IF (SELECT state FROM sys.endpoints WHERE name = N'Hadr_endpoint') <> 0
BEGIN
    ALTER ENDPOINT [Hadr_endpoint] STATE = STARTED
END
GO

use [master]
GO

GRANT CONNECT ON ENDPOINT::[Hadr_endpoint] TO [SQL\SQLServer]
GO

:Connect REPLICA1
IF EXISTS(SELECT * FROM sys.server_event_sessions WHERE name='AlwaysOn_health')
BEGIN
  ALTER EVENT SESSION [AlwaysOn_health] ON SERVER WITH (STARTUP_STATE=ON);
END
IF NOT EXISTS(SELECT * FROM sys.dm_xe_sessions WHERE name='AlwaysOn_health')
BEGIN
  ALTER EVENT SESSION [AlwaysOn_health] ON SERVER STATE=START;
END
GO

:Connect REPLICA2
USE [master]
GO

CREATE ENDPOINT [Hadr_endpoint]
    AS TCP (LISTENER_PORT = 5022)
    FOR DATA_MIRRORING (ROLE = ALL, ENCRYPTION = REQUIRED ALGORITHM AES)
GO

IF (SELECT state FROM sys.endpoints WHERE name = N'Hadr_endpoint') <> 0
BEGIN
    ALTER ENDPOINT [Hadr_endpoint] STATE = STARTED
END
GO

use [master]
```

```
GO

GRANT CONNECT ON ENDPOINT::[Hadr_endpoint] TO [SQL\SQLServer]
GO


:Connect REPLICA2
IF EXISTS(SELECT * FROM sys.server_event_sessions WHERE name='AlwaysOn_health')
BEGIN
  ALTER EVENT SESSION [AlwaysOn_health] ON SERVER WITH (STARTUP_STATE=ON);
END
IF NOT EXISTS(SELECT * FROM sys.dm_xe_sessions WHERE name='AlwaysOn_health')
BEGIN
  ALTER EVENT SESSION [AlwaysOn_health] ON SERVER STATE=START;
END
GO


:Connect REPLICA3
USE [master]
GO


CREATE ENDPOINT [Hadr_endpoint]
    AS TCP (LISTENER_PORT = 5022)
    FOR DATA_MIRRORING (ROLE = ALL, ENCRYPTION = REQUIRED ALGORITHM AES)
GO


IF (SELECT state FROM sys.endpoints WHERE name = N'Hadr_endpoint') <> 0
BEGIN
    ALTER ENDPOINT [Hadr_endpoint] STATE = STARTED
END
GO


use [master]
GO


GRANT CONNECT ON ENDPOINT::[Hadr_endpoint] TO [SQL\SQLServer]
GO


:Connect REPLICA3

IF EXISTS(SELECT * FROM sys.server_event_sessions WHERE name='AlwaysOn_health')
BEGIN
  ALTER EVENT SESSION [AlwaysOn_health] ON SERVER WITH (STARTUP_STATE=ON);
END
IF NOT EXISTS(SELECT * FROM sys.dm_xe_sessions WHERE name='AlwaysOn_health')
BEGIN
  ALTER EVENT SESSION [AlwaysOn_health] ON SERVER STATE=START;
END
GO


:Connect REPLICA1
USE [master]
GO


CREATE AVAILABILITY GROUP [WWI_AG]
WITH (AUTOMATED_BACKUP_PREFERENCE = SECONDARY,
```

```
      DB_FAILOVER = OFF,
      DTC_SUPPORT = NONE)
      FOR DATABASE [WideWorldImporters]
      REPLICA ON N'REPLICA1' WITH (ENDPOINT_URL = N'TCP://REPLICA1.SQL.LOCAL:5022', FAILOVER_
      MODE = AUTOMATIC, AVAILABILITY_MODE = SYNCHRONOUS_COMMIT, BACKUP_PRIORITY = 50,
      SECONDARY_ROLE(ALLOW_CONNECTIONS = READ_ONLY)),
          N'REPLICA2' WITH (ENDPOINT_URL = N'TCP://REPLICA2.SQL.LOCAL:5022', FAILOVER_MODE
      = AUTOMATIC, AVAILABILITY_MODE = SYNCHRONOUS_COMMIT, BACKUP_PRIORITY = 75, SECONDARY_
      ROLE(ALLOW_CONNECTIONS = READ_ONLY)),
          N'REPLICA3' WITH (ENDPOINT_URL = N'TCP://REPLICA3.SQL.LOCAL:5022', FAILOVER_MODE
      = MANUAL, AVAILABILITY_MODE = ASYNCHRONOUS_COMMIT, BACKUP_PRIORITY = 100, SECONDARY_
      ROLE(ALLOW_CONNECTIONS = ALL));
      GO

      :Connect REPLICA1
      USE [master]
      GO

      ALTER AVAILABILITY GROUP [WWI_AG]
      ADD LISTENER N'WWI_LISTENER' (
      WITH IP
      ((N'192.168.0.214', N'255.255.255.0')
      )
      , PORT=1433);
      GO

      :Connect REPLICA2
      ALTER AVAILABILITY GROUP [WWI_AG] JOIN;
      GO

      :Connect REPLICA3
      ALTER AVAILABILITY GROUP [WWI_AG] JOIN;
      GO

      :Connect REPLICA1
      BACKUP DATABASE [WideWorldImporters] TO  DISK = N'\\STORAGE\SQL_Backup\REPLICA1\
      WideWorldImporters.bak' WITH  COPY_ONLY, FORMAT, INIT, SKIP, REWIND, NOUNLOAD,
      COMPRESSION,  STATS = 5
      GO

      :Connect REPLICA2
      RESTORE DATABASE [WideWorldImporters] FROM  DISK = N'\\STORAGE\SQL_Backup\REPLICA1\
      WideWorldImporters.bak' WITH  NORECOVERY, NOUNLOAD,  STATS = 5
      GO

      :Connect REPLICA3
      RESTORE DATABASE [WideWorldImporters] FROM  DISK = N'\\STORAGE\SQL_Backup\REPLICA1\
      WideWorldImporters.bak' WITH  NORECOVERY, NOUNLOAD,  STATS = 5
      GO

      :Connect REPLICA1
      BACKUP LOG [WideWorldImporters] TO  DISK = N'\\STORAGE\SQL_Backup\REPLICA1\
      WideWorldImporters_20170310165240.trn' WITH NOFORMAT, NOINIT, NOSKIP, REWIND, NOUNLOAD,
      COMPRESSION,  STATS = 5
```

```
GO

:Connect REPLICA2
RESTORE LOG [WideWorldImporters] FROM  DISK = N'\\STORAGE\SQL_Backup\REPLICA1\
WideWorldImporters_20170310165240.trn' WITH  NORECOVERY,  NOUNLOAD,  STATS = 5
GO

:Connect REPLICA2
-- Wait for the replica to start communicating
begin try
declare @conn bit
declare @count int
declare @replica_id uniqueidentifier
declare @group_id uniqueidentifier
set @conn = 0
set @count = 30 -- wait for 5 minutes

if (serverproperty('IsHadrEnabled') = 1)
    and (isnull((select member_state from master.sys.dm_hadr_cluster_members where
upper(member_name COLLATE Latin1_General_CI_AS) = upper(cast(serverproperty('ComputerNam
ePhysicalNetBIOS') as nvarchar(256)) COLLATE Latin1_General_CI_AS)), 0) <> 0)
    and (isnull((select state from master.sys.database_mirroring_endpoints), 1) = 0)
begin
    select @group_id = ags.group_id from master.sys.availability_groups as ags where
name = N'WWI_AG'
    select @replica_id = replicas.replica_id from master.sys.availability_replicas
as replicas where upper(replicas.replica_server_name COLLATE Latin1_General_CI_AS) =
upper(@@SERVERNAME COLLATE Latin1_General_CI_AS) and group_id = @group_id
    while @conn <> 1 and @count > 0
    begin
        set @conn = isnull((select connected_state from master.sys.dm_hadr_availability_
replica_states as states where states.replica_id = @replica_id), 1)
        if @conn = 1
        begin
            -- exit loop when the replica is connected, or if the query cannot find the
replica status
            break
        end
        waitfor delay '00:00:10'
        set @count = @count - 1
    end
end
end try
begin catch
    -- If the wait loop fails, do not stop execution of the alter database statement
end catch
ALTER DATABASE [WideWorldImporters] SET HADR AVAILABILITY GROUP = [WWI_AG];
GO

:Connect REPLICA3
RESTORE LOG [WideWorldImporters] FROM  DISK = N'\\STORAGE\SQL_Backup\REPLICA1\
WideWorldImporters_20170310165240.trn' WITH  NORECOVERY,  NOUNLOAD,  STATS = 5
GO

:Connect REPLICA3
```

```
-- Wait for the replica to start communicating
begin try
declare @conn bit
declare @count int
declare @replica_id uniqueidentifier
declare @group_id uniqueidentifier
set @conn = 0
set @count = 30 -- wait for 5 minutes

if (serverproperty('IsHadrEnabled') = 1)
    and (isnull((select member_state from master.sys.dm_hadr_cluster_members where
upper(member_name COLLATE Latin1_General_CI_AS) = upper(cast(serverproperty('ComputerNam
ePhysicalNetBIOS') as nvarchar(256)) COLLATE Latin1_General_CI_AS)), 0) <> 0)
    and (isnull((select state from master.sys.database_mirroring_endpoints), 1) = 0)
begin
    select @group_id = ags.group_id from master.sys.availability_groups as ags where
name = N'WWI_AG'
    select @replica_id = replicas.replica_id from master.sys.availability_replicas
as replicas where upper(replicas.replica_server_name COLLATE Latin1_General_CI_AS) =
upper(@@SERVERNAME COLLATE Latin1_General_CI_AS) and group_id = @group_id
    while @conn <> 1 and @count > 0
    begin
        set @conn = isnull((select connected_state from master.sys.dm_hadr_availability_
replica_states as states where states.replica_id = @replica_id), 1)
        if @conn = 1
        begin
            -- exit loop when the replica is connected, or if the query cannot find the
replica status
            break
        end
        waitfor delay '00:00:10'
        set @count = @count - 1
    end
end
end try
begin catch
    -- If the wait loop fails, do not stop execution of the alter database statement
end catch
ALTER DATABASE [WideWorldImporters] SET HADR AVAILABILITY GROUP = [WWI_AG];
GO
```

EXAM TIP

Make sure you familiarize yourself with the key statements in the Availability Group creation
script for the exam.

Configure Quorum Configuration for Availability Group

One of the more important aspects of configuring an Availability Group correctly is to configure the correct quorum configuration. The default Availability Group installation might not configure the optimal quorum configuration. The quorum configuration and forming quorum is the responsible of the WSFC. Consequently, you need to control that at the WSFC level.

Quorum and quorum configuration will be discussed later in this chapter when it covers failover clustering.

Let's assume that the Availability Group with three replicas that we have configured above have the following topology:

- REPLICA1 and REPLICA2 are in one data center
- REPLICA3 is in a separate data center

Let's also assume that REPLICA3 is no longer a failover partner.

In this scenario, you do not want REPLICA3 to participate in the quorum, as it is in a separate data center. There will be a greater latency between it and the other 2 replicas. Likewise, if the network link fails between the data centers it will not be able to communicate with the other replicas. In the worst-case scenario, your entire failover cluster could shut down to protect itself. You do not want REPLICA3 to have a vote.

You are better off by creating an additional witness in the data center where REPLICA1 and REPLICA2 are located.

The following steps show how to change the quorum configuration for your Availability Group:

1. Open SQL Server Management Studio.
2. Connect to your primary replica.
3. Expand the AlwaysOn High Availability folder.
4. Right-click on your Availability Group and select Show Dashboard.
5. Click on the View Cluster Quorum Information link in the top right hand corner of the Availability Group dashboard.
6. Determine the current quorum configuration, as shown in Figure 4-27 and click on the Close button. Initially the Availability Group is using a Node Majority quorum model and replicas REPLICA1, REPLICA2, REPLICA3 all have a vote. You need to change this so that REPLICA3 does not have a vote in the quorum.

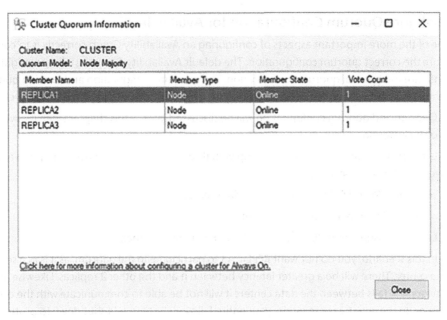

FIGURE 4-27 Initial Availability Group quorum configuration

7. Close the Cluster Quorum Information dialog box.

8. Open Failover Cluster Manager.

9. Connect to the cluster that is being used by the Availability Group.

10. Right click on your cluster, select the More Actions option and then the Configure Cluster Quorum Settings option to start the Configure Cluster Quorum Wizard.

11. Read the welcome page of the Configure Cluster Quorum Wizard and click on the Next button.

12. On the Select Quorum Configuration Option page select the Advanced Quorum configuration option and click on the Next button.

13. On the Select Voting Configuration page select the Select Nodes option, then uncheck REPLICA3 as a voting node, before clicking on the Next button, as shown in Figure 4-28.

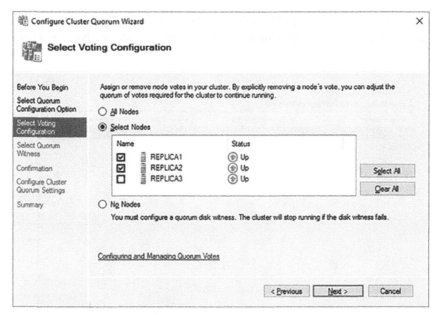

FIGURE 4-28 Select Voting Configuration

14. On the Select Quorum Witness page select the Configure A File Share Witness option and click on the Next button. In this case, you do not have an odd number of replicas in the same data center. Consequently, you need to add a witness to avoid the "split brain" problem, where a cluster cannot form quorum and effectively shuts down.

15. Click on the Browse button to create a file share witness.

16. In the Browse For Shared Folders dialog box type in the name of your file share server and click on the Show Shared Folders button to connect to the file share server and display its shared folders.

17. There are no suitable folders, so click on the New Shared folder button to create a new file share with the appropriate permissions.

18. Configure the following properties and click on the OK button:
    - Share name
    - Local path of shared folder
    - Shared folder permissions

19. Confirm that the file share path is correct and click on the Next button.

20. Review the new quorum settings are correct before clicking on the Next button.

21. Ensure that the new quorum settings have been configured correctly before clicking on the Finish button.

22. Switch back to SQL Server Management Studio and the Availability Group dashboard

23. Click on the View Cluster Quorum Information link in the top right hand corner of the Availability Group dashboard again to show the new quorum model, as shown in Figure 4-29.

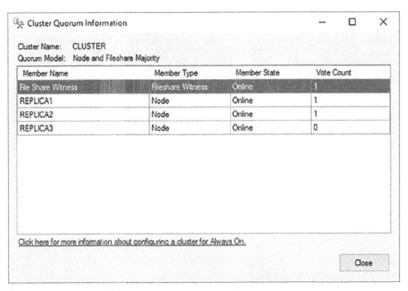

Member Name	Member Type	Member State	Vote Count
File Share Witness	Fileshare Witness	Online	1
REPLICA1	Node	Online	1
REPLICA2	Node	Online	1
REPLICA3	Node	Online	0

FIGURE 4-29 New Availability Group quorum configuration

24. Confirm that the new quorum model is a Node and Fileshare majority.

25. Confirm that REPLICA3 no longer has a vote.

EXAM TIP

Make sure you understand the different quorum models and which models to use for Availability Groups versus failover clusters for the exam.

Configure read-only routing

One of the major benefits of Availability Groups is their ability to scale out read operations or reporting to readable secondaries. Using read-only routing Availability Groups provides the capability of routing connection requests from applications automatically to a readable secondary.

The following conditions must be true for read-only routing to work:

- The application must connect to the listener and not to the replica directly.
- The application must connect with an explicit read-only request in the connection string.
- A readable secondary replica must exist in the Availability Group.
- Read-only routing rules have been defined by the database administrator.

To define the read-only routing rules you need to configure the following:

- **Read-only Routing URL**   The read-only routing URL is used for routing read-intent connection requests to a specific readable secondary replica. It needs to be specified on each replica that will potentially be running as a readable secondary. It takes effect only when the replica is running in the secondary role.

- **Read-only Routing List**   The read-only routing list. It dictates the order in which your read-only connection request will be routed. It takes effect only when a replica is running in the primary role.

Listing 4-4 shows you how to set up the read-only routing URLs

LISTING 4-4 Read-only routing URL

```
-- Execute the following statements at the Primary to configure Log Shipping
ALTER AVAILABILITY GROUP [WWI_AG]
MODIFY REPLICA ON
N'REPLICA1' WITH
(SECONDARY_ROLE (READ_ONLY_ROUTING_URL = N'TCP://REPLICA1.SQL.LOCAL:1433'));
GO

ALTER AVAILABILITY GROUP [WWI_AG]
MODIFY REPLICA ON
N'REPLICA2' WITH
(SECONDARY_ROLE (READ_ONLY_ROUTING_URL = N'TCP://REPLICA2.SQL.LOCAL:1433'));
GO

ALTER AVAILABILITY GROUP [WWI_AG]
MODIFY REPLICA ON
N'REPLICA3' WITH
(SECONDARY_ROLE (READ_ONLY_ROUTING_URL = N'TCP://REPLICA3.SQL.LOCAL:1433'));
GO
```

Listing 4-5 shows you how to set up the read-only routing list.

LISTING 4-5 Read-only routing list

```
-- Execute the following statements at the Primary to configure Log Shipping
ALTER AVAILABILITY GROUP [WWI_AG]
MODIFY REPLICA ON
N'REPLICA1' WITH
(PRIMARY_ROLE (READ_ONLY_ROUTING_LIST=(N'REPLICA2',N'REPLICA3')));
GO

ALTER AVAILABILITY GROUP [WWI_AG]
MODIFY REPLICA ON
N'REPLICA2' WITH
(PRIMARY_ROLE (READ_ONLY_ROUTING_LIST=(N'REPLICA1',N'REPLICA3')));
GO

ALTER AVAILABILITY GROUP [WWI_AG]
MODIFY REPLICA ON
N'REPLICA3' WITH
(PRIMARY_ROLE (READ_ONLY_ROUTING_LIST=(N'REPLICA1',N'REPLICA2')));
```

The following steps show you how to test whether read-only routing works:

1. Open SQL Server Management Studio.

2. Click on the Connect option in Object Explorer and choose Database Engine.

3. In the Connect To Server dialog box provide the listener name in the Server Name drop down list and click on the Options button.

4. Click on the Additional Connection Properties tab.

5. Provide the name of the Availability Group database and the read-only intention connection string parameters, as shown in Figure 4-30.

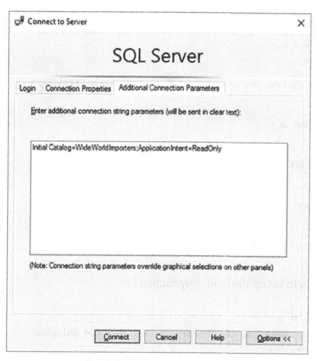

FIGURE 4-30 Read-only intention to connect to listener

***IMPORTANT* INITIAL CATALOG**

It is important to specify an Availability Group database in the Initial Catalog connection string setting for read-only routing to work. Otherwise you will connect to your default database in the primary replica. Unless of course it also happens to be a database in the Availability Group that you are intending to connect to, in which case it will work.

---

6. Click on the listener in Object Explorer.

7. Click on New Query in the tool bar to connect to your listener.

8. Execute the SELECT @@SERVERNAME query. The server name returned should be a secondary replica's and not the primary replica's.

9. Attempt to update a table in the database. You should get an error informing you that you cannot perform this DML operation in a read-only database.

SQL Server 2016 introduced the ability to load balance the read-only replicas. Load balancing uses a round-robin algorithm. To load balance between a set of read-only replica simply enclose the set of read-only replicas with parentheses in the read-only routing list option, as shown in Listing 4-6.

LISTING 4-6 Configure load-balancing across read-only replicas

```
READ_ONLY_ROUTING_LIST = (('REPLICA1','REPLICA2','REPLICA3'), 'REPLICA4', 'REPLICA5')
```

In this example the read-only connection requests will be load balanced between REPLICA1, REPLICA2 and REPLICA3. If none of these replicas are available, REPLICA4 will be used. If it fails, REPLICA5 will be used.

Monitor Availability Groups

Availability Groups support a dashboard that you can use to see the state of your Availability Groups and perform certain tasks, such performing a failover. It shows important performance indicators that will help you to make better operational decisions. Some of the key metrics that it shows includes:

- Synchronization mode and state
- Estimate Data Loss
- Estimated Recovery Time
- Time to restore log

View the Availability Group dashboard by right-clicking on your Availability Group and choosing Show Dashboard.

Figure 4-31 shows the state of the Availability Group from the primary replica. You can view at key metrics such as the send and redo queues, and how long it will take for any replica that is not synchronized to catch up.

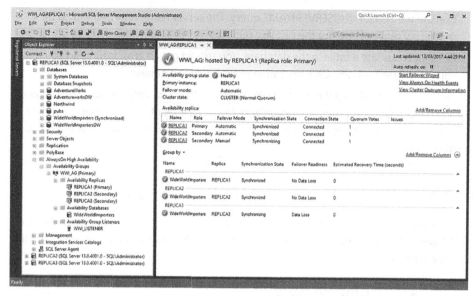

FIGURE 4-31 Availability Group dashboard at the primary replica

You can add the following metrics to the dashboard by right clicking on the column headings and selecting them:

- Issues
- Availability Mode
- Primary Connection Mode
- Secondary Connection Mode
- Connection State
- Operational State
- Last Connect Error No.
- Last Connection Error Description
- Last Connection Error Timestamp
- Quorum Votes
- Member State

You can click on the synchronous secondary replica to see its state within the Availability Group. It will not know about the state of the other replicas. It will be synchronized and ready to fall over. No data loss is possible. In the case of the asynchronous secondary replica it will indicate that data loss is possible. This is always the case with asynchronous replicas.

Manage failover

A failover is a process where the primary replica gives up its role to a failover partner. With Availability Groups the failover is at the Availability Group level. During a "normal" failover no data loss will occur. However, any transactions in flight will be lost and have to be rolled back.

During the failover process, the failover target needs to recover its instance of the databases and bring them online as the new primary databases. This process in certain cases can take a long time.

There are three types of failover:

- **Automatic failover** Automatic failover will occur when the WSFC detects that something has failed or the health of either the Availability Group or database has deteriorated sufficiently, based on the Availability Groups configuration. No data loss is possible.

- **Manual failover** Manual failover occurs when you explicitly perform a failover because you need perform some administrative task, such as patching the Windows operating system or SQL Server. You also fail over an Availability Group if you want it to run on another server's hardware resources. With manual failover no data loss is possible.

- **Forced failover** The RPO defines the maximum acceptable amount of data loss following a disaster incident. With forced failover data loss is possible.

Table 4-3 shows the failover types supported, depending on what synchronization mode the replica is using.

TABLE 4-3 Availability Group Failover options

Failover	Asynchronous MOde	Synchronous Mode	Synchronous Mode with automatic failvover
Automatic Failover	No	No	Yes
Manual Failover	No	Yes	Yes
Forced Failover	Yes	Yes	Yes (same as manual failover)

The following steps show you how to perform a manual failover.

1. Open SQL Server Management Studio.
2. Connect to your primary replica.
3. Expand the AlwaysOn High Availability folder.
4. Right-click on your Availability Group and select Failover to start the Fail Over Availability Group Wizard.
5. Click on the Next button on the Introduction page.
6. Review all of the information in the Select New Primary Replica page to ensure that you are not going to lose data due to failover. Read the warnings. Select the new primary replica, as shown in Figure 4-32, and click on the Next button.

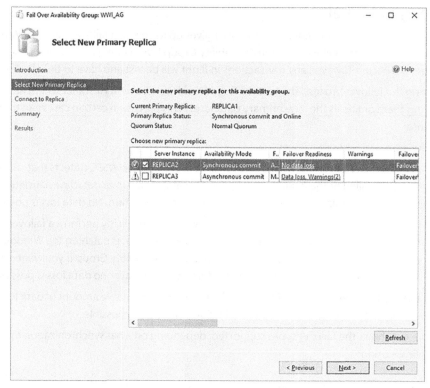

FIGURE 4-32 Specify to failover target

7. Connect to failover target replica and click on the Next button.

8. Review the choices made in the Summary page and click on the Finish button to initiate the fail over.

9. Confirm that the failover has been successful and click on the Close button.

Listing 4-7 shows you how to perform an equivalent failover in Transact-SQL. Note that it has to be performed from the failover target replica, not the primary replica.

LISTING 4-7 Manual fail over with no data loss

```
--- YOU MUST EXECUTE THE FOLLOWING SCRIPT IN SQLCMD MODE.

:Connect REPLICA2

ALTER AVAILABILITY GROUP [WWI_AG] FAILOVER;

GO
```

The following steps show you how to perform a forced failover.

1. Open SQL Server Management Studio.

2. Connect to your primary replica.

3. Expand the AlwaysOn High Availability folder.

4. Right-click on your Availability Group and select Failover to start the Fail Over Availability Group Wizard.

5. Click on the Next button on the Introduction page.

6. This time, in the Select New Primary Replica page, select the asynchronous commit replica as a failover target. The wizard shows that the asynchronous secondary replica is using asynchronous commit and that only fail over with data loss is supported. Furthermore, there are three warnings.

7. Click on the warning link and read the 3 warnings, shown in Figure 4-33.

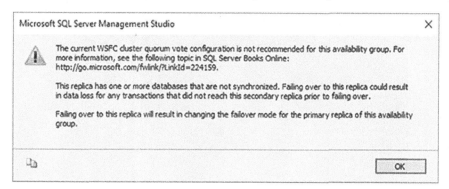

FIGURE 4-33 Fail over warnings

8. Click on the Close button to close the warning dialog box.

9. Click on the Next button in the Select New Primary Replica screen.

10. The next screen in the wizard again warns you about the potential data loss. Select the Click Here To Confirm Failover With Potential Data Loss check box and click on the Next button, as shown in Figure 4-34.

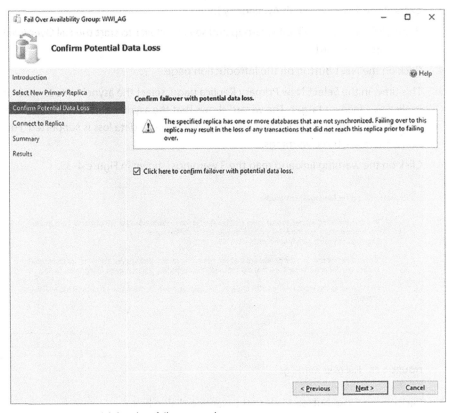

FIGURE 4-34 Potential data loss failover warnings

11. Connect to the asynchronous target in the Connect To Replica screen and click on the Next button.

12. Review the choices made and generate the failover script before clicking on the Finish button to initiate the fail over.

13. Confirm that the failover has been successful and click on the Close button.

14. Confirm on the Action Require link and read the warning, which is identical to the first error in in Figure 4-34 before closing the wizard.

Listing 4-8 shows you how to perform an equivalent forced failover in Transact-SQL.

LISTING 4-8 Forced failover with potential data loss

```
--- YOU MUST EXECUTE THE FOLLOWING SCRIPT IN SQLCMD MODE.
:Connect REPLICA3

ALTER AVAILABILITY GROUP [WWI_AG] FORCE_FAILOVER_ALLOW_DATA_LOSS;
GO
```

Create Distributed Availability Group

Distributed Availability Groups (DAGs) were added in SQL Server 2016 for a number of specific use cases. To best understand where you can use Distributed Availability Groups, it is best to start off with a diagram of what they look like.

Figure 4-35 show the architecture of a Distributed Availability Group. The DAG has the following characteristics:

- The operating system environment (OSE) for the primary WSFC (WSFC1) can be different from the secondary WSFC (WSFC2).
- The health of primary WSFC (WSFC1) is not affected by the health of the secondary WSFC (WSFC2).
  - Each WSFC is responsible for maintaining its own quorum mode.
  - Each WSFC is responsible for its own node voting configuration.
- The data is sent only once between the primary Availability Group (AG1) and the secondary Availability Group (AG2).
  - This is one of the primary benefits of DAGs, especially across WAN links, since otherwise the primary replica in AG1 would have to send the same log records across the network to the three replicas in the secondary Availability Group (AG2) .
- All of the replicas in the secondary Availability Group (AG2) are read-only.
- Automatic failover to the secondary Availability Group (AG2) is not supported.

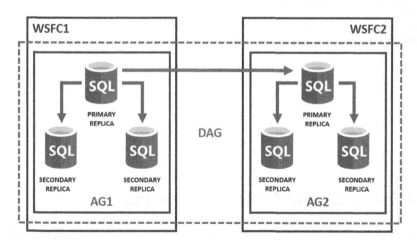

FIGURE 4-35 Distributed Availability Group

To create a distributed Availability Group, perform the following steps:

1. Create an Availability Group for each WSFC.
2. Create a listener for each Availability Group.

3. Create the DAG on the primary Availability Group using the DISTRIBUTED option as shown in Listing 4-9. Note, we will use direct seeding in this example.

LISTING 4-9 Creating an distributed Availability Group on the primary Availability Group

```
CREATE AVAILABILITY GROUP [DAG]
    WITH (DISTRIBUTED)
    AVAILABILITY GROUP ON
      'AG1' WITH (
        LISTENER_URL = 'TCP://AG1_LISTENER:5022',
                AVAILABILITY_MODE = ASYNCHRONOUS_COMMIT,
        FAILOVER_MODE = MANUAL,
        SEEDING_MODE = AUTOMATIC
      ),
      'AG2' WITH (
        LISTENER_URL = 'TCP://AG2-LISTENER:5022',
        AVAILABILITY_MODE = ASYNCHRONOUS_COMMIT,
        FAILOVER_MODE = MANUAL,
        SEEDING_MODE = AUTOMATIC
      );
GO
```

4. Join the DAG from the secondary Availability Group, as shown in Listing 4-10.

LISTING 4-10 Joining a distributed Availability Group from the secondary Availability Group

```
ALTER AVAILABILITY GROUP [distributedag]
    JOIN
    AVAILABILITY GROUP ON
      'AG1' WITH (
        LISTENER_URL = 'tcp://ag1-listener:5022',
        AVAILABILITY_MODE = ASYNCHRONOUS_COMMIT,
        FAILOVER_MODE = MANUAL,
        SEEDING_MODE = AUTOMATIC
      ),
      'AG2' WITH (
        LISTENER_URL = 'tcp://ag2-listener:5022',
        AVAILABILITY_MODE = ASYNCHRONOUS_COMMIT,
        FAILOVER_MODE = MANUAL,
        SEEDING_MODE = AUTOMATIC
      );
GO
```

Skill 4.5: Implement failover clustering

Failover clustering has been available since SQL Server 6.5, so it is a very stable and mature high availability technology. A SQL Server Failover Cluster Instance (FCI) relies on Windows Clustering, so SQL Server is effectively a cluster aware application stack. However, not all components of SQL Server are cluster aware. For example, Reporting Services cannot be installed as FCI. Always try to deploy SQL Server FCIs on the latest version of the Windows Server operating system. Microsoft is always improving failover clustering in every Windows release, making it easier to configure and manage, perform better, and more reliable.

This objective covers how to:

- Architect failover clustering
- Configure failover clustering
- Configure Quorum configuration
- Manage shared disks
- Configure cluster shared volumes

Architect failover clustering

Windows Server 2012 really saw failover clustering come of age, with improvements across the board and in particular with the release of Server Message Block (SMB) 3.0. The benefit that SMB 3.0 brings is that it gives you the ability of locating your database files on shares. SQL Server 2014 introduced the capability of running databases off shares. This capability is commonly overlooked by the industry due to a lack of education and awareness. Failover clustering no longer relies solely on Fiber Channel (FC) or iSCSI protocols.

Compared to Availability Groups, Failover Clustering is a lot easier to implement and administer. This is fundamentally due to the fact that there is only a single set of database files that are hosted by a SQL Server instance and made available to users. Microsoft will continue to invest in failover clustering, so it is a perfectly valid high availability technology that you should assess and use as appropriate.

When designing a failover cluster solution, you should aim to provide redundancy at each level including server hardware, networking hardware, and network infrastructure. Don't forget to leverage the capabilities in the Windows Server operating system, such as NIC teaming and SMB Multichannel.

The failover clustering architecture, shown in Figure 4-36, contains the following elements:

- **Node**   A node is a Windows Server instance that is participating in a failover cluster. Failover cluster instances of applications, such as SQL Server, can run on any single node at any given point in time and space. Windows Server Standard Edition only supports 2 node failover clusters. Window Server Datacenter Edition support failover clusters with up to 64 nodes.
- **Shared Storage**   Shared Storage is a single instance of a storage subsystem that is accessible by all nodes of the failover cluster. Traditionally, the Shared Storage was located on a SAN that was accessed via Fiber Channel (FC). Since then iSCSI has proved to be more popular as technology has evolved. With the release of Windows Server 2012 and SMB 3.0, you can use SMB shares instead.

- **Public Network** A public network is the network that your users will be using to access the SQL Server FCI.

- **Private Network** A private Network is typically a network solely used between the nodes of the failover cluster for cluster network traffic. Strictly speaking, you do not need a dedicated private network, but it represents a best practice that is easy to implement.

- **Windows Server Failover Clustering (WSFC)** Windows Server Failover Clustering (WSFC) is an optional Windows Server feature that you install to build a failover cluster. Think of it as the failover cluster engine.

- **Quorum** The WSFC uses the concept of a *quorum* to determine what state the failover cluster is in; whether a fail over can occur or whether the entire failover cluster should be shut down. It guarantees that only one single SQL Server FCI is accessing the database files so as to avoid data corruption and allow the FCI to start up. The following components can participate (vote) in a quorum configuration:

  - A failover cluster node

  - A disk witness, known as the quorum disk, that is located on the shared storage

  - A file share witness

  - A cloud witness (file share witness hosted in Azure)

- **Failover Cluster Instance (FCI)** A SQL Server Failover Cluster Instance (FCI) is an instance of SQL Server being installed in a failover cluster. You can install a number of FCIs per failover cluster. The number of SQL Server FCIs that are supported are:

  - 25 FCIs when using shared cluster disks

  - 50 FCIs when using SMB file shares

- **Virtual Network Name (VNN)** A virtual network name (VNN) is a virtual NetBIOS name assigned to the SQL Server FCI that is used by users to connect to the SQL Server FCI. NetBIOS names have a 15 character limit. Typically, the first SQL Server FCI that you install is a default instance that can be accessed via its computer name. All subsequent SQL Server FCIs must be named instances and are typically accessed via the computer name and instance name combination.

- **Virtual IP Address (VIP)** A Virtual IP Address is a virtual IP address bound to the VNN.

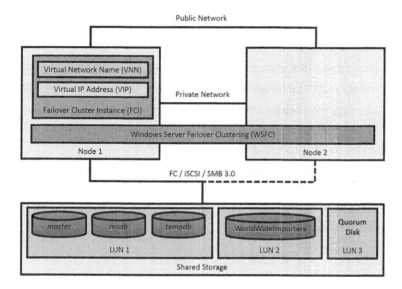

FIGURE 4-36 Failover clustering architecture

Failover in failover clustering is automatic. Being cluster aware means that a SQL Server FCI has a number of Resource DLLs that monitor the database engine's internals and communicate with the WSFC's Resource Monitors. This communication between the WSFC's Resource Monitors and the SQL Server FCI's Resource DLLs needs to ensure that a fail over is required. This can take some time in certain cases. At a high level the following steps occur in a failover incident:

1. SQL Server FCI fails on a node 1.

2. At this stage the WSFC "suspects" that the SQL Server FCI has failed.

3. The WSFC forms quorum to determine that the SQL Server FCI has failed.

4. The WSFC initiates a fail over.

5. The WSFC starts the SQL Server FCI services on node 2.

6. The SQL Server FCI services get started.

7. The SQL Server FCI's database engine connects to the databases on the shared storage.

8. The SQL Server FCI performs an automatic recovery of the databases.

   - It analyses the database's transactions logs and goes through a redo phase (replaying the transaction log after the last checkpoint).

   - It then goes through the undo phase which rolls back all uncommitted transactions.

   - Any In-memory OLTP tables are loaded into memory from the checkpoint files.

9. After the automatic recovery for a database is completed the database is accessible by users:

   - Until then the database is in the "recovering" state.

   - The database engine performs automatic recovery in order of the database's internal Database Id.

Figure 4-37 shows a high-level overview of a failover occurring in a failover cluster with a subset of the key steps from above:

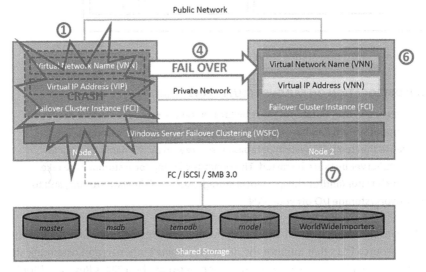

FIGURE 4-37 Failover Clustering Fail Over

The pros of using failover clustering include:

- Support for any edition of SQL Server.
  - SQL Server 2016 Standard Edition only supports 2 node failover clusters.
- Provides automatic failover.
- No data loss is possible as there is only ever a single instance of the database files. There is nothing to synchronize.

The following steps show how to configure the shared storage that the failover cluster will use.

1. Log into the storage server (STORAGE) that you plan to set up as an iSCSI target.
2. Open up Server Manager.
3. Click on Local Server in the left most pane.
4. Click on Manage drop-down in the top menu bar and choose Add Roles And Features to start the Add Roles And Features Wizard.
5. Click on the Next button in the Before You Begin page.
6. Choose the Role-Based Or Feature-Based Installation in the Select Installation Type page.
7. Ensure your local server is selected in the Server Pool and click on the Next button.
8. In the Server Roles page expand the File And iSCSI Services folder and select iSCSI Target Server. Then click on the Next button.
9. Confirm that the iSCSI Target roles is being installed on the Confirm Installation Selections page and click on the Install button.
10. Confirm that the iSCSI Target roles has been successfully installed, as shown in Figure 4-38 and close the wizard.
11. Select the Failover Clustering check box to install the Failover Clustering feature.
12. You need to set up a number of iSCSI virtual disks for your failover cluster. The SQL Server FCI will use the disks show in Table 4-4.

TABLE 4-4 Failover Cluster shared Disk Properties

Disk Number	VHDX File Name	Size	FCI disk letter	Purpose
0	Quorum.vhdx	1GB		Quorum disk for failover cluster
1	SQLData.vhdx	100GB	D:	SQL Server FCI user database data files
2	SQLLog.vhdx	50GB	L:	SQL Server FCI user database transaction log files
3	TempDBData.vhdx	10GB	T:	SQL Server FCI [tempdb] system database data files
4	TempDBLog.vhdx	20GB	U:	SQL Server FCI [tempdb] system database transaction log files

13. Back in Server Manager click on File And Storage Services the left most pane.
14. Click on the iSCSI option.
15. Click on the To Create An iSCSI Virtual Disk, start the New iSCSI Virtual Disk Wizard to start the New iSCSI Virtual Disk Wizard.
16. In the iSCSI Virtual Disk Location choose the appropriate disk volume and click on the Next button.
17. In the iSCSI Virtual Disk Name page provide the Name and Description and click on the Next button.

18. In the iSCSI Virtual Disk Size page configure a Dynamically Expanding disk that is 1GB in size for the quorum disk. You do not need a bigger size than that for a failover cluster's shared quorum disk. Click on the Next button when you are finished.

19. In the Assign iSCSI target page choose the New iSCSI target option and click on the Next button to create a target for the iSCSI disk that you are creating. The 2 nodes of the failover cluster will be the iSCSI targets.

20. In the Specify Target name page provide the following details before clicking on the Next button.

   - Name: SQLCLUSTER
   - Description: SQL Server 2016 Cluster

21. In the Specify Access Servers page click on the Add button to add the first node as an iSCSI initiator.

22. In the Add Initiator ID dialog box configure the first node as an iSCSI initiator by providing its computer name and click on the OK button.

23. In the Add Initiator ID dialog box configure the second node as an iSCSI initiator and click on the OK button.

24. In the Specify Access Servers page make sure you have added the 2 correct nodes, as seen in Figure 4-38 and click on the Next button.

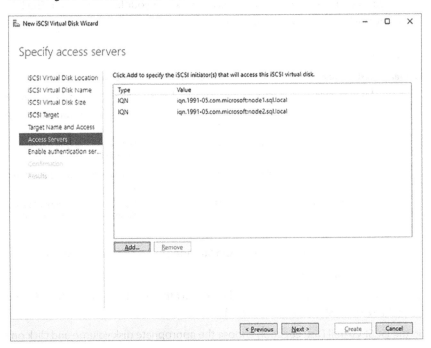

Figure 4-38 Availability Group Synchronous Commit

25. As there will be no authentication, click on the Next button in the Enable Authentication page.

26. Confirm the properties of the iSCSI virtual disk you are about to create, as shown in Figure 4-39 and click on the Create button.

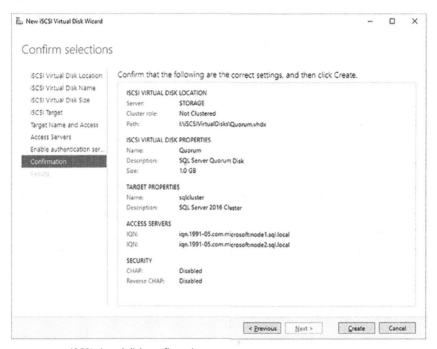

FIGURE 4-39 iSCSI virtual disk confirmation

27. Click on the Close button after the successful creation of your iSCSi virtual disk for the quorum disk of the failover cluster.

28. Repeat the above iSCSI virtual disk creation steps to create a 100GB thinly provisioned iSCSI disk for the databases' data files.

29. Repeat the above iSCSI virtual disk creation steps to create a 50GB thinly provisioned iSCSI disk for the databases' transaction log files.

30. Repeat the above iSCSI virtual disk creation steps to create a 20GB thinly provisioned iSCSI disk for the [tempdb] system database's data files.

31. Repeat the above iSCSI virtual disk creation steps to create a 10GB thinly provisioned iSCSI disk for the [tempdb] system database's transaction log.

32. In Server Manager, you should have 5 iSCSI virtual disks created for the failover cluster, as shown in Figure 4-40.

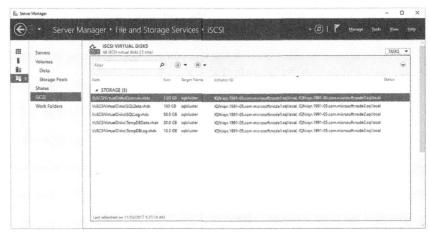

FIGURE 4-40 iSCSI disks configured for failover cluster

33. You need to configure the iSCSI Target Server to only communicate over the dedicated iSCSI network. In Server Manager click on Servers, then right-click on your storage server and select the iSCSI Target Settings option.

34. Select just the iSCSI network, as shown in Figure 4-41 and click on the OK button.

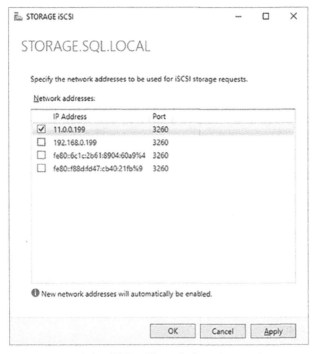

FIGURE 4-41 Isolating iSCSI traffic on dedicated network

You have now created 5 iSCSI LUNs for your failover cluster. You now need to configure your failover cluster. You need to perform the following high-level steps:

- Install and configure the iSCSI Initiator on each Node that will be part of the failover cluster.
- Format the iSCSI disks.
- Install WSFC on all the Nodes that are going to be part of the failover cluster.
- Create a failover cluster with all the Nodes.
- Create a SQL Server FCI by installing it the first Node of the failover cluster.
- Complete the installation of the SQL Server FCI by installing SQL Server on the additional Nodes of the failover cluster and joining the SQL Server FCI installed on the first Node.

The following steps show how to install and configure the iSCSI Initiator on each of the Nodes of the cluster.

1. Log into the first Node that will be part of your failover cluster.
2. Open Server Manager.
3. Select the iSCSI Initiator for the Tools menu.
4. Click on the Yes to confirm that you want the Microsoft iSCSI service to start automatically whenever the computer restarts.
5. Type in the name of your iSCSI target server into the Target text box and click on the Quick Connect button.
6. In the Quick Connect dialog box click on the Connect button and then the Done button so that the Node will be able to connect to the iSCSI Target Server LUNs as required.
7. Confirm that your Node is connected to the iSCSI target server you created earlier and click on the OK button, as shown in Figure 4-42.

FIGURE 4-42 Successfully connect to iSCISI Target Server

8. Configure the iSCSI initiator on the other nodes that you plan to add to the failover cluster

9. The next step is to format the iSCSI disks using the following properties:

- NTFS file system.
  - Although ReFS is supported, it not recommended for SQL Server database files due to performance reasons.
- 64KB allocation unit size.
  - The 1GB quorum disk can be formatted with the default (4KB) allocation unit size.
- Do not allow the files on the drives to have their contents indexes in addition to file properties.
- Assign the drive letters as per Table 4-4.

The following steps show how to format the iSCSI disks:

10. Log into the first Node that will be part of your failover cluster.

11. Open Disk Management.

12. Right click on the first iSCSI disk, which should be the 1GB quorum disk and click Online to bring it online.

13. Right-click on the same disk and select the Initialize Disk option.

14. In the Initialize Disk dialog box choose the MBR (Master Boot Record) option and click on the OK button.

15. In Disk Management, right click on the same disk and select the New Simple Volume option to format the disk.

16. In the New Simple Volume Wizard click on the Next button in the welcome screen.

17. In the Specify Volume Size page click on the Next button to format the simple volume with the default maximum possible disk size.

18. In the Assign Drive Letter Or Path screen choose the Do Not Assign A Drive Letter Or Drive path option. The quorum disk for the failover cluster does not require a drive letter to work.

19. Configure the format settings for the quorum disk and click on the Next button.

   ■ For a production environment, you should normally perform a full format to maximize performance and ensure there is no storage problems.

   ■ For your lab or development environment you should perform a quick format so as to save actual disk space.

20. Review the disk format settings and click on the Finish button to format the disk.

21. Format the remaining disks using the same steps as above. Remember to format the disks using the NTFS file system and 64KB allocation unit size. Use Figure 4-43 as a guide for the drive letters and volume names.

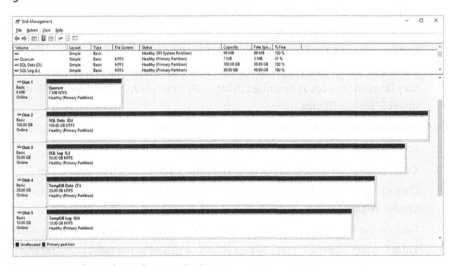

FIGURE 4-43 Failover cluster formatted volumes

You can now set up the failover cluster that the SQL Server FCI will be using. The first step is to install WSFC on all of the Nodes of the failover cluster.

Use the following steps to install WSFC on the first node of your failover cluster.

1. Open up Server Manager on the first Node.

2. Choose Add Roles And Features from the Manage drop-down list.

3. In the Add Roles And Features Wizard click on the Next button.

4. Choose the Role-Based Or Feature-Based Installation and click on Next.

5. Ensure your local server is selected in the Server Pool and click on the Next button.

6. Do not install any roles. Click on the Next button in the Select Server Roles page.

7. Select the Failover Clustering check box to install the Failover Clustering feature.

8. The Add Roles And Features Wizard will, by default, want to install the Failover Clustering tools and Powershell modules. Confirm this action by clicking on the Add Features button.

9. Confirm that you are installing Failover Clustering and the related tools before clicking on the Install button to begin the installation.

10. Confirm the installation was successful and click on the on the Close button to finish.

11. Repeat the WSFC installation on the other Nodes in the failover cluster using the same steps.

After installing the WSFC on all of the Nodes of your failover cluster you are reading to create the cluster. To install a failover cluster, you will need to have rights to modify your AD environment. Consequently, you will need to do one of the following:

- Log in as Domain Administrator when creating the failover cluster.

- Log in as yourself and get the Domain Administrator to run the setup executables as themselves using the Run As capability in the Windows OSE.

- Get the Domain Admin to pre-stage the cluster computer objects in Active Directory Domain Services as described in *https://technet.microsoft.com/en-us/library/dn466519(v=ws.11).aspx*.

The following steps show how to create a failover cluster.

1. Log into your Node as the Domain Administrator.

2. Open Failover Cluster Manager, which has now been installed on your server.

3. Click on the Create Cluster action in the right-most pane. This will start the Create Cluster Wizard.

4. Click on the Next button in the Before You Begin page of the Create Cluster Wizard.

5. Enter the name of the first Node that you want to add to the failover cluster and click on the Add button. The Create Cluster Wizard will validate the server's existence and add it to the bottom text box using its fully qualified domain name (FQDN).

6. Add all the nodes to you cluster, then click on the Next button as shown in Figure 4-44.

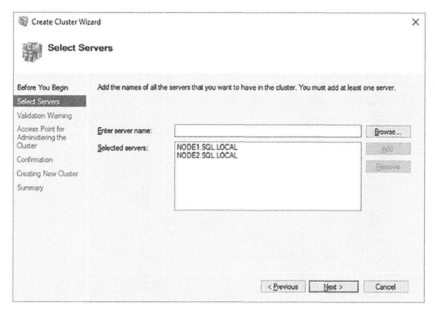

FIGURE 4-44 Selected nodes for failover cluster

7. You need to validate that your nodes are capable of running a failover cluster that will be supported by Microsoft. Click on the Next button to run the configuration validation tests.

8. The Validate A Configuration Wizard will by default automatically run all of the appropriate cluster validation tests for you. Click on the Next button in the Validate A Configuration Wizard.

9. It is a best practice to run all the cluster validation tests. Click on the Next button to start the validation tests, as shown in Figure 4-45.

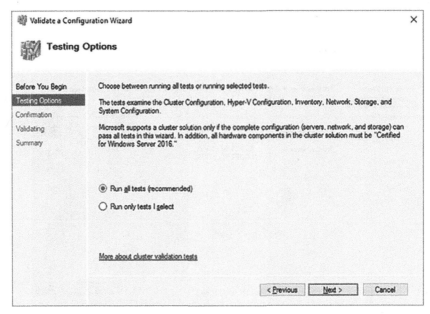

FIGURE 4-45 Running all cluster validation tests

10. Figure 4-46 shows you what tests will be run by default. Note that the Storage Space Direct tests will not be run because you have not installed and configured this feature.

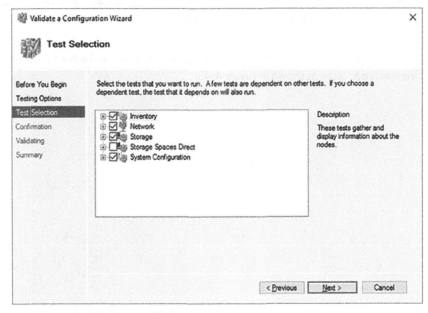

FIGURE 4-46 Possible cluster validation tests

- Name: iSCSI Network
- Do not allow cluster network communication on this network

7. Make sure you cluster networks have been reconfigured as shown in Figure 4-52

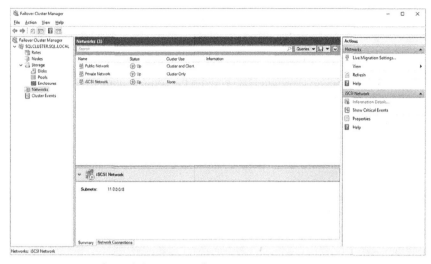

FIGURE 4-52 Re-configured cluster networks

8. Click on the Disks folder. All of the disks have also been named serially. Again, it is a best practice to rename them to help administration and minimize mistakes.

9. Right-click on the 1GB cluster disk being used as a disk witness and select Properties.

10. Rename the cluster disk to "Quorum Disk" to indicate its purpose.

11. Rename all cluster disks, as shown in Figure 4-53, to match their intended purpose.

FIGURE 4-53 Renamed cluster disks

Finally, you are ready to install the SQL Server FCI. The process to create SQL Server FCI involves:

- Run the SQL Server setup on the first node to install a SQL Server FCI on the first node
- Run the SQL Server setup on the second node to join it to the SQL Server FCI

Use the following steps to install start the installation of the SQL Server FCI on the failover cluster:

1. Log into Node 1 of the failover cluster as an administrator.
2. Mount the SQL Server Developer ISO and run the setup program.
3. Click on the Installation link in the SQL Server Installation Center.
4. Click on the New SQL Server Failover Cluster Installation link, as shown in Figure 4-54, to start the Install A SQL Server Failover Cluster setup.

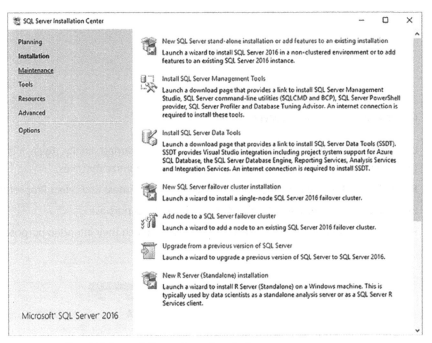

FIGURE 4-54 New SQL Server failover cluster installation

5. In the Product Key page of the Install A SQL Server Failover Cluster setup enter the product key to specify a free edition.
6. In the License Terms page accept the license terms and click on the Next button.
7. In the Global Rules page let the setup engine check to see if there are any blockers for the installation and click on the Next button.

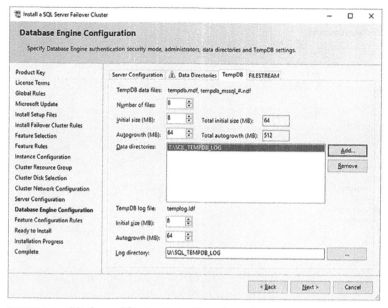

FIGURE 4-64 SQL Server FCI setup TempDB configuration

IMPORTANT **CREATING TEMPDB LOCALLY IN A FCI**

The tempdb system database can be located on local storage in a FCI, since it is automatically recreated each time SQL Server starts up. Locating tempdb on local flash storage represents a great optimization technique for database solutions that heavily utilize it.

---

22. Click on the FILESTREAM tab and configure your filestream options before clicking on the Next button.

23. In the Feature Configuration Rules page, as shown in Figure 4-65, let the setup engine run its checks and click on the Next button.

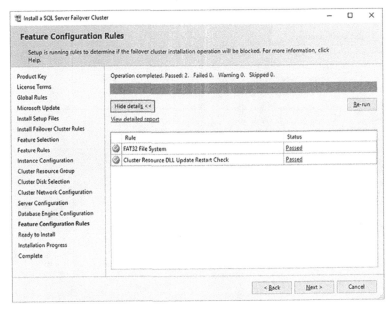

FIGURE 4-65 SQL Server FCI setup feature configuration rules

24. Review the summary of your SQL Server FCI setup and click on the Install button to initiate the installation procedure.

25. Once the setup has completed, review the summary to ensure nothing has gone wrong. Save the summary log for support reasons and click on the Close button to complete close the installer.

You now need to complete the installation of the SQL Server FCI by installing the same configuration on the second Node. Fortunately, this is a lot easier as the installation on the first node has most of the information needed to complete the installation on the second Node, barring the service account passwords.

Use the following steps to complete the installation of the SQL Server FCI on the failover cluster:

1. Log into Node 2 of the failover cluster as an administrator.

2. Mount the SQL Server Developer ISO and run the setup program.

3. Click on the Installation link in the SQL Server Installation Center.

4. Click on the Add Node To A SQL Server Failover Cluster link, as shown in Figure 4-54, to start the Install A SQL Server Failover Cluster setup.

In the Product Key page of the Install A SQL Server Failover Cluster setup enter the product key to specify a free edition, like for Node 1, and click on the Next button.

1. In the License Terms page accept the license term and click on the Next button.

2. In the Global Rules page let the installer check to see if there are any blockers for the installation and click on the Next button.

3. In the Microsoft Update page, like for Node 1, click on the Next button for Node 1.

4. Click on the Next button in the Product Updates page, for Node 1.

5. In the Install Setup Files page let the installer install the required setup files and click on the Next button.

6. The Add Node Rules page, shown in Figure 4-66, runs a number of checks to see if anything would block the Node being added to the FCI. Review and warnings and correct any errors as required. Click on the Next button when you are done.

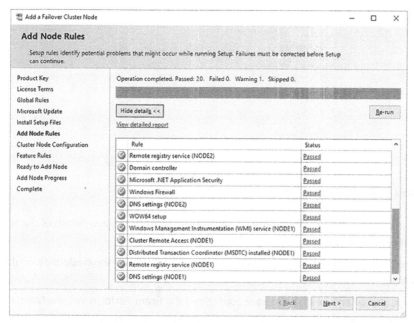

FIGURE 4-66   SQL Server FCI setup install add node rules

7. In the Cluster Node Configuration page, shown in Figure 4-67, the installer shows you details of the SQL Server FCI you are going to become part of. Remember that you can have multiple SQL Server FCIs in a failover cluster. In this case, there is only one SQL Server FCI. Click on the Next button when you have reviewed the page.

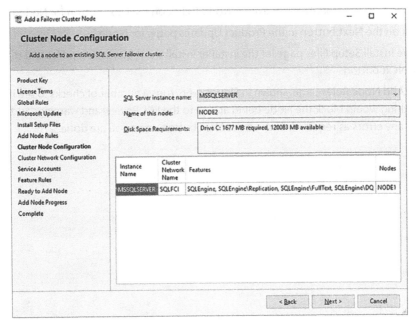

FIGURE 4-67 SQL Server FCI setup cluster node configuration

8. In the Cluster Network Configuration page the installer shows you details of the SQL Server FCI's network configuration Click on the Next button.

9. In the Service Accounts page provide the same passwords for the credentials configured for Node 1 and click on the Next button.

    ■ You should ensure that you have configured the Grant Perform Volume Maintenance Task Privilege To SQL Server Database Engine Service all Nodes of the failover cluster.

10. The Feature Rules page, shown in Figure 4-197, checks to see if there are any blocking processes for configuring the SQL Server FCI. Click on the Next button to proceed to the next step.

11. In the Ready To Add Node page review what will be installed and click on the Install button to engage the completion of the SQL Server FCI installation.

12. Save the setup log for support reasons and click on the Close button.

In general, there is nothing further to configure after you create your SQL Server FCI. However, you should familiarize yourself with the failover cluster and SQL Server FCI, especially if they have been deployed using new versions of Windows Server and SQL Server.

Figure 4-68 shows the SQL Server FCI that you have created. The bottom pane shows all the resources of the SQL Server FCI.

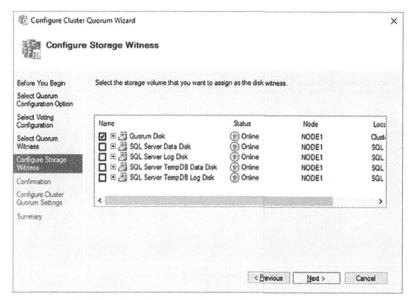

FIGURE 4-72 Configuration of disk witness in WSFC

Figure 4-73 shows the file share witness option. In the case of a file share witness the cluster database is not stored there. The file share witness only keeps track of which Node has the most updated cluster database in the witness.log file. This can lead to a scenario where only a single Node and the file share witness survive, but the failover cluster will not be able to come online if the surviving node does not have the most up to date version of the cluster database because this would cause a "partition in time." That is why the disk witness was recommended over the file share witness. You should use the file share witness when you do not have shared storage or where you have a multisite cluster with replicated storage.

FIGURE 4-73 Configuration of file share witness in WSFC

Figure 4-74 shows the cloud witness, which was added with Windows Server 2016. It is fundamentally a file share witness, except that it is hosted in Microsoft Azure. Its primary use case is where you have two data centers and ideally need to place the witness in a third data center.

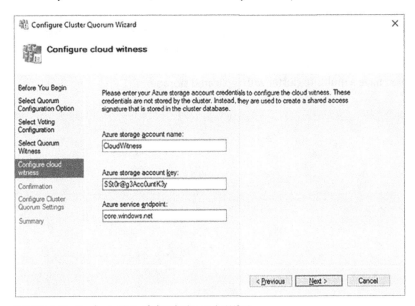

FIGURE 4-74 Configuration of cloud witness in WSFC

Manage Shared Disks

Disks (LUNs) attached to a failover cluster work differently from disks attached to a stand-alone server environment. A number of health monitoring checks are performed on a failover cluster managed disks. If any of these checks fail the WSFC will assume there is a problem and take appropriate action, including:

- Try to restart the resources and mount the disk on same node.
- Assume failover ownership of the disk.
- Try to bring the disk online on another Node.

The following file system level checks are performed on disks managed by WSFC:

- **LooksAlive** A quick check is performed every 5 seconds to verify the disk is still available.
- **IsAlive** A complete check is performed every 60 seconds to verify the disk and the file system can be accessed.

Additionally, the following device level checks are performed by the Clusdisk.sys driver:

- **SCSI Reserve** A SCSI Reserve command is sent to the LUN every 3 seconds to ensure that only the owning node has ownership and can access the disk.
- **Private Sector** Perform a read/write operation to sector 12 of the LUN every 3 seconds to ensure that the device is writable.

Sometimes you need to perform certain administrative or maintenance tasks on your clustered disks that require exclusive access to the disk, such as with the CHKDSK /F or FORMAT operations. In such cases, you do not the health monitoring checks to fail and trigger a failover.

To perform such administrative or maintenance tasks on your failover cluster's shared disks you first need to place the disk into maintenance mode. This can be done in Failover Cluster Manager by right clicking on the disk, selecting More Actions and then Turn On Maintenance Mode.

Configure Cluster Shared Volumes

Clustered Shared Volumes (CSV) is a new clustered file system in Windows Server that is a layer of abstraction above the NTFS file system in a WSFC environment. It allows all Nodes in the failover cluster to read and write to the CSV volume. CSV leverages the investments Microsoft have made in SMB 3.0, such as SMB Direct and SMB Multichannel.

SQL Server 2014 was the first version of SQL Server to support CSVs. However, CSVs are not commonly deployed with SQL Server in the industry. This poor adoption is mostly like due to a lack of awareness in the industry of CSV and its related benefits.

The Cluster Shared Volume architecture, shown in Figure 4-75, contains the following elements:

- **Coordinator Node** The Coordinator node is the node of your failover cluster on which the NTFS volume is mounted. All meta data operations from the other nodes in your failover cluster are orchestrated through this coordinator node using SMB 3.0. Meta data operations in SQL Server include opening and closing a database, creating a database, and auto-growing a database. Such meta data operations are relatively rare.

- **CSV Proxy File System** The CSV Proxy File System is mounted on all nodes of the failover cluster. All read and write operations are sent directly through these proxies to the shared storage. This direct I/O is not even hitting the NTFS stack. If a Node cannot communicate directly to the shared storage it can communicate with the CSV Proxy File System using SMB 3.0 at the block level.

- **CSVFS** The Clustered Share Volume File System (CSVFS) is the clustered file system that spans all nodes of the failover cluster. It is effectively the layer of abstraction that sits on top of the NTFS file system.

- **NTFS Stack** The NTFS stack is used for all meta data operations to maintain consistency at the file system level.

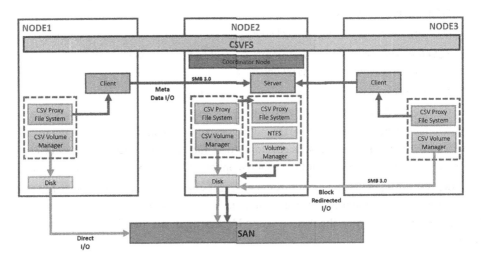

FIGURE 4-75 Cluster Share Volumes architecture

The benefits of CSV include:

- Faster failover times because there are no physical disks that need to be unmounted/mounted by the WSFC.

- Improved resilience in the case a data path fails. A Node is now able to redirect its block level I/O to the coordinator node. With the benefits of SMB 3.0, including SMB multi-channel and SMB Direct (RDMA), there should be no/minimal performance impact.

- Your failover cluster no longer relies upon drive letters. You can only have as many cluster disks as the alphabet allows (24 in most cases). In the case of CSVs you are no longer replying on drive letters.

- Zero downtime with CHKDSK operations. Effectively you can provide disk repairs without any SQL Server down time.
- Easier administration as you are able to manage the underlying storage from any node. CSVFS provides the same abstraction layer across all nodes of the failover cluster.

The following steps show you have to implement CSVs in your SQL Server FCI.

1. Log into your storage server as administrator.
2. Provision another 2 iSCSI virtual disks as your iSCSI targets.
3. Log into Node 1 of the failover cluster as an administrator.
4. Open Disk Management.
5. Online, initialize and format the two new disks as NTFS volumes.
6. Open Failover Cluster Manager and connect to your failover cluster.
7. Right-click on the Disks folder and select the Add Disk option.
8. Select both new disks in the Add Disks To A Cluster dialog box and click on the OK button.
9. Rename both new cluster disks to something more meaningful.
10. Convert the cluster disks to Cluster Shared Volumes by right clicking on each cluster disk and selecting the Add To Cluster Shared Volumes option.
11. Confirm that the disks are not Cluster Shared Volumes and the they are using the CSVFS filesystem, as shown in Figure 4-76.

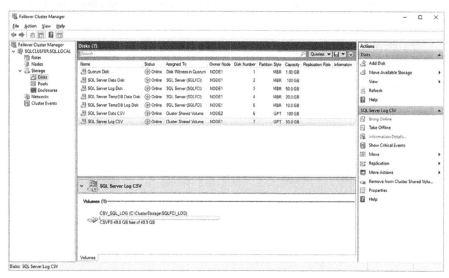

FIGURE 4-76 Cluster Shared Volumes and CSVFS filesystem

12. Open File Explorer and navigate to the C:\ClusterStorage root CSV folder as shown in Figure 4-77.

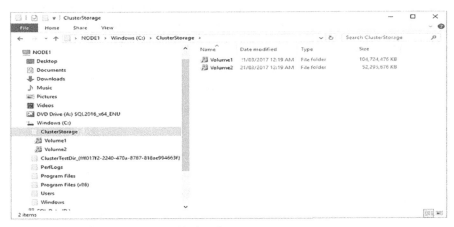

FIGURE 4-77 C:\ClusterStorage root CSV location

13. Rename the two volume folders to something more meaningful.

14. Create a subdirectory under both mount points for the SQL Server FCI to store the database files.

15. Open SQL Server Management Studio and connect to the SQLFCI instance.

16. Create a new database using the CSV database paths, as shown in Figure 4-78.

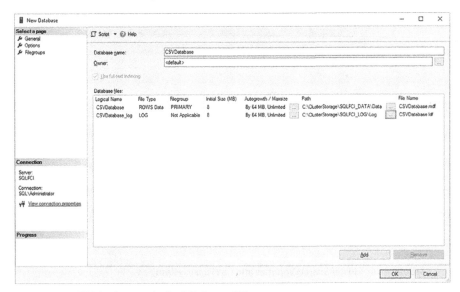

FIGURE 4-78 CSV database paths for SQL Server FCI

17. Switch to File Explorer and confirm the database files have been created in the CSV folder namespace.

18. Log into Node 2 of your failover cluster.

19. Open File Explorer and navigate to the same directory location used in Step 16.

20. Confirm you can see the database files there as well.

21. Switch back to Node 1.

22. Switch back to Failover Cluster Manager.

23. Generate a new Dependency Report.

24. Confirm you cannot see the CSVs in the dependencies, unlike the physical disks.

Consider using CSVs in your next SQL Server 2016/2017 failover cluster solution because they offer a number of advantages over traditionally deployed shared disks.

Thought experiment

In this thought experiment, demonstrate your skills and knowledge of the topics covered in this chapter. You can find answers to this thought experiment in the next section.

You work as a Database Administrator for World Wide Importers. You need to design a disaster recovery and high availability strategy for your multi-database solution that is used internally. Your company has a primary office in Sydney and another office in Wagga Wagga.

The multi-database solution has the following characteristics:

- The main OLTP database is 400GB in size
- There is a 200GB database which is used for auditing and logging records
- There are 5 more databases that are used. They are all under 50GB in size.
- All databases currently use the full recovery model.
- All databases are hosted on a single SQL Server instance
- OLAP and real-time reports are impacting performance of the OLTP transactions

You have an existing 2 Node failover cluster based in Sydney that hosts a vendor database solution. This database solution does not support Availability Groups.

Management has asked you to solve the following business problems:

- The business requires a high availability solution that supports automatic failover.

- The databases should be highly available in Sydney's data center.
- If that data center in Sydney fails the disaster recovery solution should have Wagga Wagga with an RTO of 2 hours and RPO of 15 minutes.
- Management wants to reduce the impact of running reports on the OLTP transactions. Analysts in Wagga Wagga want to report off a "snapshot" of the database at close of business on the previous day.

Question 1

Management wants you to create a high-availability solution strategy for the multi-database solution that meets their requirements. What high availability solution should you use:

1. Create an Availability Group with 4 replicas:

   - 3 replicas in Sydney
   - 2 synchronous replicas in Sydney will be used as failover partners
   - 1 readable synchronous replica in Sydney for OLAP reporting
   - 1 asynchronous secondary replica in Wagga Wagga

2. Create an Distributed Availability Group with 4 replicas:

   - 3 replicas in Sydney
   - 2 synchronous replicas in Sydney will be used as failover partners
   - 1 readable synchronous replica in Sydney for OLAP reporting
   - 1 asynchronous secondary replica in Wagga Wagga

3. Create a 3 node failover cluster:

   - 2 nodes will be based in Sydney
   - 1 node will be based in Wagga Wagga

4. Create an Availability Group in Sydney. Use log shipping between Sydney and Wagga Wagga:

   - 3 replicas in Sydney
   - 2 synchronous replicas in Sydney will be used as failover partners
   - 1 readable synchronous replica in Sydney for OLAP reporting
   - Perform log backups every 15 minutes

Question 2

Management wants to extend the failover cluster to Wagga Wagga. They plan to add two more nodes to the cluster in Wagga Wagga. What quorum configuration should you use?

1. Use a node majority quorum with no witness.
2. Use a node majority quorum with a file share witness.
3. Use a node majority with a cloud witness
4. Use a node majority with a disk witness.

Index

A

actions 206
Activity Monitor 182–183, 188
administrative accounts
    Azure SQL Database 49
Advanced Encryption Standard New Instructions
        (AES-NI) 21
alerts
    custom 245
    SQL Agent 243–245
ALLOW_SNAPSHOT_ISOLATION isolation level 186
ALTER DATABASE statement 93, 104
ALTER INDEX DISABLE statement 225
ALTER INDEX REBUILD statement 220, 226
ALTER INDEX REORGANIZE statement 220, 225–226
ALTER INDEX statement 220
ALTER TABLE REBUILD statement 220, 226
Always Encrypted (AE) 9–20
application roles 36
asymmetric keys 3, 4, 27
    encrypting backups with 25
asynchronous commit mode 289, 291–292
auditing
    Azure SQL Database 57–61
    blob 59–60
    configuration 50–61
    database audit specification 51
    implementing 54–55
    management of 56–57
    policies 57–58
    querying SQL Server audit log 55–56
    server audit specification 51
    SQL Server 51–58
audit logs 55–56, 57, 60–61

authentication
    Azure Active Directory 49
    Azure SQL Database 49
    SQL 29, 49
    Windows 29
authenticator parameter 6
Auto Create Incremental Statistics 232
Auto Create Statistics 232
automatic failover 268, 293, 327
Auto Update Statistics 231–233
Auto Update Statistics Asynchronously 232
availability 266–267. *See also* high availability
Availability Groups 269
    architecture 287–298
    automatic failover in 293
    backup preferences 310–311
    Basic 293–294
    configuration 307–319
    creating 304–318
    Distributed 331–332
    enhancements to 296–297
    failover management 327–330
    implementing 287–332
    Initial Catalog connection 324
    listener preferences 311–312
    listeners 288
    log stream compression 293–294
    monitoring 325–326
    pros and cons of 293–295
    quorum configuration 319–322
    readable secondary replicas 297–298
    read-only routing configuration 322–325
    synchronization modes 289–293
    use cases 296–297
    Windows Server Failover Clustering 298–304
avg_page_space_used_in_percent 219

Clustered Shared Volumes 371–375
data access 28–50
database mail 235–241
data collector 188–196
dynamic data masking 47–48
encryption 2–28
Extended Events 205–214
failed backup alerts 131–140
failover clustering 338–367
log shipping 275–284, 286
maintenance plan 116–131
operators 131–132
policy based management 247–253
Query Store 198–202
quorum 319–322, 367–369
read-only routing 322–325
row-level security 41–46
Windows clustering 298–304
Configure Management Data Warehouse Wizard 190
connections
  encryption of 26–27
CONTINUE_AFTER_ERROR option 81
Coordinator node 371–372
COPY_ONLY option 81
CREATE INDEX statement 220
cross-database ownership chaining 32
CSV. *See* Cluster Shared Volume
CSV Proxy File System 372
CTEs. *See* common table expressions (CTEs)
current sessions
  monitoring 180–183
custom roles 36–37

D

DAGs. *See* Distributed Availability Groups
damaged databases
  tail-log backups on 100
data
  querying. *See* queries
data access 1
  Azure SQL Database 49–50
  configuration 28–50
  custom roles 36–37
  database object permissions 38–41
  dynamic data masking 47–48
  row-level security 41–46
  user creation 29–35

database activity monitoring 180–196
  current sessions 180–183
  data collector 188–196
  identifying sessions causing blocking activity 183–186
  identifying sessions consuming tempdb
    resources 186–188
database audit specification 51
database backups. *See* backups
database checkpoint 74
database consistency checks 163–167
Database Console Command (DBCC) 164–167, 170
database corruption
  identifying 167–169
  recovery from 169–173
database encryption key (DEK) 22
database files 68
database integrity
  consistency checks 163–167
  database corruption 167–173
  management of 163–173
database mail
  components of 236–237
  configuration 235–241
  logs 241
database mail accounts 236, 238
database mail profiles 236
Database Master Key (DMK) 3
database mirroring 269, 293
Database Properties page 94–95
database recovery models
  configuration 91–95
database roles 29, 32, 34–35
  Azure SQL Database 49–50
  user-defined 36
databases
  emergency repairs 171–173
  indexes 218–226
  maintenance plan for 116–131
  number of 268
  partial availability 89
  restoring 141–163
  size 268
  very large 87–90
database size 68
database snapshots
  performing 84–85
  reverting 148
database user mappings 33–34

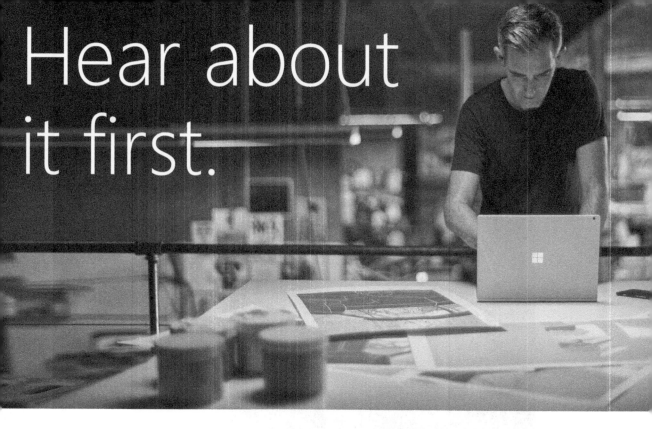

Hear about it first.

Get the latest news from Microsoft Press sent to your inbox.

- New and upcoming books

- Special offers

- Free eBooks

- How-to articles

Sign up today at MicrosoftPressStore.com/Newsletters

 Microsoft

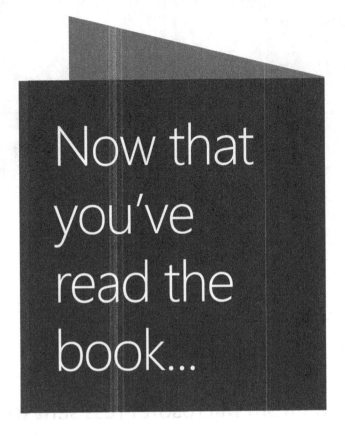

Now that you've read the book...

Tell us what you think!

Was it useful?
Did it teach you what you wanted to learn?
Was there room for improvement?

Let us know at https://aka.ms/tellpress

Your feedback goes directly to the staff at Microsoft Press,
and we read every one of your responses. Thanks in advance!